Full Leadership
Development

Advanced Topics in Organizational Behavior

The **Advanced Topics in Organizational Behavior** series examines current and emerging issues in the field of organizational behavior. Written by researchers who are widely acknowledged subject area experts, the books provide an authoritative, up-to-date review of the conceptual, research, and practical implications of the major issues in organizational behavior.

Full Leadership
Development
Building the
Vital Forces in
Organizations

Bruce J. Avolio

Advanced Topics in
Organizational Behavior

SAGE Publications
International Educational and Professional Publisher
Thousand Oaks   London   New Delhi

For information:

SAGE Publications, Inc.
2455 Teller Road
Thousand Oaks, California 91320
E-mail: order@sagepub.com

SAGE Publications Ltd.
6 Bonhill Street
London EC2A 4PU
United Kingdom

SAGE Publications India Pvt. Ltd.
M-32 Market
Greater Kailash I
New Delhi 110 048 India

Printed in the United States of America

Library of Congress Cataloging-in-Publication Data

Avolio, Bruce J.
  Full leadership development: Building the vital forces in organizations / by Bruce J. Avolio.
      p. cm. — (Advanced topics in organizational behavior)
    Includes bibliographical references and index.

    ISBN 0-7619-0602-9 (acid-free paper)
    ISBN 0-7619-0603-7 (pbk.: acid-free paper)
    1. Leadership. I. Title. II. Series.
    HD57.7 .A95 1999
    658.4'07124—dc21   98-51235

This book is printed on acid-free paper.

05   7

Acquisition Editor:	Marquita Flemming
Editorial Assistant:	MaryAnn Vail
Production Editor:	Denise Santoyo
Editorial Assistant:	Stephanie Allen
Typesetter:	Christina M. Hill

Contents

Hello, Dolly,/this is Louis, Dolly,/we're so glad to have you back where you belong./You're lookin' swell, Dolly,/I can tell, Dolly,/you keep glowing, you're still growing, you're still going strong.
(From Louis Armstrong's rendition of "Hello, Dolly")

For Dolly, who taught me as her son that the most vulnerable people in this world often possess the greatest strength in their ability to love others with all their heart and with little expectation for any return. I have come back to where I started, realizing how important your kindness was to my development. Every year of my life, your light is much brighter for me than the last.

Forever your follower in both my mind and heart.

Preface

Give your difference, welcome my difference, unify all difference in the larger whole—such is the law of growth. The unifying of difference is the eternal process of life—the creative synthesis, the highest act of creation. Mary Parker Follett

In all the discussions I have had about leadership, one issue seems to come up time and time again. The issue involves discussing leadership as a process, as a person, or as some aspects of both. When discussed as a process, we can explore the context in which leadership occurs, the characteristics of followers, the timing of events, the history in which leadership is embedded, and so forth. When discussed as persons, we get into names, personality characteristics, values, whether they are "born versus made," how their intelligence plays a role in successes and failures, experience, and so forth. In rare instances, some groups may even talk about the culture and its relevance to understanding and explaining leadership, which means they are focusing on process. Often, this creates sort of a grayish look in people's eyes because those who thought about leadership as a person try to understand it now as being embedded within some abstract cultural process.

One of my goals in writing this book was to help followers, starting with readers of this book, begin thinking about leadership as a system, one that has a very broad range and depth. I refer to the range as a "full range of leadership" potential. To think about leadership as a system, one needs to consider the *inputs,* which for now we can say are the people, timing, and resources; the *process,* which we can describe as the system/context in which these people and resources interact over time; and the *outcomes,* which are the levels of motivation and performance we expect to achieve after optimizing the full potential of the leadership system. By optimizing the leadership system, we intend to enhance each individual's "vital force" and, in turn, the "collective force" of the group or organization.

Together, we need to build a full range leadership development system by working from the inside out. This is where the depth of the system becomes relevant to our discussion. Specifically, we start with the various perspectives that both leaders and followers must have to perform at the top of their game and to avoid the end of the range, where levels of performance are sub-optimal. Once we have clarified this range of perspectives, including our own, we can then move to external factors that compose the system and context in which leaders and followers interact. Together, we can then build a leadership system, which encompasses a full range of leadership styles from those leaders who are highly avoidant and the reasons for being so, to those who are inspiring and *idealized* by their followers, *not idolized!* We can then take those styles and perspectives and apply them to even more complex forms of leadership when we discuss *shared leadership* in teams and building a *leadership culture* within an organization. In the end, we can develop a framework of leadership that will be applied to all three levels, as it should be, if one is to build an organizational system that can sustain its performance at optimal levels by maximizing the collective force of its members.

So, for whom is this book written? For any level of leader, follower, team member, in any organization large or small, that is operating in any culture. The principles associated with a full range of leadership potential are expected to be universal across levels, organizations, and cultures.[1] Of course, I leave the wisdom of this conclusion to your judgment.

Before proceeding with our journey along a full range of leadership potential, I should probably say something about the overall orientation for this book. During the last year and a half, this book had several titles before the current one was chosen. The "vital forces" included in the subtitle has symbolic importance to our discussion of leadership systems in that it helps us focus on the relationship between leader and follower as the basis for generating the "vital forces" in any group or organization.

The concept of *vital forces* comes from African humanistic philosophy.[2] Basically, one's vital force is either enhanced or diminished by the relationships one has with others.[3] Each of us has our own force and energy that is enhanced (and sometimes diminished) by our relationships with others. Simply watch what happens to a married couple as their relationship goes downhill. Ever work with a group that was hell-bent on eating its young? How was your vital force when you worked in an organization where every relationship was politically motivated? Relationships can either enhance or diminish our vital force. And leadership represents the relationship between at least two people. Full leadership development works to enhance the individual and collective force in groups and organizations.

According to African humanistic philosophy, in one's family the grandfather's vital force is seen to be greater than the father's and the son's, given the grandfather's proximity to the family's ancestors. Yet, each family member derives a share of this vital force because of her or his unique relationship with other members and because of the unique talents they each represent. In some ways, the vital force is a perfect blend of collectivism and individualism, which for many people, especially current leaders, would seem quite paradoxical. I will have more to say on this "collective-individualism" distinction shortly.[4]

We use the concept of *vital force* to represent what great leaders are attempting to accomplish in building "ideal" relationships with their followers or peers or both. Leaders, followers, and peers are enriched in terms of what they can accomplish through the quality of relationships they have developed with each other. If we examine the quality of each relationship in an organization and continuously work to improve those relationships, the chance is good that the organization will achieve its full potential. I say "chance" because many other factors affect the success and/or failure of an organization's leadership system, including timing, resources, and luck.

Great leaders are great because someone contributed to their greatness whether they were the heads of state, social movements, religious institutions, companies, schools, and/or communities. I believe that, by fully understanding what is going on in the relationship between a leader and his or her followers, a much deeper appreciation can be developed for what constitutes a highly effective and more fully developed "leadership system." Being added to the current discussion here is the idea of looking at this relationship along what I call a full range of leadership potential.[5]

Taken together, people derive their vital forces through the relationships they have with each other at all levels of an organization. Relationships built on trust provide the basis for building the vital force that differentiates the average team from the highly developed one;[6] the average organization from the market leader; and the exemplary leader from one who simply gets a job done. The task before us is to provide a clear idea of how to build relationships between leaders and followers that can enhance the vital force of each in achieving one's highest aspirations. So, it doesn't matter whether you are a leader, a follower, or both. In fact, in any 1 day, it is rare that most people are not both leader and follower, and it is in the optional exchanging of these roles that the best organizational systems and teams are built.[7]

As you will discover while reading this book, the task of building a full range system is one we will work on together. To do so any differently would detract from each of our vital forces. I'd also hate to start out a new book by being a bad role model.

Oh, by the way . . .

If you finish listening before I finish talking, please feel free to leave.
   (Adlai Stevenson)

Acknowledgments

Numerous people have had both a direct and an indirect impact on the thinking that formed the basis for this book. In addition, many hands have helped put this book together. So, in the interest of being inclusive, I list here the names of people whom I thank personally for helping me along toward completing this book. Many thanks to all of you for bringing me to a point where I felt confident enough to put my ideas into words for others to use in developing their full leadership potential: Beth Avolio, Fran Yammarino, Boas Shamir, Jane Howell, Bill Gardner, Taly Dvir, Dov Eden, John Sosik, Dong Jung, Danie Maritz, Ralph Alexander, Howard Powell, Galen Kroeck, Yair Berson, Bernie Bass, Mike Dean, Donna Dennis, Micha Popper, Ruevan Gal, Eliav Zakay, Casey Avolio, Jake Avolio, Sydney Avolio, Glenn Poveromo, Jim Burns, Paul Crookall, Frank Farley, Mike Cannetti, John Cannetti, Kevin Harrington, Harry Greenspan, Sammy Greenspan, Sam Goldenberg, Esther Avolio, Barry Goldenberg, Gerry Barrett, Giovanni Testa, Harvey Sterns, Sheri Poveromo, Diane Thomas, Surinder Kahai, Marty Freedman, Rich Gelman, Robb Most, Charles Simonson, and Cathy Gelman.

I also thank the people who helped me put this book together in the very literal sense. I extend my appreciation to all of you for your help, smiles, and patience throughout these last few years: Cheryll Hague, Wendy Kramer, Bernie Cencetti, Juliette Monet, and Sally Bowers.

In addition, I thank the people at Sage who made this a very enjoyable process for me and, in particular, the editor of this series, Julian Barling. Your encouragement, critical insights, and timely feedback made many of the ideas presented in this book more understandable and user-friendly.

Finally, although many, many people have contributed their ideas to what I included in this book, in the end what I have said is based on my opinion, and therefore, like any good leader, I am the one who is accountable for what has been included in this book.

1

Building a
Leadership Relationship

---

*How an entity becomes constitutes what that actual entity is . . . It's being
constituted by its becoming.* (Alfred North Whitehead)

M any, many books have been written on the subject of what constitutes
effective leadership. In running training programs around the world, I
can almost guarantee that one will get asked the question, "What does it take to
be an effective leader?" Of course, this question typically follows the debate on
what the differences between a leader and manager are, which is usually more
about the person than about processes. "How can one be a manager and also a
leader?" is the typical question being asked. At the risk of sounding somewhat
disinterested, I leave this debate for others to work out and instead concentrate
on those individuals or groups who engage in the *process of leadership,* whether
they are first-line managers, CEOs, project leaders, teammates, teachers,
coaches, parents, siblings, shop stewards, or counselors. Let me add, for empha-

sis, *especially parents.* The most important leader in any society is the parent, next the teacher, and coming in a close third are the manager and the adminis- trator. What the parent doesn't develop, the teacher handles, and what the teacher falls short on becomes the responsibility of the manager to develop in his or her followers. And if the manager fails, the developing leader goes to trainers.

The process of leadership can be observed from all these sources; it can be highly effective, mediocre, or in some cases, absolutely disastrous. Many faces contribute to the leadership development process, not least of which is the person many authors have labeled "the leader." In this book, I attempt to broaden the focus regarding leadership to go beyond the figure—the leader—to also include the background—the follower and the context in which both are embedded over time. Why focus on the follower now? Lorraine Matusek,[8] in her book *Finding Your Voice,* suggests that "leaders should think of themselves as individuals surrounded by mirrors of many kinds" (p. 17). What they do and say is often reflected back to them in the behavior of their followers.

Imagine a situation where you are unable to meet with a particular leader of some large organization but are given the opportunity to meet with the person who reports to that leader, someone we might call the "second in command." What can we learn from this meeting in terms of understanding the leadership system and dynamics in this organization? Could we possibly learn everything we need to know about the leader's role in the leadership process by just talking with the leader's "follower"? I believe that the answer to this question is often yes, but in reality it is also great to talk with both because each will add something unique to describing the leadership process that is quite valuable— each of his or her own perspectives. In the spirit of being provocative, however, let's set a standard that if we were to talk with the second in command, we would learn everything we needed to know about the leadership system in that organi- zation. Now, I didn't say that it would necessarily be good, but that we would learn what constitutes the leadership system by talking with the individual most directly affected by the leader (for lack of a better term that is broadly under- stood, let's simply say "the follower").

I say "observe leadership" here because I realize that you are watching exactly what I'm saying, even perhaps more than would typically occur with the average "leader-follower" interaction. And like that interaction, I, too, don't always know what you're thinking, whether you are reflecting on what I've just said, whether you're annoyed, bewildered, concerned, or inspired. (Okay, I, too, may be prone to exaggeration from time to time.) Like many leaders, I am trying to keep in mind that if I don't get my messages through to you, then subsequent interactions you have with others will be neither positively nor negatively affected by my influence on you. Simply put, to fully lead, I cannot do it without your engagement. No leader leads without followers. And almost all leaders must shift between being a follower and a leader on a daily basis, and in some cases on an hourly basis. This is even more true today with trends toward flattened, networked organizations that are establishing shared leadership systems.[9,10]

Leaders must also be keenly aware of their vulnerabilities. The first concern is that, absent followers, leadership is very limited and, more important, not really that interesting. The second concern is that being aware of the way one follows and leads will, to a large extent, determine the way one's followers lead and follow. Perhaps this is what R. D. Laing meant when he said, "The range of what we think and do is limited by what we fail to notice. And because we fail to notice that we fail to notice, there is little we can do to change until we notice how failing to notice shapes our thoughts and deeds." (I also had to read this several times to get the full meaning of his message.)

So, to meet people in the second level of command in any organization can be an interesting reflection of an absent leader. One might even say a mirror image, in many cases, and this can be good or bad, depending on the reflection that appears in the mirror.

Being aware of these vulnerabilities (and I address more vulnerabilities later on in our discussion) helps me in my role to adjust my interactions with you, which I hope will add some positive value to our relationship. Indeed, at the outset of building any leadership relationship and broader system of leadership, we must establish a framework for working together. This requires that we discuss the parameters we must establish for our relationship to enhance its ultimate effectiveness, or as the subtitle of this book indicates, to achieve our "vital forces." If we can agree to examine leadership as a process, at the core of this process we must then examine how relationships are built that involve leaders and followers. And here we hardly know each other, so what better place to start than to establish the groundwork for building our relationship? For example, as a basis for our relationship, from time to time I'll ask you, and even challenge you, to give further consideration to what I've said and how you might apply it to your own leadership development with your second in command, peers, and/or supervisor. We can then discuss what each of us requires in terms of our own needs, level of recognition, "redlines," and how we desire to work together over time.

Let me state one of my redlines up front: I would never be satisfied with a passive follower. This would be inconsistent with the basic philosophy expressed throughout this book and the research used to support the full range model of leadership. Being a passive and dependent follower is completely inadequate and would certainly be inconsistent with what my colleagues and I have described countless times as more effective, if not exemplary, leadership. At its core, leadership and the system(s) it is a part of involve development, or helping people grow to their full potential at which, eventually over time, they can effectively lead themselves.[11] Stated another way, the legacy of any great leader is typically witnessed in the ability of his or her second, third, and fourth in command to assume the responsibilities of the first—and that is, of course, to lead in new directions. In today's world, the turnover of responsibility between the first and second level and so on down the line occurs almost on a daily basis through delegation, empowerment, and shared leadership processes emerging in teams. In fact, it becomes even more difficult to consider what constitutes the first and second level in flattened, networked organizations. Even the mere use of the term *second in command* or *follower* may raise those tiny hairs on the back of some people's necks, perhaps even yours!

When recently asked to draw a metaphor of my conception of a follower, I immediately drew a person in a cape, with a tight blue outfit and boots. Taking into consideration my artistic limitations, it resembled my image of a hero. I consider the best followers my heroes. They have helped me fly much higher in my work as a consequence of their efforts, and that represents one basic aspect of my philosophy of leadership. When I say "basic," I mean fundamental and essential to my way of thinking about developing a full range of leadership potential. To some extent, what better reflection of oneself than someone who is an exemplary follower? Such a person is the true indicator and bottom line of one's success as a leader. And I will admit up front that I have had some dismal failures on these indicators as well. More on that later, and please nudge me if I forget to discuss these points even though revisiting them is often painful.

Regardless of the context, be it at work or otherwise, to develop others to their full potential requires continuous input, and where the input is filtered and poorly edited, the leader is placed in a position of extreme vulnerability. Not knowing what one doesn't know makes any leader extremely vulnerable in the most negative sense. Thus, if this book is to have any real impact on your development, input is required from you for each of us to be optimally effective. It is no different in any other leader-follower interaction, so I hope to practice what we preach within this context while fully realizing that I have to lead you at a distance, with a larger span of control than I have been used to in the past

---

BOX 1.1. Outcomes of Team Development Programs

Salas, Mullen, Rozell, and Driskell (1997) completed a meta-analysis of research testing the effects of team building on team development. (A *meta-analysis* is a study of studies, wherein the researchers aggregate the effects of all studies to produce the average relationship.) Team-building efforts that emphasized role clarification were more likely to enhance performance and team development. Emphasis on building a base on how the team was to transact with itself seemed to be an important contributor to team development. *It's not what you tell them; it's what they understand is required of them, that really counts.*

---

and in an environment that is constantly changing, depending on whom I am working with at any one point in time. Does this sound familiar? Rest assured that I have some idea what your questions might be because many a great hero (follower) before you has taught me a great deal about what it takes to be an exemplary leader. Let me add that it is something I can typically describe, but perhaps like yourself, I still personally have a lot of work to do to achieve what will be described here as exemplary leadership.

Because we are unable to sit down across from each other and talk, we will each have to rely on our inner voices to communicate using some anticipation and, whenever necessary, what we will call "strategic redundancy" to catch our communication disconnects and/or mistakes. Thinking about this issue with communication, I have always tried to keep in mind what coach Red Auerbach of the Boston Celtics once said: "It's not what you tell them, it's what they hear that's important" (see Box 1.1). This is a very important principle for anyone assuming the role of a leader. Yet, when mistakes occur—and they certainly will occur, given the fragile nature of our communication systems—let's try to pick them up along the way, to learn from them, and to resolve them so that we both can benefit from our exchange. This is certainly a "stretch goal" by anyone's estimation, and that would be true in any context, including the current one.

To be specific, one of my challenges and central goals in writing this book was to engage you in the process of leadership development in parallel with writing about the processes of leadership. I guess you could call it "just in time application." Engagement represents an active involvement on your part to learn and apply what is being discussed and to challenge it when it doesn't make any sense to you. If you are willing to consider such a role (notice that I have not assumed you would, nor mandated it), then perhaps we can start building a full range of leadership potential and the vital forces that result. All along the way, when we talk about leadership, we should also be trying to practice it through its description and in our own philosophy and behavior. Frankly, my personal and perhaps self-interested view in writing this book was to make myself a better leader and follower. It has made me reflect on instances I have experienced in my life and the work of many colleagues and, in the end, to reconsider how I've influenced others. My hopes are that it will do some of the same for you as well.

You may have noticed Box 1.1, where I present a brief review of a study conducted by Salas, Mullen, Rozell, and Driskell (1997). Throughout the book, I refer to leadership research that either directly or indirectly supports the points I raise in the text. I have tried to place similar boxed summaries at points in the book where I hoped you would reflect on my message and also find that some research out there corroborates what is being said here. I said "may" because one research study only provides evidence that we *may* or *may not* be correct. Once you implement what I've suggested, however, you will know whether it's correct.

To engage you as an exemplary follower, we need to clarify what we expect from our relationship. That's a very important first step that works well with individuals and with teams.[12] I intend to call this our *compact of understanding,* which will form the basis or framework for the next chapter, as well as a later chapter on building shared leadership in teams. This will become an evolving document of sorts that details what we expect from each other to maximize the full potential of our collective development and performance. (Your inner voice may have just said, "Our development?") Yes, I believe that what I later refer to as "idealized leadership" is a process where *both* leader and follower develop to their full potential, often changing roles, depending on the contingencies and challenges being addressed at any one moment in time.

Contained in the philosophy of African humanistic thinking are two sayings that capture this point directly: "Together each of us accomplishes more successes" and "We are all together on the inside." Let me propose that we set a standard for ourselves to engage in a "knowledge generating partnership" from which both of us should benefit over time. If we continue to generate new and interesting knowledge, then we have a good chance of renewing our relationship over time and of achieving the full potential of our leadership system. We can call this CPI (for *continuous personal, people,* and *process improvement).*

Some Things Worth Repeating

- My goal is to demonstrate that the principles contained in this book can also be demonstrated in parallel in helping each of us develop as we work through this material together.
- At the outset, we use a full range framework to examine leadership as a total system, with particular emphasis on the context in which leader and follower interact and are embedded over time.
- Although often neglected in prior discussions of leadership, the follower will play a prominent role in how we examine and develop the vital forces contained in a *total* leadership system, with our second in command being a reflection of the first.
- Consider the following: "There are two types of organizations: those that see the cliff coming, and those that don't" (Mike Walsch, former CEO of Tenneco). I would like to make you part of the former organization.
- I briefly summarize research findings that are directly and indirectly related to our discussions of a full range view of leadership. I highlight research here because I believe that leadership development is both science and art.
- How do you feel about your new role as an active reader?

2

Developing a Compact of Understanding

---

*There are many objects of great value to man which cannot be attained
by unconnected individuals, but must be attained, if at all,
by association.* (Daniel Webster)

The reason for developing a compact of understanding between us is that
leadership is a process that typically requires two individuals, one who is
disproportionately influencing another, although I realize that people can also
lead themselves out of difficult situations, and this has been called "self-leadership" by some of our colleagues.[13] I do not intend to ignore the process of
self-leadership in this book by any means. To the contrary, sometimes the best
leader and follower is you! Just you. In fact, in a high-performing team,

organization, or community, you need to be both, and the ability to shift back and forth between one and the other is crucial not only to your own success but also to the success in building an effective and sustainable leadership system.

Taking the situation I raised in Chapter 1 regarding the absent leader, if we talk with the second in command, who is used to assuming the first in command's roles and responsibilities, then how much would we be missing by talking with the second about her or his leader's leadership? Very little indeed, I believe, suggesting as I did in Chapter 1 that the follower can be a mirror image of effective leadership. The mirror can also be cracked under circumstances representing less exemplary leadership.

The term *understanding* in the compact assumes that you will not be a passive follower in the process of learning more about leadership. To understand requires both active engagement and self-reflection. If you say to me, "You're the expert; tell me the best ways to lead. Come on, I have 5 minutes here, so let's get on with it," my response will be, "Please read another book, one that does not require your active involvement in the process of your own leadership development." To have someone disengaged in the process of learning about leadership is just not good leadership; it is not even good followership. For *us* to be successful, you must ask questions of *yourself,* and *you* will need to spend time reflecting on those questions throughout this book. In some sense, the process of reflection is the basis I have used in selecting what is included in this book. You will use reflection to determine what you think is worthwhile pulling out from this book for future reference, and perhaps what you think was missing. Paraphrasing R. D. Laing, there are likely to be many instances where I failed to notice what I didn't notice and should have noticed. If you take on the role of an exemplary follower, however, those areas I neglected can be captured in your feedback to me.

My first specific request I ask of you is 300 seconds of your time every day, anytime, anywhere. If you don't have 5 minutes right now in your life to "sacrifice" for some self-reflection, please wait to read this book at some future point in time. Much greater sacrifices than allocating 5 minutes will be asked of you as you fully engage in the process of leadership development in vivo. I therefore strongly recommend that you embrace the leadership development process when you have the time and are ready developmentally. If you say, "Yes, I have 5 minutes," then we can work with each other allocating 5 minutes each day for your own development or, in some cases, the development of others. That gives us 1,800 seconds of quality time per week to dedicate to reflecting on how you perform as a leader. You see, I am trying to be reasonable. I could

---

BOX 2.1. The Power of the Voice: Pygmalion Effects on Performance

---

> Eden (1990) has confirmed numerous times, in both laboratory and field settings, that what we say to ourselves or others can become "self-fulfilling" prophecies. When they are positively set expectations, they can represent positive improvements in performance. Negative effects, however, have also been observed in performance when the expectations were not positive in the form of Golem effects. Let's work on your inner voice and its potential impact on you and others.

---

have asked for the full 2,100 seconds! And those 1,800 seconds will contribute to the 10,080 minutes per week that I would expect you to be in your leadership role. The message: *Leadership comes from who you are, what you do, and how it affects people's ability to achieve their full potential.*

Let me be very specific here because, in the formation of relationships, one major failing that occurs is a lack of clarity in what is initially expected from each person. (This is one conclusion we can take away from the team research I cited in Box 1.1.) I'd like to avoid this trap. Consequently, I am asking that, as you work your way through this book, you write down a question or questions you think are important enough to reflect on and to give deeper consideration to for your own development as a leader or follower. Our compact of understanding is that we agree to allocate, minimally, 5 minutes each day for some deep reflection on these questions. (I am obviously making an assumption here about "our agreement," which we can test out as we work together over time.) These 300 seconds will constitute your personal debriefing time in active engagement with your inner voice.[14] Your inner voice will walk you through what you did, how you did it, how you could have done it, what the consequences were, and how you felt about your choices, decisions, and/or actions (see Box 2.1). Like most things applied to leadership, some people's inner voices can be real task masters or screamers, whereas others are very quiet, if not too reserved. We are going to work on the tone of your inner voice, as well as on the content in terms of your full leadership development. Recall that what you say to yourself can potentially be seen in your own actions over time, as well as be reflected in the behavior of others. Your mirrors.

My fondest hope is that you will find the issues, incidents, or observations you jotted down to be important enough to discuss with someone else for her or his feedback and reflection. My compact with you is that I expect a minimum of one provocative question per chapter and of 5 minutes a day to reflect on each of those questions. The question(s) will form the basis for your engaging in a process that most famous leaders in history engaged in, and those current ones we say are the "real deal" . . . *they really reflected on what's important.* Honestly, would you respect a leader who wouldn't spend 5 minutes contemplating your most significant problem at work?

Thus far, the compact represents a preliminary basis for engaging you and me in some specific actions that lead to your reflecting on issues, examples, and crucial points being raised and then to considering, through reflection, how it has affected your perspective about the leadership process and system you are attempting to build over time. What I am asking you to do represents a very important aspect of your leadership development, summarized in the following statement:

To lead means to step back before moving forward.

By the way, if you need a little more help than your inner voice can provide for you, access the Mindgarden Web site at http://www.mindgarden.com. E-mail your questions, and we can discuss them. The Web site is a learning and developmental site where you can go to discuss, with me and others, issues regarding the full range of leadership development—maybe even "fuller" than I myself have realized in our work. Developmental tools are also available there for your use to help you develop as a leader and as a follower. You see, it is not as lonely as you might have thought at first to be a leader and follower.

As you read on, at certain places in this book I refer you to additional points to include in our compact of understanding. Also, by working together, we should try to anticipate, as often occurs in the process of leadership, something you might not understand by offering current examples, a story, a parable, a historical moment, or . . . and I hesitate to say this, knowing the reaction of many managers . . . research evidence. To make it easy on you, I present research evidence in boxes or at the ends of chapters so that you can read on if you think you already understand the main points being made. You will notice that I have already slipped in some research along the way. I also use these boxes to highlight other messages along the way.

Again, consistent with one aspect of what we will now call a "full range" model of leadership, we attempt throughout this book, not to address the "average" needs of readers, but rather the individual needs, with the goal of enhancing each individual's full potential. So, for some readers, the research evidence will provide further reassurance and comfort concerning what I am suggesting for you to consider in your own leadership development makes sense. For others, it may be unnecessary, and I would simply say, read on. Ultimately, my goal is to provide information that "grows with the learner," and the Web site is one form of technology that will be used to accomplish this core objective. The other form is the "software" you carry around in your head. I would like to think that we can make it self-adaptive, with updates to address new problems and opportunities confronting you over time and different circumstances.

My internal voice also indicates that research evidence reassures me that what I am suggesting as a personal intervention has some support that your efforts will ultimately be productive. So, as a follower, bear in mind my needs as well. My need for research support as a basis for helping you achieve your full potential is, in my mind, similar to any situation where a treatment is being recommended. In leadership development, the treatment is a suggestion to change some aspect of the way you think or your perspective and some aspect of what you do as a leader, a follower, or both. We can also suggest a need to change the context. In another context where treatments are frequently considered, could you imagine an official from the U.S. Food and Drug Administration saying, "Why don't you try this particular drug? It's blue and a very nice color. Our chemists have made its taste very enjoyable, and I *think* it will have the impact you desire"? Okay, raise your hand if you would take the drug. What, no hands? Having seen no hands raised, I'd like, with your permission, to refer from time to time to the broad research literature that forms the basis for many recommendations contained in this book. So, if the "leadership pill" is blue and tastes good, it actually has some proof that it works!

I would also like to add that I have consciously selected research that supports the recommendations made in this book. I intentionally make "a strong inference here" because I believe that what I'm suggesting will work for you and provide what I consider supportive evidence for my recommendations.

BOX 2.2. Leadership at the Base of Leadership Effectiveness

> The bulk of research on establishing positive transactions and exchanges between leaders and followers indicates that followers who work with leaders who set clearly defined expectations and agreed-on levels of performance are more likely to achieve these goals than are followers who work with leaders who do not clearly define goals and expectations. Positive transactions in the form of contingent reward leadership positively relates to follower satisfaction and performance (see, e.g., Podsakoff, Todor, Grover, & Huber, 1984). Effective transactional leadership can create the "conditions" on which deeper levels of trust are formed.

Let's revisit what I am asking of you. (This is my way of demonstrating strategic redundancy!) First, I need your active engagement in the process of developing leadership potential. Second, to gain that active involvement, we are building a compact of understanding that delineates a framework and agenda for establishing our mutual expectations. And at least for the moment, these expectations are quite simple: Ask a question and step back and reflect on it for *no more than 5 minutes per day.* That's it! I said for the moment these expectations were rather straightforward; however, as any relationship evolves and develops, one's expectations may become more complex, yet still doable, if they are in line with one's developmental trajectory and potential. If they are impossible or too simple, they will not be very good expectations.

A significant aspect of developing leadership potential is knowing the expectations one should have of others and stretching them when an individual or group of individuals is prepared to be stretched (see Box 2.2). Stated another way, development of your full potential as a leader has some building blocks, including first and foremost an articulation of the expectations you have of yourself and of others you are attempting to influence over time. Through your expectations and your collective achievements, identification and trust are built.[15] This is a connection often missed by newcomers to leadership development, who are beginning to explore and learn the leadership development process, an issue we take up in much more detail throughout this book because, without trust, you can never achieve the full potential of your leadership or the vital force. Yes, I meant to say "never."

In this chapter, we have discussed the importance of developing a set of mutual expectations, with a goal of clarifying our understanding of what underlies those expectations and their impact on relationships over time. If you extend this process with your own followers, peers, or supervisor, the development of expectations clarifies what you seek from each other. As a leader in this process, it also tells you something about the developmental level of the people who work with you over time. Some expect a lot of direction and support and clarify those levels for you through their expectations, suggesting a less mature level of development. Others want more discretion and will require or expect more self-direction, indicating a more mature level of development or that their expectations exceed their abilities. It is perhaps obvious but worth restating that the second in command, third, forth, and so on are quite varied in their needs, expectations, and capabilities, which also change for each group over time. This makes the establishment of expectations both informative and instructive for relationship-building purposes—your relationship with others.

Investing in the development of effective transactions with others will pay off to a great extent later in the relationship-building process, as we move from simple transactions based on agreements and contracts to trust being the internal basis for our expectations of each other. It is important to understand that if you consistently honor your expectations with others, you build the conditions for trust, and trust is the credit in the bank that leaders acquire and use in situations where they don't have the time to clarify the rationale for their choices.[16] Simply put, they expect and hope that they have the trust to do what is required. You must build identification with your main purposes and trust in every calm moment because when a crisis occurs, you have to hope that enough time is available to reflect before acting. Frequently, however, there isn't enough time, and everyone, including yourself, has to *trust* that you are heading in the right direction. Why would anyone do so? Because she or he identifies with you as a leader, and identification breeds trust, and trust gets people to work much harder than compliance.

To summarize, for many years my colleagues and I have argued that transactional leadership was the basis for developing transformational leadership.[17,18,19] This, in part, explains the high correlation between the transformational and transactional leadership ratings often found when people report their results using the Multifactor Leadership Questionnaire (MLQ) (see Box 2.3).[20] The relationship between these two leadership orientations is discussed through-

---

BOX 2.3. Exchange Tactics and Transformational Leadership

Tepper (1993) had followers of managers in a financial institution rate the leadership of their managers. Those leaders who were seen as more transactional tended to employ exchange and pressure tactics to influence followers, whereas those leaders who were rated as more transformational frequently employed legitimating tactics that resulted in higher levels of follower identification and internalization of values.

---

out this book. Here, we introduce the concepts to underscore that both are important to achieving the maximum potential along the full range of leadership development. Without the transactional base, expectations are often unclear, direction is ill-defined, and the goals you are working toward are too ambiguous. It is certainly possible, however, to get people inspired in this context, but it is difficult to align them around what their focus should be and who does what when. Transactions clearly in place form the base for more mature interactions between leaders over time.

In terms of reflection, consider your most successful attempt at building people's identification with what you were striving to accomplish at some point in your life, going back as far as you can recall. What was the first thing you did? What did you do next? And what made this particular situation stand out in your mind?

Some Things Worth Repeating

- A compact provides the basis for building a clear sense of what each of us wants to derive from our relationship.
- The compact is a living document that must be revisited periodically to determine whether it is still relevant.
- Transactions are the basis for building trust and identification and for launching a sustainable full range leadership system.
- There is no stronger force toward compliance than identification (see Box 2.4).

BOX 2.4. Taking More Responsibility—Maybe Call It Empowerment

---

Empowerment may be viewed as a psychological mind-set, according to
Conger and Kanungo (1988). Relevant to anyone asking you to take responsibility for your own development, you will feel more empowered to the
extent that you see meaning in what the person is suggesting and have a clear
idea of the direction and ability to achieve what has been asked of you. People
we will call transformational leaders attempt to make the challenges meaningful for you, ones you feel capable of handling and encouraged to persist
at until you have been successful.

3

Many Sides and Levels to Leadership Processes

Leaders are dealers in hope. (Napoléon Bonaparte)

The most useful thing I learned was to be humble and listen.
(Larry Bossidy, CEO of Allied Signal)

Effective leadership is not limited to the heads of organizations or to one best way of leading.[21] Recall that we are talking about a process of influence and building a relationship that can include anyone, at any level, and in any organization. I recently came across an elementary school teacher who exemplifies many aspects of what on anyone's scale would be considered exemplary leadership and followership. I discuss her style of leadership in some detail because, beyond parents, the teacher is the second most important leader in any society.

Stacey (a fictitious name) is an elementary school teacher who taught second graders. Her capabilities as a teacher were well known not only to her colleagues, students, and the parents in her district but also to the state examiners, who evaluated her for the "best teacher award." She was also known to the federal examiners, who evaluated her as one of the runners-up for the "best teacher award" in the United States. A little more about Stacey being a runner-up for this prestigious award later.

On the last day of school this year, a stream of fifth graders who were leaving the elementary school to go on to the middle school were stopping by to wish Stacey a great summer. Many students had been in Stacey's class several years earlier, and now that they were leaving for the middle school, they just wanted to wish her well. It was interesting to observe the young boys coming up to her and hugging her without reservation in front of other students. If you have a 10- or 11-year-old boy at home or know one even from a distance, I think you can understand the significance of this interaction, gender typing notwithstanding.

What makes Stacey so different from other teachers? One aspect is that she continues to search, with her students, for what might be an avenue to help them achieve their full potential on both an individual and a collective level. When one talks with her, one gets the feeling there is a development plan in her head for each student, one that can ignite the fire inside each student to learn to his or her potential. (Having asked many managers around the world whether they have such plans for each of their followers, I can tell you this is a rare situation indeed. Although in a recent interview with Steven Kerr, Vice President for Corporate Leadership Development at GE, Kerr indicated that Jack Welch keeps track of nearly 1,000 managers at all levels of GE in terms of how they are progressing in their careers, often asking very specific questions about one particular individual's progress and status.[22]) Stacey's plan includes each student as an active participant in his or her own development. It is clearly not seen as a one-way street or as being just Stacey's responsibility to develop students. (You may begin to see some parallels to our emphasis in developing a compact of understanding.)

It is evident from her behavior that Stacey respects her students, values their opinions, seeks out their views on tough issues, and follows up when she is unsure how a student feels or when students appear not to understand something they should have learned the first, second, third, or fourth time. She truly believes in her students and inspires them to believe in themselves. In a final letter sent home at the end of the year, she closed the letter by saying, "Please remember the times I asked you to repeat, 'I am the best, therefore I will do my best' . . . I believe you are the best, and I hope you do, too!" Quite a Pygmalion effect in vivo.

Stacey is both demanding and fair, and often she structures her class so that more controls for behavior reside in the children and what eventually becomes their own control system. By the way, I find this to be a very common characteristic among exemplary teachers who are highly respected by students. One example is her infamous jar of beads. On the left-hand side of her desk sits a jar filled with beads. On the right-hand side sits an empty jar. Generally, by the end of the day, the right-hand jar has gained some advantage, and on a really difficult day, it's brimming with beads.

At the beginning of each year, Stacey works to clarify her expectations of students, as they do of each other and of her. The jar is there to remind everyone when expectations were or were not met. A full jar on the right is one clear indicator of missed expectations, and a near empty one is something to celebrate because the expectations that were set were met and typically benefited everyone in class. She provides positive recognition (see Box 3.1) for achieving a very skimpy right-hand jar of beads. Stacey's approach on the surface appears to be a simple behavioral reinforcement strategy that one might observe in some other classroom or in a work setting where certain rules for safety are set and the organization keeps track of how many days the rules have been violated. It also is similar to any sports team, which must work within the expectations and rules set for the members' behavior. Indeed, I have recommended to several companies that if they really want to use the sports analogy for building teams, which many do, then they should place a referee in the hallway, calling violations. For example, let's say that you had a really bad meeting with someone; why not call in a referee to throw a flag for "roughing the leader"? Why do we think we can build teams anymore effectively than sports organizations do, usually without the aid of experienced coaches, referees, and rules—very clear rules? Okay, I'm deviating, but it's an irony I wanted to share with you early on in this book.

And now, back to Stacey. Some core lessons for building a leadership system underlie her constructive approach to dealing with aberrant or "unexpected" behavior in class. Stacey's focus goes beyond simple reinforcement toward building internal control and accountability for one's actions, as well as learning and support through feedback. We can identify three clear components of the leadership system that are external to Stacey. On the *inputs* side are the students and Stacey working on the establishment of the rules and expectations. In terms of *process* are the behaviors exhibited by the class and Stacey and how they relate to the rules. On the *outcomes* side are the consequences associated

---

BOX 3.1. Recognition From Employees

In an article "The Magnificent Seven" (Butler, 1997), which refers to the top seven CEOs in the United States, Mary Kay Asch commented on the importance of recognition: "What is it that people say—that the first thing a baby does when it comes into the world is cry for attention and recognition? I believe this is true. That is how I've worked for thirty-one years—give attention and recognition where needed."

---

with behavior. A feedback mechanism is also very clear in terms of the jar of beads, a simple system that appears to work quite well over time in helping develop students to their full potential.

Over time, we can observe in Stacey's class students giving each other feedback to avoid a situation where another bead "bites the dust." Through this and many other clever systems, Stacey builds a structure or process for her class that is considerate of their needs yet provides a framework concerning what is and is not considered appropriate behavior. As noted above, we are again back to setting clear expectations. I clarify and honor my expectations, and therefore I can eventually build trust with you. It's a very fair system, with clear redlines established for behavior. The expectations set are clear, mutually agreed-to over time, and most important become owned by the entire class, including Stacey. This is evident when you see the class work together on a really good bead day, to beat the all-time "low" in terms of the number of beads transferred to the right!

Interestingly, a recent large-scale analysis of the last 30 years of research on team building noted in Box 1.1 would support Stacey's approach. Eduardo Salas and his colleagues found that the most important effect in the early development of teams was learning how to structure roles and expectations. This was seen as the foundation for building effective teams and could apply to a classroom, battlefield, or any workplace. One might query the difference among the three. Okay, I won't deviate again. We must set a quota on deviations lest we run out of book. Hearing no objections, I will stay on track for the moment, but I will return to my deviations shortly. As a Gemini, I almost have no choice in the matter.

Until the early 1980s, what was described above may have been the end of the story for many of us on what constitutes effective leadership. The leader or group creates a structure in which expectations are then clarified. The needs of the group are considered and folded into those expectations, and from there it's all about implementation, consistency, feedback, and in some cases rewards or recognition for achieving expectations. But let's continue the story beyond what has traditionally been labeled "transactional leadership."[23]

Stacey has actually demonstrated much more in her leadership style and perspective than a simple transaction based on setting clear expectations. Her "deep" perspective or frame of reference on how to treat students is not simply to get students to meet "her" expectations. The leadership system she is creating is there as a basis for building respect and commitment with each other, for taking the initiative to do the right thing, and ultimately to offer the second in command an increased share of responsibility for achieving the group's objectives. Students learn to be active, responsible followers and leaders. Very early in the school year, the necessity to point out missed expectations has fallen into the hands of the second in command, or students. They are in command of monitoring expectations they have agreed to for the class. Control goes where it belongs and will do the most good—on the inside, looking out.

One question you might have is, "Are we talking about leadership here, followership, peer influence, or something else?" For the moment, let's just say we are talking about all three and that each is a component of the leadership system taking shape in the classroom. This leadership system can parallel the formation processes that goes on each time a group gets together and decides, either consciously or not, to form a team by using as a foundation for team development each other's expectations. Let me add here that if we are talking about developing a leadership system, then by definition we must discuss both leading and following, especially when it applies to the same person.

Stacey is highly respected by her colleagues and trusted by her students. People who know her often describe her in "idealized" terms. She demonstrates a true passion for learning and a commitment to her students achieving their full potential. As I indicated at the outset of this story, Stacey had won the best teacher award in her school district and was in the running for the national award. During the evaluation process, however, she suddenly pulled herself out of competition. During her interview with the board of examiners, she was asked how she planned to spend the 50% of her time teaching her other colleagues around the country her methods of instruction. Up to that point, Stacey was unaware she would have to travel so often during the school year, which was a newly established requirement for the award. On hearing this, she politely finished the interview, excused herself, and told the head examiner on her way out that she was removing herself from the competition.

There was no way Stacey would begin the school year with a new class of students, telling them that they should expect her to be around only 50% of the time because of her travel schedule. This was a tremendous sacrifice for her. Yet, she did not appear to have a moment's hesitation on making the "right" decision, nor apparently any regrets. If not for the principal of her school and a close friend who was involved in the selection of the best teacher award recipient, no one would have known about her decision to excuse herself from the competition. Her perspective on which decisions she should make appears to come from an internal set of standards, which represent a compass for taking what she considers the right course[24] (see Box 3.2). Some say in leadership that the very best leaders know the difference between choosing something that is "right" versus "less right." You may have heard the expression "the leader's moral compass." This expression is exemplified in Stacey's choice. She knew what she needed to do *on brief reflection,* and the criterion for that decision was not a set of external standards or expectations, like the one described above for her class. It was a much higher set of standards that makes a significant difference in both a leader and follower's accomplishments over time. It is their mutual or core beliefs, which are often born out of expectations set and reinforced through numerous interactions, that has led them to conclude, "Now this is the right course of action to take."

Although Stacey didn't win the national award for teaching, later in the year she was nominated for and won the opportunity to carry the Olympic torch for the 1996 summer Olympic games in Atlanta, Georgia. Consistent with her style, she decided that this privilege should not be given to just one individual. She started a contest in school: Any student who read a certain number of books would be eligible to sign the sneakers she would use to run with the torch. The sneakers would be put in the school's trophy display cabinet to celebrate how they all had carried the Olympic torch a little closer to Atlanta. By the time Stacey ran with the torch, very little white space was left on her sneakers for additional signatures.

At the end of each year, Stacey approaches several parents and asks whether it would be okay for their children to meet with her periodically over the summer. Her objective is to continue with some of the work she had begun with those students during the school year, to help them attain their next level of development. These are students who are dealing with a very broad range of issues, from being able to organize themselves in their work, to difficulties with concentrating, reading, and/or comprehension. It is not a planned summer program, nor do

---

BOX 3.2. High Moral Compasses and Transformational Leadership

---

Lucius and Kuhnert (1997) examined the moral development levels of 32 cadets at a large military institute, using Jerome Kegan's interview procedure (Lahey, Souvaine, Kegan, Goodman, & Felix, 1991). This procedure is based on constructive-developmental theory, which indicates that as people mature, they go from making decisions based on external standards (e.g., Will I be punished?) to higher internal standards (e.g., How do my actions affect the welfare of people I work with here?). Lucius and Kuhnert reported that those cadets rated higher on transformational leadership by their peers were also evaluated as having higher perspective-taking capacity and/or moral development as measured by interviews and James Rest's Defining Issues Test (Rest, 1986).

---

all parents know about this offer. Those who do, however, know that Stacey is simply trying to continue her work with children to help them achieve their full potential and that, for her, the end of the school year is merely an arbitrary and temporary point of closure in this process. Stacey spends her summer continuing her work with children in a very individualized way. If students or their parents do not wish to meet with her, then that's as far as the offer goes.

My inner voice asks, "What parent in his or her right mind would turn down such an offer?" Well, some parents do because they themselves are not ready to appreciate her extra effort, do not see the need for it, and may be unwilling to sacrifice "their time." In some cases, the students choose not to meet with her. The varied reactions of either parents or students are not unlike what one typically observes in any leadership context.[25] Some parents are deeply indebted to her for offering this option and appreciate her loyalty to their children. Some do not see it positively at all; they may even see it as a negative regarding her ability to accomplish in the year "what she should have accomplished." This very straightforward gesture on Stacey's part and the range of reactions it receives is a very important lesson about leadership that you may want to allocate 5 minutes to reflect on today. The true and most accurate interpretation of leadership always rests in the "eye of the beholder." What constitutes accuracy must be based on each individual's perception of leadership, and using the term *leadership* suggests that perceptions are based on what the leader does and how the follower interprets the leader's actions or, in some cases, inaction within a particular context over time.[26]

One last point about Stacey's behavior relates to her interactions with peers. Typically, she meets with teachers who will be working with students from her class during the next academic year; she briefs them on the individualized plans she has developed, activities that worked well with each child, options to avoid, and in special cases detailed plans regarding where Stacey and the student left off in their work together. It is not her way simply to throw students "over the wall" to the next class, captured in the phrase, HEY, IT'S NOT MY DEPART-MENT! I can't say that this is a typical behavior I have observed in many companies around the world, but one that is clearly necessary for building a learning-centered culture based on collaboration.

I hope, by not using a typical corporate example, I can convey to your inner perspective and voice that "leadership can occur in all the right places" (see Box 3.3)! Restating an earlier comment, the three most important leadership roles in any community are, in order of importance, parent as leader, teacher as leader, and manager or supervisor as leader. Like many other leaders I will discuss with you, and their followers, Stacey exhibits four essential ingredients to exemplary leadership, whether it occurs with individuals, groups, or at the level of an organization's culture. Those four components are what my colleagues and I refer to as the four I's of transformational leadership: *idealized influence, inspirational motivation, intellectual stimulation,* and *individualized consideration.*[27]

Stacey is *idealized* in her efforts to build trust, *inspiring* in the degree to which she is willing to sacrifice her own time for the good of others, *stimulating* in the way she challenges students to be actively engaged in creating expectations and the creative use of beads, and *individualized* in her constant attention to what each student most needs and desires to develop to his or her full potential.

I wonder whether you have thought of a parent in the role of leader. Have you thought of the family as a high-performing team? I suspect that we all have thought about children as followers, willing or otherwise, and sometimes even exemplary. I think, too often, that many parents create a dependent followership until around age 13. Then a battle occurs for who will set expectations, and the conflict that ensues is not always adaptive[28] (see Box 3.4). This statement presupposes that conflict can be very productive, so productive that it is actually developmental. Although more complicated than the average team working on NASA'S space shuttles, the transference of authority and accountability in families is very much the same challenge that one observes in high-performing

---

BOX 3.3. Transformational Leadership and School Performance

Silins (1992) examined the relationship between transformational and transactional leadership and its effects on schools, teachers, students, and programs in a sample of 256 elementary schools in British Columbia undergoing reform. Results indicated that transformational leadership had a more significant and positive relationship with school effects than transactional leadership, supporting the "full range" model of leadership. Transformational leadership in school systems has been shown also to have a positive impact on levels of trust, commitment, citizenship behavior, and satisfaction levels of teachers (Koh, 1990). Most significant about Koh's study was that transformational leadership augmented transactional leadership in predicting levels of commitment, trust, and satisfaction, which, in turn, predicted hard measures of school performance in a large sample study of Singaporean principals. More recent results reported by Philbin (1997) in secondary schools showed a strong and positive relationship between the transformational leadership of the principal and how effective he or she was perceived to be, satisfaction with his or her leadership, and the willingness among teachers to put in extra effort. Transformational leadership was shown to have a greater impact among more capable students in terms of their overall scholastic performance, something we can also see in Stacey's work with students.

---

teams. If the challenge is ignored, the team and the child both suffer in their mutual potential and development.

I should note here that I do think conflict represents the highest order of human interaction. But in this instance, it is a battle over "who" versus "what." In *A World Waiting to Be Born,* Peck writes, "[C]onflict is only uncivil when it is either hidden or unnecessarily blown out of proportion."[29] Who are you to tell me what to do versus what are we are trying to discuss and work out here? Let me state this point again because most people think I am a little crazy when I say it for the first time. (Okay, I may be underestimating how much they think I am crazy.) *Adaptive conflict represents the highest order of human interaction and the essential basis on which truly profound insights are generated and deployed.* Now, don't run out to cancel those conflict management programs just yet, before you have reflected on this point and heard more about it in subsequent chapters. Elliott Lehman, former cochairman and founder of FelPro, Inc., one of America's most well respected companies, approaches this issue in the

---

BOX 3.4. Conflict as the Basis for Profound Transformation

Ron Heifetz, in his 1994 book *Leadership Without Any Easy Answers,* views the creation of adaptive conflict or challenge as being central to the leadership process. He advocates creating the dilemma for leaders and followers and keeping the level of distress at a tolerable level to clarify the issues and to move toward a new level of understanding and, ultimately, resolutions. Heifetz suggests that, without contradictory impressions, there appears to be little to awake reflection. The adaptive part of the challenge is that we learn from conflict if handled properly, which allows us to move to higher levels of understanding and perspective.

---

following manner with his employees: "There is only one silly question, the one you don't ask. There is only one silly comment, the one you don't make." Questions and comments will inevitably create conflict in organizations with leaders and followers who truly want to have continuous learning and improvement. And not asking the "wrong" question can be disastrous for an organization.

Going back to the most important leaders in our society—and followers, I suspect—I discuss parallels between parenting and leadership in the next chapter (see also Box 3.5). For the moment, it is sufficient simply to say just consider the type of person who enters a leadership training workshop, and you will understand quite well how parents serve as good and bad leaders. Take the highly self-assured, secure individual who respects others and is willing to listen to what others have to say. "Born to be considerate?" or, developed to a state of high self-confidence? How about the more anxious one, who is defensive and unwilling to bend to anyone else's views. "Born to be obnoxious"? A hard truth is that some people who come to these workshops are damaged by a parent or parents or their absence and require a great deal of recovery before effective leadership development can actually begin. Other attendees have already had exemplary leadership training from a parent or parents, and often I personally think, as a trainer, that I am simply reaffirming and extending what they already know and do in their roles as leaders or followers. To put a label on a "methodology in use," they have already been developed from the "inside out," and my role is to refine the style and enhance their perspective even further, often through adaptive challenges and conflict. This goes along with General Colin Powell's comments about leaders having the gut instinct that we end up honing

---

BOX 3.5. How Well "Attached" Are Your Leaders?
Attachment Level and Leadership Development

Bowlby (1969, 1973) posits that humans have a survival need to be attached to caregivers who can provide security. Attachment is a lifelong need characterized by individual differences in the level of security that people require in their relationships with significant others. Micha Popper recently reported that "securely attached" leaders were also rated by their followers as more transformational. Such securely attached leaders have the ability to attend to another person's needs because they are not so consumed by their own. Those people classified as "insecure-avoidant" were not evaluated as transformational. Following along the same line of research, others have also reported that individuals' implicit models of ideal leaders and followers were affected by their level of attachment. What you see as ideal is based, in part, on your own foundation and/or development (Berson & Yammarino, 1997; Popper, Mayseless, & Castelnovo, 1998).

---

and shaping through training. At the other end of development, the foundation work on the person's perspective of how to relate to others must first be developed. Stylistic considerations come later, in the "life" training program.

Something I find helpful in my own work on leadership development that may be of some help to you is a metaphor I call the "life stream." When I meet a group of people for the first time in a leadership development workshop, I try to visualize a life stream for each person. For some, the stream is very narrow, straight, and perhaps not so deep. For others, it is quite turbulent, dramatic, and circuitous. For the remaining members, the streams have their waterfalls, but for the most part they are not so unique nor all that dramatic. By using this metaphor, I realize that I am just a point along their life streams, charged with building on the *in vivo* leadership training they've already received from a parent, coach, teacher, former manager, and/or friend (see Box 3.6). Now, we are engaging in *in vitro* training, and I must build on what they've developed thus far to help them understand the process of developing themselves and others to their full potential. In the best instances, we can add value to the established base. In the worst, we may not have a clue of how much anxiety or damage we caused in their development.

You may now want to take a step back and look at your own life stream. How fast has it brought you to this point in time, and how far downstream can

---

BOX 3.6. Early Antecedents to Leadership Development

Gibbons (1986) compared the life history profiles of senior managers at a Fortune 100 high-technology company on the basis of the following leadership ratings breakdown: high high transformational and transactional; high transformational; high transactional; and high laissez-faire leadership. These leaders also completed the Personal Orientation Inventory, which measures a person's degree of self-actualization. Gibbons found that transformational leaders tended to be more self-actualized but not significantly so. The high high leader group had significantly higher scores on Self-Regard and Capacity for Intimate Contact than all other groups. As children, transformational leaders were expected to be the best and to do the best, with moderately high levels of responsibility given to them by parents. These individuals were stretched but in a balanced way. The individuals learned how to deal with conflict, stress, and disappointment. The best leaders had a pattern of many prior leadership experiences that they reflected on over time to improve themselves. They had a very strong desire to engage in development work, and it was so much a part of them that it was seen as automatic. Role models, workshops, and training were all incorporated into improving the personal development of these leaders. They had a very strong tendency toward self-reflective learning and to integrate what they had learned to improve themselves. "Born versus made?"

---

you see? What have you learned that was fundamental to developing your perspective about how you treat others, including yourself, and your life in general? I must admit that, in some workshops, after interacting with a group of people for some time, I keep hearing those famous words ringing in my ear: "Houston, we have a problem here." The problem, from the ill-fated Apollo 13 mission, is us.

Exemplary leadership is a process whereby we continuously develop people to their full potential. To do so, we must be very conscious of the past, but not so tightly bound to it that we can't move in new directions with equally new challenges. We must know where we want to go, which may take time and some data collection. Knowing the depth of the stream, its speed, and points where it might flood over if given too much pressure are crucial issues for developing all people, or as Ron Heifetz alluded in Box 3.4, creating adaptive versus maladaptive challenges/conflict. And perhaps most crucial is for you to know what you intend to leave behind. I have no doubt that Stacey would understand

---

BOX 3.7. The Power of Observation for Leadership Development

We need to train others to observe how they observe themselves and others. We learn to observe by distinguishing certain information from its background. We make it distinctive, and often create stories to capture and summarize our observations. Learning is the act of learning new distinctions that we otherwise wouldn't notice.

"Water is fluid, soft and yielding, but water will wear away rock, which is rigid and cannot yield. As a rule, whatever is fluid, soft, and yielding will overcome whatever is rigid and hard . . . what is soft and strong." (Lae-tzu, cited in Matusek, 1997, p. 127)

---

this metaphor in her work with students. They come back to thank her because the intervention she made in each of their life streams caused them to change course, to deepen their positions, to address the waterfalls, and to do so with the intent of building perspective about who they are and what they can accomplish. Knowing oneself at each stage along the life stream is the absolute basis for knowing others (see Box 3.7). "You develop yourself in order to develop others"; therefore, you must jump into your own stream before attempting to change others. Actually, this statement is based on Confucius' view on leadership development.

Unfortunately, not all "great leaders" had the wisdom or the belief system to either know or understand what they were leaving behind. They didn't consider how they were affecting the life streams of individuals and, in some cases, entire societies. So, when someone asks you whether Hitler, Mussolini, Pol Pot, or Stalin were great leaders, you might simply answer with a resounding NO! They were NOT great leaders. Why? The legacy they left behind was much worse then the conditions in which they started their leadership journeys. Among many things, their followers were no closer to achieving their full potential than they were before those individuals came into power. (Here I am referring to the followers who were still alive!) In fact, they were often much farther away, having been completely suppressed by these leaders in terms of personal development. Using the criterion of what they left behind, if you want to consider them leaders, then do me a favor and insert the adjective *lousy* up front, and we may be near agreement. Okay, I am sure some neo-Nazis and fascists would disagree with me on this point. As my 14-year-old daughter often says to me when she wants to end our conversation . . . FINE! I am not writing this book necessarily to agree or disagree with others, but if one is going to write a book on leadership, then at times one needs to take a strong stand. We are at one of those points in time.

Ralph Waldo Emerson once wrote, "An institution is the lengthened shadow of one man [or woman]." (I will keep adding *woman* to somewhat "outdated" quotes.) It is the criterion I always keep in mind when judging the full leadership potential of people, and with leaders like Stacey the conclusion on her leadership legacy is very clear to me. Her shadow will be long and deep and reflected positively in the lives of many children who will become more effective adults over time as a consequence of her efforts. Some trainers will feel and sense her shadow if, years from now, they ask participants who had her as a teacher to identify leaders in their lives who had a profound impact on their development. No doubt, her shadow will emerge on the flip charts and through the perspectives demonstrated by those people as they work to influence others.

The emphasis on building one's shadow is strong at Motorola. Leaders at Motorola are asked to articulate what they want their legacies to be over time. The whole idea is to present what one wants to leave behind in the future so that one can begin to develop it now.[30]

When I started this chapter, I thought I would also have time to talk about Sam. It is easy to spend a lot of time talking about quality people like Stacey. At the risk of exceeding the senior executive's attention span of "you have 5 minutes to make your point," permit me to say a few words about Sam. I met Sam, a technology supervisor in the Canadian Correctional Services, back in the early 1980s, when I first went out to train "transformational leadership." At that time, books on the topic by Tichy and Devanna,[31] Bass,[32] and Bennis and Nanus[33] had appeared in the literature. To a large extent, these books talked about transformational leadership among senior executives in a very broad range of organizations. I don't think any included prisons. In this period, and in meeting people like Sam, I discovered that transformational leadership was much more pervasive than my colleagues had noted in their excellent books. I found it occurring in many strange places, such as Sam's shop and in the correctional services root cellar.

Sam's unit in the correctional services had one of the lowest recidivism rates in the country. Let me say just a few words about Sam, and then I'll add more about him later in this book.

Sam worked with inmates in a metal-working shop, a shop filled with very sharp devices. He was a very short man, in his late 50s or early 60s. I recall walking into his shop for the first time and seeing a large group of men standing around a machine. I could hear someone in the middle of the group talking but could not see who it was at first. Sam was in the middle of the circle and was instructing the group how to operate a particular machine. They all had tools in their hands . . . really sharp ones! With his back to the group, he described the process of working on the machine. Because this was a maximum security prison, the inmates were there for often very brutal crimes. I was nervous, and they had their backs to me!

While Sam was talking, I noticed on the wall four pieces of metal. One was a raw piece of metal. The second was severely scratched and bent. The third looked a little better. The last one had a high-gloss finish and was perfectly cut to specs. After the group left the room, I had some time to talk with Sam alone. I asked him about the "metal art" on the wall. He explained that he needed a way to convey to his "students" what they could do in Months 1, 2, 3, and 4 if they were willing to work with him and trust his directives. He laughed and then said, "A limited vision of sorts." Because many of his students were illiterate, Sam needed some visual indicator of future potential and progress that could be achieved by his followers. A vision statement pasted on the wall wouldn't have worked. This is one of many examples Sam used to frame what he was trying to accomplish with people. He treated his followers with respect and dignity, and they, in turn, did the same with him. Of course, the ones who didn't were handled by the group, so to speak. Sam had the best protection in the correctional facility: He had the full commitment and trust of his closest "employees"—big, strong employees.

I can say with some degree of confidence that neither Sam nor Stacey would describe themselves as leaders; in fact, Sam said this to me at one point in our conversation. It suggests the problems we have with the term *leadership* (see Box 3.8) because, without a doubt, both were not only leaders but also exemplary in their leadership styles and the impact they had on their followers over time. They were the best of leaders in the sense that they really knew who they were and what their real work was all about. They had built a set of internal standards and perspectives that helped guide them through their work with others. What may have started at some point in their life streams as a set of external expectations had clearly become internal standards and principles that guided their actions and behaviors.

In *Lightening Bolt,* Storm (yes, I know what you're thinking) says that "the greatest battle in life is subtle. The reality of self ignorance is obvious to be learned, but the person who is ignorant cannot see the truth about the self. The ignorant seek to conform."[34]

BOX 3.8. Training Transformational Leadership

Crookall (1989) conducted a training impact study of prison shop supervisors, comparing the impact of transformational leadership training to situational leadership training on inmate performance. Three groups of supervisors were involved: Group 1 received situational leadership training; Group 2 received transformational leadership training; and Group 3 received no training. Measures were taken on work group productivity and inmates' personal growth for a 3-month period before the onset of training and after the close of the training intervention. Both trained groups improved on an order of 10% to 50%, depending on the measures. Although both training programs had a positive impact on performance and personal growth, the transformational training had a more significant effect on personal growth and development, whereas situational leadership training had greater effects on productivity levels. Transformational leadership significantly improved inmates' respect for their managers, potential skills, and good citizenship behavior as rated by case managers in the correctional services.

Barling, Weber, and Kelloway (1996) examined the impact of transformational leadership training in a "true" field experiment. The study was conducted with bank branch managers who received individual coaching and training in transformational leadership that was extended over time with booster sessions. Barling et al. reported significant differences in ratings of intellectual stimulation in the experimental versus the comparison group. Significant effects were also shown with the performance of bank branches comparing these two groups.

Let's leave this chapter with a question for you to consider. Look back over the last several months and ask yourself, *What have I done in my transactions with others to build trust? Identification? Commitment?*

Can you turn your back and be assured that people will continue to work with you, and for you, so to speak?

Some Things Worth Repeating

- Get to know your own life stream and those of others to help focus you on the individual needs of others.
- Think about your leadership legacy now so that it can fruitfully unfold during the course of your life span. It's never too early.
- Transformational leaders can be found at all organizational levels and in all cultures.

4

A "Full Range" View
of Leadership Development
and Potential

*To be an effective leader, "You must become yourself. To know how other
people behave takes intelligence, but to know myself takes
wisdom."* (Lorraine Matusek)

In the title of this chapter, I refer to developing a "full range" of leadership
potential. One question that may immediately arise is whether I am saying
"a" full range or "the" full range. I will say "a" full range, suggesting that other
aspects of leadership yet to be discovered will enhance the range of leadership
processes in organizations. Nevertheless, I have set out to challenge you and my
colleagues to think about a broader or "fuller" range than is often associated with
leadership measurement and development. To simplify matters, our focus is on
three broad classifications of leadership processes: *transformational, transactional,* and *nontransactional leadership.*

BOX 4.1. Feedback Gaps and Leadership Development

Atwater and Yammarino (1997) addressed a crucial area in leadership development; it concerns the growing popularity of using upward and 360-degree feedback for leadership development. The controversy stems from the fact that the agreement between self and other ratings is often rather low. The gap between self and other ratings has implications for effective leadership specifically. Atwater and Yammarino (1992) demonstrated that self-other agreement was a predictor of the leadership performance relationship. Research evidence indicates that "over-" and "underestimators" of their own leadership styles vary in terms of how effective supervisors rate their leadership potential and performance. Recently, Atwater, Ostroff, Yammarino, and Fleenor (in press) demonstrated that simultaneous consideration of self ratings, other ratings, and their gap was important to predicting leadership effectiveness.

Some global distinguishing characteristics of *transformational leadership* are worth stating up front. Transformational leadership involves the process whereby leaders develop followers into leaders (see Box 4.1). This is a conscious goal; the leader has a development plan in her or his head about each follower. Transformational leadership is fundamentally "morally uplifting." Such leaders stimulate challenge, as opposed to suppressing it when it arises. They are deeply trusted and exhibit the moral perspective to warrant such trust. Their willingness to be vulnerable and to self-sacrifice builds tremendous trust among followers, along with identification in their mission or cause. Their willingness to self-sacrifice is often associated with similar patterns of self-sacrifice among their followers in a sort of "falling dominoes" effect. They desire to leave behind something in their organization, community, or even society, something that is more positive than when they first began their work. For these reasons, Burns,[35] Bass,[36] and Sergiovanni[37] referred to transformational leaders as moral agents who focus themselves and followers on achieving higher-level missions and purposes. The higher levels of identification result in higher levels of commitment, trust, loyalty, and performance.

How can I describe such leaders to you in more practical terms? They are people who come to their tasks not only willing to listen but also determined to know what others are thinking and can contribute to the challenges being

---

BOX 4.2. Honest Appraisal

"Part of the change equation demands we let employees know how they're doing, that means that management must learn to appraise employees in a constructive manner . . . we tell them what their development needs are and help them overcome problems." Lawrence Bossidy, of Applied Signal (cited in "Jack's Men," 1997)

---

confronted. They take the time to get to know the people they work with, what these people need to know to perform at their best, and how far they can be stretched, challenged, and supported (see Box 4.2). They are role models of the expectations they have of others.

> *If the troops are cold, you're cold. But make sure you don't look or act cold.*
> (General Colin Powell)

If cost cutting is required, these leaders don't protect their offices from the ax. If they think training is important, then they will go to it first and often take on the role of delivering training to their followers and colleagues in both a formal and informal sense. They frequently struggle with what is the right thing to do, and they keep in the forefront a set of standards that makes the execution of their principles predictable. You get to know what they think is right and wrong through their words and their actions. Novel idea, huh? Many want to emulate them because they are respected for taking a stand on important issues, for championing someone's cause, for taking on difficult challenges others have avoided, for being concerned, and for doing something about those concerns. They encourage those around them to question, to use their full intellectual capitol, and to not fear questioning those things that are most established nor those issues with which they are most closely aligned (see Box 4.3).

Instead of moving those led to go beyond their self-interests, a *transactional leader* addresses the self-interests of those being influenced by them. Transactional leaders offer inducements to move in the direction desired by the leaders, which often is a direction that would also satisfy the self-interests of the followers. They exchange promises of reward for cooperation and the compli-

---

BOX 4.3. Levels of Commitment/Loyalty and Transformational Leadership

---

Pitman (1993) provided evidence to show that the commitment level of white-collar employees in six organizations correlated positively with the transformational leadership ratings of their supervisors. Niehoff, Eng, and Grover (1990) surveyed 862 insurance employees, reporting that commitment to the organization was positively affected by the extent to which top management was inspirational and encouraged innovativeness from employees. Similarly, employee ratings of their shop stewards' leadership styles predicted members' loyalty, sense of responsibility, and actual participation in union activities (Kelloway & Barling, 1993). In fact, the strongest predictor of levels of loyalty to the union and participation in union activities was the shop steward's transformational leadership.

Shamir, Zakay, Breinin, and Popper (1998a, 1998b) reported that, with Israeli Defense Force companies, group morale, cohesiveness, and level of potency were each positively related to trust in the platoon leader, identification with the unit, notification, willingness to sacrifice for the leader, and the leader's charisma. The level of agreement among members of the company about the leader's charisma also augmented the positive relationships reported above between charismatic leadership and company culture, indicating that agreement on how the leader influenced the unit had a positive impact on motivation and performance. Finally, Curphy (1992) showed that transformational and transactional leadership positively predicted performance that required interdependent effort among cadet squadron members and produced higher levels of motivation and cohesiveness in platoons.

---

ance from their followers to get the task done. The best transactions are *constructive,* and evidence cited earlier would suggest these are usually reasonably effective in achieving desired levels of performance. Many examples of this type of leadership behavior may be found in almost any organization, even in my initial interactions with you in formulating a *compact of expectations* and understanding on how best to develop leadership potential. At the base of our understanding, we've established a transaction that will help us, over time, move up to the higher end of the full range, where we will focus on transformational leadership. Thus, we must take into consideration a "walk"-before-we-"sprint" philosophy, and for some people it will be very appropriate for them to take "baby steps" at the start to make sure their expectations and target outcomes are clearly understood.

You may wonder how transactions are at the base of transformations. At least I think you may wonder. We already have identified one example of how this might occur. Specifically, if you honor all your various transactions with people, over time they come to trust you; and it is higher levels of trust versus compliance that transformational leadership uses as its base for achieving exemplary performance. But of course, lifelike leadership is not always that simple, meaning that even though you believe you have been absolutely consistent, some followers, peers, or even your supervisor may not concur with your opinion. So, being consistent in the eyes of all your followers who are close and at a distance will be a very difficult challenge that is renewed each time you work with a new group of followers.

Farther down the range, transactional leadership can also be an *active* or *passive* engagement in terms of being a *corrective exchange* or transaction. Here, the exchange involves a desired change in behavior, learning level, cooperation, or compliance of followers to avoid censorship, reproof, negative feedback, punishment, or disciplinary action. For example, if too many beads are shifted from the left jar to the right in 1 day, then certain privileges are lost by students in Stacey's class (see Chapter 3). The same applies to the number of defects in rejected products, poor customer service, and errors made in deliveries by suppliers.

Both constructive and corrective transactions can be set to be contingent on each follower's performance or, in some cases, the leader, if follower-directed. Some leaders emphasize constructive promises, praise, and rewards that are contingent on achieving expected performance (see Box 4.4). Other leaders manage by exception and pay attention to their followers "only" when their behavior is off the mark and a correction is needed. Even though such *constructive* transactions are reasonably successful and effective, *corrective* transactions are less so, particularly in terms of developing greater learning potential in followers. How well would you learn if you only had someone who always built a list of things for you that you *shouldn't do?* What about the long list of things you *should do,* should try, and be encouraged to explore, and even fail at over time. In all, transactional leadership is not enough for people to achieve their full potential, whether they are leaders or followers, individuals or in groups. And as a culture, this style of leadership creates an environment that is often risk averse and quite low in innovation.

One example of creating a low-risk culture comes to mind. I was at a senior management retreat for a large medical supplies company. The company was very conservative and embedded in a culture that constantly tried to avoid

---

BOX 4.4. Mission/Purpose and Transformational Leadership

Keller (1992) reported that effective leaders in R&D project teams tended to inspire a sense of mission and purpose about the importance of the work being done by the team; they stimulated new ways of thinking and solving difficult problems; and they got members to contribute the extra effort needed to achieve exemplary performance levels. Such transformational leadership was also shown to be more predictive of project quality in research versus development teams.

---

mistakes. In that business, it was quite important to avoid making mistakes that would place customers at risk. Yet, the company had taken an extreme position on avoiding any mistakes after being caught by the Federal Drug Agency (FDA) for putting out a product that was not properly tested. This led to a huge fine for the company, several indictments, a dramatic loss in market share, and a very tarnished image with customers. The "event," as it was called internally, also became the turning point in creating a culture that was very paranoid about making any mistakes. The key words in the culture became *control* and *comply,* which do not go too well with a third word—*innovate.* During the second day of the retreat, the CEO was challenging the group to give him feedback: "Help me. . . . Don't you guys have any passion!" A young Italian manager spoke up finally and said, "I was told by my regional manager that under no circumstances am I to say *anything* interesting at the meeting." Here, the company had spent tens of thousands of dollars to bring in its senior managers from around the world, and they were being coached to not be innovative, creative, and above all else, say anything interesting. I found *that* interesting. And you?

When leadership is needed, any leadership is likely to be more successful and effective than avoidance of responsibility to provide leadership (see Box 4.5). *Laissez-faire leadership (LF)* is the behavior of those individuals in a group who, in the extreme, don't care what happens, avoid taking responsibility, cannot make up their minds, and are satisfied to sit and wait for others to take the necessary initiatives imposed by the tasks at hand. We can call these types of individuals "social loafers." Our descriptions of Stacey or Sam (Chapter 3) should suggest that this style is not the one either of them exhibited very often, but still they probably exhibited it once in a while, as we all do at various points

---

BOX 4.5. Thinking the Unthinkable

Thinking against the crowd has been one key ingredient in Motorola's long-term success. It is the basis on which the company was founded by Paul Galvin. Taking risks before competitors do is, paradoxically, considered the basis for long-term security. Conventional wisdom suggested that radios were defined as the "home set." When Galvin decided to put a radio into everyone's car, many thought it was a crazy idea and dangerous. Galvin persisted, and history has proved him correct. Some might also say that the same visionary leadership put Motorola ahead of its competition in the cellular phone business when it cost four to six times as much to call using a cellular phone (Winston, 1997).

---

in time. It is quite human to avoid certain decisions, yet it is ineffective leadership to be seen over time by your peers, supervisor, or followers as primarily avoidant.

Ask yourself, *Have I ever* not *avoided a problem or delayed taking action on a particular decision beyond what others thought was reasonable?* If your answer is yes, you may want to consult your physician, as it is very likely your parents lied to you about your origin (I believe that you must be an android).

Seriously, we all must admit that we have avoided making a decision, and therefore the answer is always no! Consequently, someone has certainly seen all of us at some point exhibiting laissez-faire leadership. In terms of building the full range of leadership potential, how often you exhibit a certain set of behaviors along the range ultimately determines how effective you are over time as a leader. And the frequency with which you exhibit behaviors depends on your perspective or frame of reference of what you consider important. What is important to you will influence where you place more or less emphasis in terms of your choice of actions and decisions. For example, if you understand the importance of identifying the needs of people who report to you and that it can have a positive impact on their development as well as your own, then you are more likely to spend time trying to understand each individual's needs.

Think about the last time you were confronted with a choice of sitting back and waiting for someone else in your group to say what was needed to be said for the group to move forward or for you to take the initiative. Why were you reluctant to act? What made you finally do what you did? We all are laissez-faire about certain things, and, in fact, it may be used to our advantage. For example, an article appeared in the *Wall Street Journal* several years ago about Lou Gerstner 6 months after he was selected to lead IBM out of its worst slump. The article described Gerstner as laissez-faire. This is a label no one today would ascribe to Lou Gerstner's leadership of IBM. With some *reflection,* one might say he chose not to act before he was prepared to act, despite the fact that employees, stockholders, investors, and competitors may have seen him as laissez-faire. By the way, he apparently spent the first 6 months closeted with IBM's customers, finding out what they liked, didn't like, and needed from IBM. Yet, in his employees' eyes, he may have been seen as avoidant. Realize that part of IBM's problem was the company's avoidance of its customers in terms of really listening to their needs, succumbing to its own long history of success. Heeding the words of Alvin Toffler, "Nothing is so dangerous as yesterday's success."

And the Research Says . . .

For the past decade, research has supported the idea that, on average, transformational leadership is far more effective than transactional leadership in generating the higher levels of extra effort, commitment, performance, and satisfaction of those led (see Box 4.6). This has been true almost regardless of the level of leadership position, the type of organization, and the culture in which both are embedded.

Constructive transactional leadership is reasonably effective under most circumstances. *Management-by-exception (MBE),* also a transactional style, is more corrective than constructive. But actively correcting a follower for failure to perform as expected is more varied in effects. And corrective leadership that is passive (please don't fix it if it ain't broken) tends to be generally ineffective across most conditions and situations.

You must be willing to address a follower's sense of self-worth to engage her or him in being committed and fully involved in the challenges at hand. And that is one thing transformational leadership adds to the transactional exchange. People don't comply with what needs to be done; at the higher end of their potential, they are more committed to achieving it because they believe in what they are doing and therefore identify with the effort. Identification provides the high-octane for achieving exemplary performance. Think about anything you

---

BOX 4.6. Linkages Between a Full Range of Leadership and Performance

---

Gasper (1992) conducted a meta-analysis of prior literature on transformational leadership. Results indicated that transformational leadership was the more preferred style among followers and was associated, as noted with single sample studies, with perceived leadership effectiveness, follower satisfaction, and a greater willingness to put forth extra effort.

Coleman, Patterson, Fuller, Hester, and Stringer (1995) reported the results of a comprehensive meta-analysis. The average relationship (which can vary from −1.0 through +1.0) across studies for the transformational leadership factors and performance ranged from .45 to .60; for transactional, .44; for management-by-exception active, .22; for management-by-exception passive, .13; and for laissez-faire, −.28. These meta-analyses included 27 studies. A similar pattern of results also emerged in the relationships with satisfaction and rated effectiveness.

Lowe, Kroeck, and Sivasubramaniam (1996) conducted a parallel meta-analysis confirming that the transformational leadership factors were more highly correlated with work performance and that this pattern held up across two levels of leadership and with both hard (number of units) and soft (performance appraisals) measures of performance. The total number of samples, including both published and unpublished works, was 47. Lowe et al. did find some differences attributable to moderator effects in the relationships observed. For example, some differences were found in comparing public and private organizations and when examining the type of performance measure. For example, in terms of performance measures, the following results were noted for relationships between the leadership scales and follower ratings versus organizational measures: Idealized/Charisma, .81 versus .35; Individualized Consideration, .69 versus .28; Intellectual Stimulation, .68 versus .26; Contingent Reward, .56 versus .08; Management-by-Exception, .10 versus −.04, respectively.

---

do that you fully identify with right now. Now think about how you function when you are involved in something that either you have no identification with or you are "anti-identified" with, so to speak.

Transformational leadership involves motivating others to do more than they originally intended and often even more than they thought possible. This can happen when a person goes from doing a task for "the money" to doing it because she or he identifies and takes pride in what is produced. What is good enough to be paid for is not always good enough to take pride in, and this gap is what transformational leadership often narrows. Such leaders set more challenging expectations and typically achieve higher performance as a consequence. Transformational leadership involves tapping into the full potential of those being led. Transformational leadership is a significant expansion of transactional leadership. Transactional leadership emphasizes the transaction or exchange that takes place among leaders, colleagues, and followers. This exchange is based on the leader discussing with others what is required and specifying the conditions and rewards that others will receive if they fulfill those requirements. Such exchanges are only the base to build on, however, rather than the ceiling for the leader's efforts.

In sum, "true" transformational leaders raise the level of identification, moral maturity, and perspective of those they lead. Over time, they develop their followers into leaders. They broaden and enlarge the interests of those they lead. Their shadows are much deeper and longer in terms of their effects on others, and by and large they are very positive shadows over time.

Components of Transformational Leadership

Transformational leaders do more with colleagues and followers than set up simple exchanges or agreements. They behave in ways to achieve superior results by employing one or more of the four components of transformational leadership briefly mentioned above (see Figure 4.1). Let me reiterate those four components here because, before going on to the next chapter, I will ask you to reflect on how they can be developed in you.

Leadership is *idealized* when followers seek to identify with their leaders and to emulate them. The leadership *inspires* followers with challenge and persuasion by providing meaning and understanding regarding the actions required. At the core is *identification,* which drives people to achieve the vision. The leadership is *intellectually stimulating,* expanding the followers' use of their abilities to question not only other people's perspectives but also their own, even the most deeply rooted ones. Finally, the leadership is *individually considerate,* providing followers with support, mentoring, and coaching. Each of these components is assessed with a survey called the Multifactor Leadership Questionnaire (MLQ; see Box 4.7).[38] The MLQ comprises all the components of transformational, transactional, and nontransactional leadership that we have referred to as a full range of leadership potential (see the sample MLQ profile at the end of this chapter).

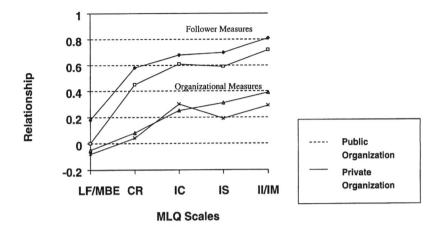

Figure 4.1. Evidence for Impact on Performance

SOURCE: From "Effectiveness Correlates of Transformational and Transactional Leadership: A Meta-Analysis Review," by K. Lowe, K. G. Kroeck, & N. Sivasubramaniam, 1996, *Leadership Quarterly, 7.* Reprinted with permission.

Idealized Influence

Transformational leaders behave in ways that result in their being role models for followers to emulate over time (see Box 4.8). They are admired, respected, and trusted. Followers identify with the leader and the cause or mission the leader is advocating and over time come to emulate the leader, but in a true idealized sense they never learn *not* to question the leader. Bass (1998) indicated that followers' goals become more meaningful as the goals become more consistent with their self-concepts. Followers attribute their own extra effort to internal self-related causes rather than to extrinsic rewards further adding to the followers' commitment to the cause, and to vague and distant goals. (p. 24)

Napoléon Bonaparte once said about great leaders that they must "speak to their eyes," as perhaps opposed to their wallets!

Among the things leaders do to earn idealized credit is to consider the needs of others over personal needs, often willingly sacrificing personal gain for the sake of others. Leaders share risks with followers and are consistent rather than arbitrary in their actions over time. They can be counted on to do the right thing, demonstrating high standards of ethical and moral conduct. Principles and standards provide the base of consistency for how leaders are perceived, not

---

BOX 4.7. Measuring a Full Range of Leadership Styles:
How Many Factors Compose This Model?

Den Hartog, Van Muijen, and Koopman (1997) conducted a study in the Netherlands, involving 1,200 employees from eight organizations. The authors used the *M*ultifactor *L*eadership *Q*uestionnaire (MLQ) Form 8Y with followers of supervisors completing these ratings. The MLQ was translated into Dutch for this study. Results supported a 4-factor solution of a global transformational factor, transactional contingent reward, active management-by-exception, and passive leadership factors.

Avolio, Bass, and Jung (1999) completed a comprehensive analysis of the MLQ (form 5x) by using data collected from 14 samples. Avolio et al. provided evidence for a 6-factor structure in the first nine samples and confirmed the six factors in the second collection of samples. The six factors were Idealized/Inspiring, Intellectually Stimulating, Individualized Consideration, Contingent Reward, Management-by-Exception Active, and Passive/Corrective Leadership.

Bycio, Hackett, and Allen (1995) conducted a confirmatory factor analysis of the MLQ, involving hospital nurses; 97% of the participants in this study were female. Moreover, the mean average ratings on transformational leadership at the high end were only 2.08 out of a possible 4.0, showing a restriction of range on these measures. The 5-factor model was composed of the following: Idealized/Inspiring, Intellectual Stimulation, Individualized Consideration, Contingent Reward, and Passive Management-by-Exception. The authors also found that transformational leadership was associated with a lower level of intentions to quit. The laissez-faire scale was omitted from their study.

BOX 4.8. Executive Leadership and Performance

Agle (1993) examined 250 CEOs of primarily major U.S. companies. The 250 executives were rated by their direct reports in terms of their idealized or charismatic leadership qualities, achievement level as CEOs, and performance of their organizations under their tenure. Findings indicated that the more charismatic leaders led more effective organizations as seen by their direct reports, as well as on the basis of stock performance. Ratings of idealized leadership also correlated with sales increase, market share, earnings, and ROI.

BOX 4.9. Relationships Between Transactional/Transformational
Leadership and "Soft" Measures of Performance

Gottlieb (1990) examined the relationship of self-reported transactional-transformational leadership styles of 49 chief and 106 associate chief nurses with 545 follower ratings of job satisfaction, effectiveness, and extra effort. The self-reported idealized charismatic leadership of the nurse leaders accounted for a high percentage of variation in ratings of job satisfaction and effectiveness, whereas inspirational leadership had the strongest relationship with amount of extra effort followers were willing to put forth in their jobs.

---

each behavior. Specifically, leaders can be very difficult and challenging to some and highly empathic and supportive for others all within their range of principled leadership (see Box 4.9).

Transformational leaders avoid using power for personal gain but will use sources of power at their disposal to move individuals or groups toward accomplishing their mission, vision, and cause. They are the leaders whom people describe when asked to reflect on their life by describing someone who has had a profound influence on their personal development. In the Israeli military, I came across a great description of these types of leaders in a book on exemplary platoon leadership. The book was entitled *Leading With Them and Ahead of Them.* Often, an idealized leader is perceived as being the central force in moving a group forward and the person who sees what she or he should be doing next: *With Them and Ahead of Them.*

Inspirational Motivation

Transformational leaders behave in ways that motivate and inspire those around them by providing meaning and challenge to their followers' work. Team spirit is enhanced. Such leaders display enthusiasm and optimism. They get followers involved in thinking about various attractive future states or scenarios, considering sometimes very different and desirable alternatives. They can inspire others by what they say, by what they do, and at the highest end of the range, by both (see Box 4.10).

BOX 4.10. Transformational Leadership and Sales Performance

Garcia (1995) examined the relationship between transformational leadership and sales performance. The field study was conducted in two large U.S. companies serving a nationwide market. The context in which these sales-people operated could be classified as high-complexity buying centers. Using the MLQ, 101 salespersons were rated by their supervisors. Transformational leadership of the salespeople significantly correlated with the performance rating they received, as well as a sales/quota ratio generated to compare the performance of salespeople across the two organizations included in this sample. For the transformational factors, relationship between Charisma/Inspiring, Intellectually Stimulating, and Individually Considerate Leadership with sales were .27, .29, and .19, respectively. Transformational leadership accounted for 37% of the variance in sales performance effectiveness as rated by the sales managers.

Intellectual Stimulation

Transformational leaders stimulate their followers' efforts to be innovative and creative by questioning assumptions, reframing problems, and approaching old situations with new methods and perspectives. Creativity is encouraged as a high norm for conduct. There is no public criticism of individual members' mistakes. New ideas and creative problem solutions are solicited from followers, who are included in the process of addressing problems and finding solutions. Followers are encouraged to try new approaches, and their ideas are never criticized simply because they differ from the leaders'. Often, the leader focuses on the "what" in problems, rather than on the "who," where blame might be assessed.

Followers, in turn, stimulate the leader to reconsider her or his own perspective and tried-and-true assumptions. The leader is observed advocating "the retirement" of a system that is no longer useful, even a system the leader developed her- or himself. Nothing is too good, too fixed, too political, or too bureaucratic that it can't be challenged, changed, retired, and/or abandoned (see Box 4.11). It is quite likely that what you refuse to question that is essential to your business' survival will be successfully questioned by your competitors, who will, no doubt, be delighted you left the questioning to them. Paul Galvin built into the culture of Motorola the idea that to take risks with new ideas was,

---

BOX 4.11. Champions of Innovation and Transformational Leadership

---

> Howell and Higgins (1990) provided results to corroborate Keller's findings with R&D teams (cited in Box 4.4). Specifically, Howell and Higgins reported that the champions of innovation who, in a variety of Canadian organizations, were identified by using a rigorous peer nomination and interview process also displayed the high end of the full range of leadership exhibited by transformational leadership. Such champions generated innovative ideas and approaches, which were synonymous with being more intellectually stimulating.

---

paradoxically, the basis for long-term security in business. Maybe this is also what Andy Grove of Intel meant when he said in his book that one must run a business by being absolutely paranoid. Of course, to be paranoid is to worry without cause. So, perhaps we should label this "healthy, constructive, and adaptive paranoia."

Individualized Consideration

The transformational leader pays special attention to each individual's needs for achievement and growth by acting as coach, mentor, teacher, facilitator, confidant, and counselor. Followers and colleagues are developed to successively higher levels of potential on a continuous basis, paralleling the type of continuous process improvement sometimes observed in highly effective total quality systems. Here at the Center for Leadership Studies, however, we call it *continuous people improvement* (CPI). Individualized consideration is practiced as follows: New learning opportunities are created, along with a supportive climate for learning to occur. Individual differences in terms of needs and desires are continuously recognized (see Box 4.12). The leader's behavior and affect demonstrate not only acceptance of individual differences but also a desire to attract them to enhance creativity and innovation (e.g., some people receive more encouragement, some more autonomy, others firmer standards, and still others the needed attention in the summer, as described in Chapter 3 with Stacey's students).

A two-way exchange in communication is encouraged, and "management by continuous engagement" is the norm in practice. Interactions with followers

---

BOX 4.12. Transformational Leadership and a Culture of Empowerment

---

Masi (1994) reported a positive relationship with army personnel between transformational leadership and individual empowerment and motivation. Motivation to achieve was also related to transformational leadership. Reports of empowering organizational cultural norms across organizations were modestly positively related to ratings of transformational leadership.

Bryce (1989) set out to describe the leadership styles of senior executives in major Japanese companies. In her study, 132 managers and senior executives were rated by their 194 respective followers from 14 Japanese corporations. Senior Japanese leaders did exhibit a high level of transformational leadership, which was also reflected in the leadership styles of their direct reports. This finding supports the idea of the "falling dominoes effect," whereby the leadership displayed at the top cascades to lower organizational levels. Although the transformational leadership styles received the highest frequency scores, the results did vary considerably across companies.

Kane and Tremble (1998) analyzed survey data collected from 3,216 soldiers from 41 battalions in the U.S. Army. More frequent transformational leadership was exhibited by senior officers, such as company and battalion commanders. Generally, ratings of transformational leadership augmented transactional leadership ratings in predicting levels of extra effort, job motivation, and moral commitment. The magnitude of the augmentation effect was greater at higher officer levels.

Spreitzer and Janasz (1998) reported that empowered managers tend to be perceived by their followers as being more intellectually stimulating and charismatic. What we need now is an examination of the leaders' style of thinking with respect to empowering others and their actual behaviors in doing so over time.

---

are personalized (e.g., the leader remembers previous interactions, is aware of individual concerns, and sees the individual as a "whole" person, rather than as "just" another student, soldier, employee, or customer). The individually considerate leader listens effectively and could be heard saying, "It's not what you tell them, it's what they hear." We must make sure that what was heard was what the speaker intended us to hear. Such leaders may not always get the concerns right, but you have to give them credit for trying.

Such leaders delegate tasks as a means of developing their followers. Delegated tasks are monitored to see whether followers need additional direction or support and to assess progress; ideally, followers do not feel that they are being checked on at all. Why? How can this be? Simple. They trust their leader's intentions. Stated in their terms, "This person is trying to help me by pointing out mistakes, as opposed to pointing a finger at me in some accusatory way." If you asked such leaders, they could most likely tell you in fairly specific terms where their people are in terms of achieving their full potential and the plan they have in mind to close the gap between the "as is" and the "what could be."

Have you known anyone in your life who displayed the four components of transformational leadership? If so, how did you feel toward the person, and how did you perform as a consequence of that person's efforts toward you? Do you agree with the research findings and descriptions?

Components of Transactional Leadership

Transactional leadership occurs when the leader rewards or disciplines the follower, depending on the adequacy of the follower's behavior or performance. Transactional leadership depends on laying out contingencies, agreements, reinforcement, and either positive contingent reward or the more negative active or passive forms of management-by-exception (MBE-A and MBE-P).

Contingent Reward

Such constructive transactions have been found to be reasonably effective, although not typically as much as any of the transformational components in motivating others to achieve higher levels of development and performance. With this approach, a leader assigns or secures agreements on what needs to be done and promises rewards or actually rewards others in exchange for satisfactorily carrying out the assignment.

Management-by-Exception

The management-by-exception form of corrective transaction tends to be more ineffective, particularly when used in excess. In many situations, this style of leadership may be required. We find, for example, in combat military settings that corrective leadership in its active form is seen as being much more positive and effective by followers and leaders (see Box 4.13 and Figures 4.2a and 4.2b). In fact, in most environments where risk is high, the interpretation of corrective transactions is much different than in contexts where risk is low or negligible.

BOX 4.13. Leadership and Platoon Performance

In a 2-year project codirected by myself and Bernie Bass, one can see from Figures 4.2a and 4.2b that the management-by-exception leadership of both platoon leaders and platoon sergeants positively predicted the platoon's readiness. Platoon readiness was evaluated on the basis of its performance with a 2-week field exercise called Joint Readiness Training Corp. (JRTC). JRTC is a 2-week simulated exercise in which platoons are taken through near-combat missions to evaluate their performance. The transformational and transactional leadership of both the lieutenants and the sergeants positively predicted platoon performance over a 3-month period, with correlations in the .3–.6 range. (This project was funded by the Army Research Institute 1996-1997, Contract #DASW01-96K-008.)

The corrective transaction may be active or passive. When active, the leader arranges to actively monitor deviations from standards, mistakes, and errors in the follower's assignments and to take corrective action as necessary. Such leadership involves a constant vigilance for possible mistakes. As suggested above, it is easy to imagine many situations where such behavior is highly desirable, including in emergency settings and in any process where the risk of failure is extremely high in financial cost, physical costs, loss of life, and so forth. When passive, the leader waits for deviations, mistakes, and errors to occur and then takes corrective action. Now, here comes another one of those reflective questions.

Do you think you spend too much or too little time in your leadership role, focusing on mistakes? What is your ratio of recognition to reproofs? How do you think this affects people's willingness to be creative and innovative, which by definition is a deviation from standards?

Nontransactional/Laissez-Faire Leadership

Nontransactional/laissez-faire leadership is the near avoidance or absence of leadership and is, by definition, most inactive, as well as most ineffective, according to almost all prior research on this style of leadership. In the very extreme, nothing is transacted between a "leader" and a "follower" with this style.

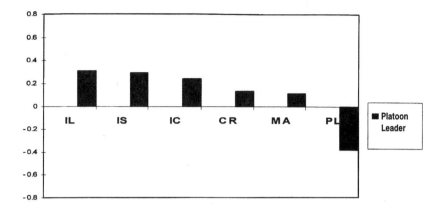

Figure 4.2a. Platoon Leader Effectiveness in JRTC Predicted by 360° MLQ Ratings of 18 Platoon Leaders in Garrison

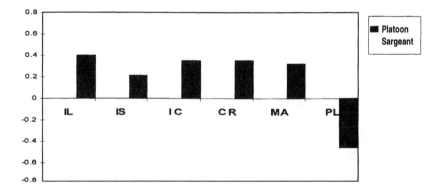

Figure 4.2b. Platoon Sergeant Effectiveness in JRTC Predicted by 360° MLQ Ratings of 18 Platoon Leaders in Garrison

NOTES: IL = Idealized Influence; IS = Intellectual Stimulation; IC = Individual Consideration; CR = Contigent Reward; MA = Management-by-Exception (Active); PA = Passive Corrective

Fundamental to the full range leadership model presented here is that every leader displays each style to some degree. An optimal profile is shown in the right side of Figure 4.3. The third dimension of this model (*depth*) represents how frequently a leader displays a style of leadership. The *active* dimension is self-evident in that I have shared with you examples of active or proactive leadership. The *effectiveness* dimension is based on research results that have shown active transactional and proactive transformational leadership to be, by and large, far more effective than other styles of leadership and/or nonleadership. The left side of Figure 4.3 portrays the sub-optimal profile in that the higher frequency of occurrence occurs at the lower end of the full range of leadership.

In the right side of Figure 4.3, the leader infrequently displays laissez-faire leadership, higher frequencies of the transactional leadership styles of passive and active management-by-exception, and more contingent reward, and the most frequently observed are the transformational leadership components. In contrast, and as shown in the left side of Figure 4.3, the poorly performing leader tends toward exhibiting more laissez-faire leadership, passive management-by-exception, and much less, if any, transformational leadership. By the way, you could replace *leader* with *team* and, on the basis of our current results with teams in industry, education, and the military, thus far this statement would be accurate.

In a recent study of team leadership, Sivasubramaniam, Murry, Avolio, and Jung[39] reported that the collective transformational leadership of self-directed teams positively predicted its performance over a 3-month period. Team laissez-faire and management-by-exception leadership negatively predicted performance (see Box 4.14).

Many research studies have been conducted in business/industry, government, the military, educational institutions, and nonprofit organizations, showing that transformational leadership, as measured by the MLQ derived from the full range model, was more effective and satisfying than transactional leadership, although the best of leaders frequently do some of the latter and more of the former. Follow-up investigations have shown that developing transformational leadership by training its four components also increases the potential to enhance effectiveness and satisfaction. These studies are described in more detail in Box 4.15.

Among the components of transformational leadership, *idealized influence* and *inspirational leadership* are most effective and satisfying; *intellectual stimulation* and *individualized consideration* are a bit less so. But, in turn, all

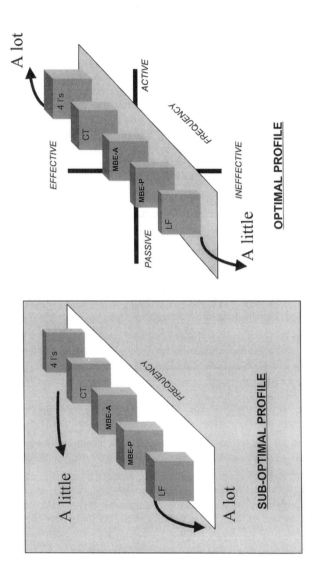

Figure 4.3. Contrasting Leadership Profiles

BOX 4.14. Team Transformational Leadership and Performance

Sivasubramaniam, Murry, Avolio, and Jung (1997) contrasted the higher-order factor of transformational leadership and corrective transactional leadership in teams to predict how potent the teams perceived themselves to be over time, as well as to predict performance over a 3-month interval. Student teams participating in this study rated themselves at 1 month and at 3 months on how they perceived the collective leadership of their respective teams. Leadership ratings taken early on were highly predictive of subsequent leadership ratings for both transformational leadership and corrective management-by-exception. Transformational leadership directly predicted the performance of these groups and also predicted performance indirectly through levels of group potency. A similar pattern emerged for avoidant leadership.

BOX 4.15. Examining a Range of Leadership and Performance Outcomes

- Executives who were seen to champion projects in 28 different organizations were shown to display more transformational behaviors than 25 matched nonchampions (Howell & Higgins, 1990).
- Transformational leadership among Methodist ministers was associated with greater Sunday church attendance and membership growth (Onnen, 1987).
- Transformational leadership was higher among presidents of MBA teams completing complex simulations with greater financial success (Avolio, Waldman, & Einstein, 1988).
- Transformational leadership was higher among strategic business unit managers whose departments achieved greater future financial success (Howell & Avolio, 1993).
- Managers who were seen as transformational by their followers earned better performance evaluations from committees composed of their superiors (Hater & Bass, 1988).
- American presidential productivity was seen as being related to leadership evaluations of their charisma and how they performed in office. Charismatic presidents were more proactive in building coalitions and overcoming barriers to address obstacles to new initiatives set forth by their administrations (Deluga, 1997).
- Naval officers who were rated as more transformational by their followers earned from their superiors recommendations for early promotion and better fitness reports (Yammarino & Bass, 1990).
- German bank unit performance over longer versus shorter time periods was higher in banks led by leaders who were rated by their followers as more transformational (Geyer & Steyrer, 1998).

BOX 4.16. Transformational Leadership and
Project Unit Performance

Thite (1997) examined the extent to which transformational leadership was better suited for leading technical project teams as compared with transactional leadership. Respondents were from 36 organizations involving 225 teams and 70 project leaders. Results indicated that the most versus least successful project teams, using company criteria for determining performance, had project leaders who were rated as more transformational and also active transactional. All the transformational scales and the contingent reward transactional scale were positively correlated with team outcomes.

Carless, Mann, and Wearing (1995) obtained MLQ follower ratings of 695 middle-level branch managers employed by a large Australian bank. The focus of their study was to examine whether self-efficacy predicted transformational leadership and whether, in turn, group cohesion mediated the relationship between transformational leadership and performance. Self-efficacy was a significant predictor of transformational leadership and performance. Group cohesion was a significant mediator of leadership and performance. Transformational leadership predicted both individual and group performance.

---

four I's of transformational leadership are more effective than constructive transactional leadership. However, constructive transactions remain reasonably effective and satisfying for most situations except where a leader has no control over the ways a follower may be rewarded for satisfactory performance. Actively taking corrective action—that is, *managing by exception* and arranging to monitor the performance of followers—is generally less effective and satisfying. Waiting for problems to arise or remaining oblivious until a mishap occurs is seen as poor, ineffective leadership and is typically highly dissatisfying for followers. Most ineffective and dissatisfying is *laissez-faire leadership,* wherein the individual avoids leadership and abdicates responsibilities.

As noted above, transformational leadership adds or augments transactional leadership in its effects on follower motivation, satisfaction, and performance (see Box 4.16).[40] Transformational leadership does not replace transactional leadership. Constructive and especially corrective transactions may have only a marginal impact on followers unless accompanied by one or more components of transformational leadership. For getting the most out of transactions, the follower needs to feel valued by the leader; the follower needs to find meaning in what she or he is doing; and the follower needs a sense of ownership in what is being done.

Linkages to Older Models of Directive Versus Participative Leadership

Transformational leadership can be directive or participative, as well as democratic or authoritarian. Sometimes, transformational leadership is misunderstood as elitist and/or antidemocratic. Since the 1930s, democratic and participative leadership has been pronounced as the "modern" way to build the intelligent, learning organization. Indeed, most managers have learned that, before making a decision, it pays to consult with those who will implement the decision, although fewer pursue a democratic vote or strive for consensus in a participative discussion with all those involved and affected by their decisions.

There are many good reasons for encouraging shared decision making, empowering followers, and self-managing, not least of which is that it is your job as a leader to develop followers into leaders. The quality of followers you leave behind is part of your legacy. Yet, many circumstances call for a leader to be decisive and directive. Novices may wish direction and advice on what to do and how to do it. Even when no leader is appointed, someone must begin to take initiative, and that person may soon come to be seen as a leader.

Many have confused transformational leadership with democratic or participative leadership. It often may be similar, but at times it can also be directive, decisive, and authoritative. The *idealized* leader, by providing radical solutions to address her problems, can direct followers who are counting on her to help them get out of a crisis. Perhaps they are at a stage of learned helplessness, not knowing which way to turn, and only a directive transformational leader will make things happen in a positive direction. Again, the *inspirational* leader can be highly directive in her appeals. The *intellectually stimulating* leader may directly challenge her followers. The *individually considerate* leader could rise above the demands for equality from her followers to treat them differently according to their different needs for growth, challenge, and development (see Box 4.17). At the same time, the transformational leader can share in building visions and ideas that could result in a more democratic and collective enterprise. She can encourage follower participation in the change processes involved. In the same way, transactional leadership can be either directive or participative.

BOX 4.17. Nine Faces of Leadership at Federal Express

On the basis of some initial research conducted by Hater and Bass (1988), Federal Express now identifies a list of attributes its best leaders share in common. The nine "faces," or attributes, represent the core components of transformational leadership, often using the same titles as used in the MLQ.

MLQ	*FedEx Attributes*
Idealized Attributes/Charisma	1. *Charisma*—Instills faith, trust, and respect
Idealized Behaviors	2. *Integrity*—Does what is morally and ethically right. Is a role model for others. Conveys a strong sense of mission.
	3. *Dependability*—Follows through on commitments. Takes responsibility for actions taken.
Inspiring	4. *Courage*—Willing to stand up for ideas even if they are unpopular. Will do what's right for the company.
Intellectual Stimulation	5. *Intellectual Stimulation*—Gets others to use reasoning and evidence, rather than unsupported opinion. Encourages others to think about problems in new ways and to rethink ideas never questioned before.
	6. *Judgment*—Reaches sound judgment and objective evaluations of alternative courses of action by using past experience and knowledge to shape perspective for current decisions.
	7. *Flexibility*—Handles more than one problem at a time. Changes course when the situation warrants it.
Individualized Consideration	8. *Individualized Consideration*—Coaches, advises, and teaches people who need it. Gives newcomers a lot of help. Honors and respects others' opinions.
	9. *Respect for Others*—Honors and does not belittle the opinions of others, regardless of their status and position.

How Others Describe the High End
of the Full Range of Leadership

When we have asked in numerous workshops and interviews what constitutes transformational leadership, many respondents have offered the following
descriptions. So in their words, or perhaps in your own, we can see the following
attributes and behaviors associated with the four I's of transformational leadership.

Idealized influence leadership was attributed to leaders who set examples
for showing determination, displaying extraordinary talents, taking risks, creating in followers a sense of empowerment, showing dedication to "the cause,"
creating a sense of a joint mission, dealing with crises, using radical solutions,
and engendering faith in others.

Inspirational leadership included providing meaning and challenge, paint-
ing an optimistic future, molding expectations that created self-fulfilling prophe-
sies, and thinking ahead. Taking the first step, often with risk to oneself—the
Ahead of Them part, described earlier in the chapter, on exemplary platoon
commanders in the Israeli Defense Forces.

Intellectual stimulation was judged present when the leaders questioned
assumptions, encouraged followers to employ intuition, entertained ideas that
may have seemed silly at first, created imaginative visions, asked followers to
rework the same problems they thought they had solved, and saw unusual
patterns, and for those who used humor to stimulate new thinking.[41]

Individualized consideration was apparent for leaders who answered followers with minimum delay, showed they were concerned for the followers'
well-being, often assigned tasks on the basis of individual needs and abilities,
encouraged two-way exchanges of ideas, were available when needed, constantly encouraged self-development, and effectively mentored, counseled, and
coached peers and followers (see Box 4.18).

A Full Range Leadership Development Program, developed by Avolio and
Bass,[42] begins with participants describing their implicit models of leadership,
as evidenced by an ideal leader each participant has known during her or his life
span. Invariably, and for thousands of trainees in all cultures, the characteristics
of their *ideal leader* has included the four components of transformational and
constructive transactional leadership (see Box 4.19). The general consistency in
these descriptions has led to the idea that some leadership attributes may be
universal even when comparing the most collective to the most individualistic
cultures.[43]

BOX 4.18. Peer Ratings of Cadet Transformational Leadership

When peers of military cadet leaders were asked what characterized the most important traits of a good leader, they described traits associated with inspiration, intellectual stimulation, and individualized consideration, such as having self-confidence, having persuasiveness, showing concern for the well-being of others, having the ability to articulate one's ideas and thoughts, providing role models to be emulated by others, holding high expectations for himself and others, keeping others well informed, and maintaining high motivation in himself (Atwater et al., 1994). As noted earlier, these same leaders were also evaluated (by using an interview procedure for assessing moral development developed by Kegan and his associates [Lahey et al., 1991]) as being more highly morally developed then their peers at the same institution.

BOX 4.19. Implicit Models, Attachment Level, and Transformational Leadership

---

An important aspect of the nature of leader-follower relationships is followers' implicit models of leadership (Lord & Maher, 1993). Berson and Yammarino (1997) investigated the basis for follower implicit models of leadership by using attachment theory (see Bowlby, 1969, 1973) to predict both implicit leadership and followership perceptions, leadership style, and performance. These authors argue that highly "secure" versus "insecure" followers will have markedly different views of what constitutes their ideal models of leadership and followership. Results indicated that insecure participants ranked the attributes of their ideal leaders as first laissez-faire leadership, whereas charismatic leadership and considerate leadership were ranked last out of 52 attributes. The complete opposite rankings were reported for secure individuals. Differences in their views of "ideal" followership were also noted. How subjects perceived their relationships with others according to attachment theory was also related to perceptions of leadership and followership.

Another type of leader Bass has labeled the "pseudo-transformational leader." These are leaders who act like transformational leaders from an impression management perspective, but they are not really transformational leaders. Why? They have no intention of sacrificing their self-interests for the good of others. In fact, they typically do just the opposite, taking advantage of other people's interests for their own good, if not their survival. Pseudo-transformational

TABLE 4.1. Examples of Pseudo-Transformational Versus Transformational Leaders

Pseudo-Transformational	Transformational
Idi Amin	Andrew Carnegie
Jim Bakker	Charles DeGaulle
Nicolae Ceausescu	Dwight Eisenhower
François Duvalier	Mahatma Gandhi
Jimmy Hoffa	Dag Hammarskjöld
Adolf Hitler	Nelson Mandela[a]
J. Edgar Hoover	Edward R. Murrow
Joseph Goebbels	Abdel Nasser
Howard Hughes	Erwin Rommel
Benito Mussolini	Marshal Tito
Ferdinand Marcos	Bishop Desmond Tutu
Pol Pot[a]	Lech Walesa

Some Distinguishing Attributes	
Self-aggrandizing	Envisions a more desirable future
Dominating	Seeks consensus and is empathic
Exploitative of others	Respects differences and develops independent followers
Manipulative	Unites though internalization of mission and values
Unites through fear/compliance	Is self-sacrificing and trustworthy

SOURCE: From "Charismatic Leaders and Destructiveness: An Historiometric Study," by J. O'Connor, M. D. Mumford, T. C. Clifton, T. L. Gessner, & M. S. Connelly, 1995, *Leadership Quarterly, 6*. Reprinted with permission.
NOTE: [a]Not originally included in the O'Connor et al. (1995) article.

leaders are self-oriented, self-aggrandizing, exploitative, narcissistic, and power oriented. Such leaders openly preach distorted utilitarian and immoral principles. Hitler, Pol Pot, and Stalin enslaved and murdered millions they declared enemies of the state. The labor provided was cheap and the imprisonment and deaths regarded as deserved for the good of all of their countrymen. The 1997 trial of Pol Pot in Cambodia and his conviction for participating in the murder of millions of Cambodians indicate that his conclusion was far from the truth. Table 4.1 lists examples of good and bad leaders, along with some distinguishing attributes that look like they are transformational and those that are labeled pseudo-transformational.

Where do these leaders come from in terms of their life streams, and how can we know when they are for real and when they are just full of impression management behavior, hell-bent on deceiving us for self-aggrandizement?

In this chapter, I have discussed the basic components of the full range model of leadership and have demonstrated the hierarchical ordering of these components in the full range sub-optimal and optimal model profiles. I have shown where the full range model links up to more traditional styles of democratic and participative leadership. Finally, I have made an important distinction between transformational leaders who look like and behave like transformational leaders but who are not because of the perspective they maintain, which is that they come first in their desires to dominate others and most often take advantage of the goodwill of the people who follow them.

Some Things Worth Repeating

- Transactions often form the basis for effective transformational leadership to augment.
- The full range model has received a broad range of empirical support demonstrating the hierarchical ordering of effects of transformational, transactional, and laissez-faire leadership on performance.
- Further work on impression management and moral development will no doubt help differentiate the pseudo-transformational leaders from the "real deal."
- For your own reflection, consider where your leadership strengths and weaknesses fall with respect to the optimal and sub-optimal profiles presented earlier. What area should you concentrate on right now to move toward a more optimal profile?
- By using the term *a full range,* we intended to stimulate you and our colleagues to think about what was missing in our model that now needed to be included. So, what can you recommend that will make it "the" full range model of leadership?

Sample Profile Below.

OBSERVATIONS:

POINTS TO WORK ON AND DEVELOP:

REACTIONS:

Graphs of Leadership Styles

The two charts below show the average of how you and your raters perceived the frequency of behaviors you exhibit for each leadership style.

You completed the MLQ to generate this report. The MLQ was also completed by the following number of raters:

One rater at a higher organizational level than you.
Three raters at the same organizational level as you.
Three raters at a lower organizational level than you.
Three raters marked None of the Above.

Transformational Leadership

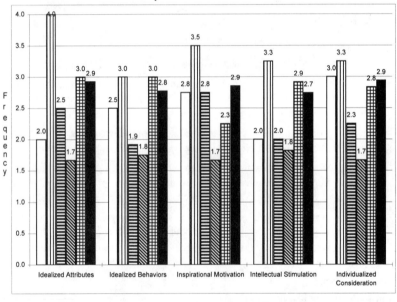

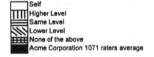
Self
Higher Level
Same Level
Lower Level
None of the above
Acme Corporation 1071 raters average

The average frequencies for the MLQ scales can be interpreted with the scale below.

0 = Not at all
1 = Once in awhile
2 = Sometimes
3 = Fairly often
4 = Frequently, if not always

Figure 4.4. Graph of Leadership Styles

5

Are Leaders Born Versus Made? Well, Yes

A happy man [person] is too satisfied with the present to dwell too much on the future. (Albert Einstein)

I am going to put my reputation on the line at this point and say from my research, I now believe that training can play a vital role in leadership development. (Jay Conger)

Usually, in a workshop, after one completes the debate on whether leaders and managers are different, someone will typically ask (usually with an answer already in mind), "Are leaders born versus made?" The answer, of course, is yes! Have you ever met a leader who wasn't born? Well, okay, for some leaders out there, people might question whether they are truly human or not, and often not in the most positive sense (see, e.g., the pseudo-transformational leaders in Table 4.1). At the same time, what type of learning experiences

63

BOX 5.1. Interview With Colin Powell

In an interview, General Colin Powell, former Chairman of the U.S. Joint Chiefs of Staff, said, "I think leaders can be shaped. You have to have the fundamental instincts for working with people. But the instinct can be improved upon through training and education, so that you understand what works for you. In my career I've come across people who were terrible leaders because they had no gut instinct for leadership and no amount of training helped them. I've also come across brilliant natural leaders who became even better when they developed their skills, pp. 56-57." ("Colin Powell's Thoughts," 1998)

---

beyond an individual's genetic endowments are required to be an effective, if not an exemplary, leader? Recall our discussion of the life stream. Perhaps genetics is what you enter the stream with, but the real question is what you come out with downstream in the life course (see Box 5.1).

To what extent do you think leaders are born versus made?

You are being asked to consider this question at the outset of our discussion here because it affects the way you perceive what can be developed in terms of leadership and followership, which is based, in part, on the implicit model of leadership in your head. It is one indicator of your perspective about leadership, but only one, and I cover many others as we work through the remainder of this book together.

What do I mean by an indicator? If you believe that leadership is something you are born with, then your expectation about yourself and others is that leadership is relatively fixed at birth in the form of "natural leaders." So, if I were asked to develop leadership in myself or to develop it in others, my expectation would be that I can do very little to develop someone's leadership much further than it already has been developed. Such expectations alone can affect the degree to which you are going to be successful as a leader. Simply put, your expectation about leadership not being able to be nurtured and developed is exactly right, but unfortunately it may be based on the wrong reasons. You can't develop it because you believe it can't be developed; therefore, your beliefs become a self-fulfilling prophecy. Yet, a positive lesson for leadership here is worth stating: Be careful what you expect and believe; it may very likely come true! Recall Dov Eden's work on both the Pygmalion and Golem effects.[44,45]

Another individual who believes that leadership can be continuously developed actively seeks out development opportunities to enhance his own or someone else's leadership potential. In searching for such opportunities, he signals to others that this competency can be developed with the right mix of opportunities and experience. It doesn't necessarily mean he believes that there are no limits to development. To the contrary, he may expect that, within certain limits, a considerable degree of leadership potential can be developed, and that's as far as one can realistically go. One might say that certain predispositions set boundaries within which leadership potential can be developed. With this perspective in mind, one can then develop each person's leadership potential to full potential, even one's own.

So, what's the position taken here? This is a fair question. At the risk of sounding sarcastic, however, why would anyone write a book on leadership development if he or she thought leadership potential was *preordained* versus *predisposed?* I firmly believe that leadership development is, to an extent, predetermined by the nature of one's personality, intelligence, and emotional makeup. Evidence accumulated over the last decade has indicated that personality and intelligence are, to some degree, genetically transferred from one generation to the next.[46] Yet, most evidence on personality predispositions indicates that about 50% of the similarity in personalities with identical twins is attributable to genetics, whereas 50% is not. Thus, one could say we have at least 50% to work with in terms of developing the situation, and then let's allocate the rest to the individual's predispositions. Notice that I said "individual" and "situation" because we believe the individual and the situation must be considered to assess leadership, to develop it, and to enhance one's ability to achieve one's potential. Here again, we must keep in mind an important distinction between leadership as a *process* and the leader as a *person* embedded within that process.

A basic premise that I have attempted to thread throughout this book is that we must consider both the individual and the situation in order to develop a deeper appreciation of the full range of leadership potential. Leadership is almost always affected by prior events in the situation and the time period in which leaders and followers are operating. This statement reminds me of a comment one of my students made about Genghis Khan. He said, "If you look at his behavior within the time period he 'ruled in,' it wouldn't appear to be so barbaric or nearly as autocratic." This student was suggesting that one should not judge the behavior of a leader in isolation of the context and time period in which it occurs. It caused me to pause for some reflection on how I judge the leadership of leaders in the present and the past, as well as to consider what we need in the future "life" context.

We may witness a leader's behavior during crisis, and under those conditions we may think the behavior is not only appropriate but highly desired and may even label the leader as inspiring. Under normal day-to-day circumstances, the leader's behavior would seem completely unacceptable and inappropriate, but in crisis we are thankful someone took the first step and perhaps, most important, a step to resolve the crisis.

One example of such a situation comes to mind from a story I read recently concerning an Israeli colonel. Colonel Eli Geva had grave reservations about the role of the Israeli military in the Lebanon War. Part of his reservations stemmed from the fact that the Israeli military was not adequately trained to be an occupying force and that it was being asked to occupy Beirut, Lebanon. When told to move his troops into Beirut, Colonel Geva indicated to his superior that he couldn't comply with the order. In not complying with this order, Colonel Geva knew full well that his career in the military would be over. Unlike in most other military organizations, the Israeli officer is often trained to improvise and to question, yet in this situation Colonel Geva's commander was adamant about his response to this directive. Colonel Geva had no other choice but to either comply with the order or relieve himself of his command. He made the latter choice, which ended his career in the military. This type of decision for a young rising star would never have occurred in another situation, the Yom Kippur War. Ironically, officers in the Israeli army today learn about Colonel Geva's case and are asked to analyze the situation and to understand why he made the difficult choice he did and its implications for developing military leaders who should question authority when such questioning is warranted. Over time, the context may very well become the figure of our attention.[47]

In many contexts, we now find managers saying in today's organization that a manager is much more a coach and facilitator than a director and commander. Mort Meyerson, former CEO of Electronic Data Systems (EDS), said after taking over his new appointment at Perot Systems following several years of retirement, that almost everything he learned as a CEO at EDS about leading had to be abandoned or retired for this "new" work situation. Such conclusions are now more commonplace among senior executives who find themselves embedded in a workforce that is technically more sophisticated and competent and that requires less oversight and day-to-day direction. Now, the leader must coach, facilitate, and gain control through commitment (see Box 5.2).

BOX 5.2. Crisis and Charismatic Leadership

Rivera (1994) examined in a laboratory setting whether there were two types of charismatic leadership—crisis induced and non-crisis visionary leadership. Followers' performance under both types of charismatic leadership was superior to that under transactional leadership. An assessment of performance over time indicated that crisis-induced charismatic performance was not sustained at the same levels over time as visionary and transactional leadership with a second task performed by followers.

Pillai (1993) examined how followers and leaders coming from health care organizations responded to crisis situations. Specifically, this author was interested in examining a basic question often raised in the charismatic leadership literature: Is a crisis required for the emergence of charismatic leadership? The author reported that the perception of a crisis did not relate to emergence of charismatic leadership in the investigation.

We now return to the "born versus made issue." Specifically, preliminary evidence parallels the results noted above regarding the link between personality attributes and genetic predispositions (see also Box 5.3). A study conducted on identical twins found that self-ratings or perceptions of leadership had a 50% overlap with identical twins, as compared with fraternal twins. Specifically, by using the MLQ (self-ratings) discussed earlier,[48] a strong relationship was found in how twins rated themselves with respect to leadership styles along the full range of leadership.

For example, if a member of a twin pair thought he was inspirational with followers, it was likely that his twin thought the same was also true for himself. Because most personality instruments use self-ratings, these results parallel those findings obtained by using a similar methodology to assess personality. So again, if it's 50%, then what value can we add in terms of promoting leadership development? A great deal, both within and across generations, to the extent that genetic predispositions are eventually carried across generations partly because of the experiences accumulated within a generation. These are streams that go back a long, long way (see Box 5.4).

You might be thinking, Where is the evidence for the impact of experience on leadership development? This is an excellent question in the light of the main focus of this book. First, let's be clear on what we mean by experience and its connection to leadership and the development of an individual's perspective-

---

BOX 5.3. Environmental Stability and Leadership Performance

Brown (1994) set out to identify the leadership competencies associated with superior performance in times of turbulence versus stability. Superior and average performers were pooled from some Fortune 500 firms that had engaged in transformative processes within the last 5 years. Conducting behavioral event interviews resulted in the identification of four clusters of competencies that differentiated the top and average performers. The competencies represented four components of leadership similar to the components of transformational leadership discussed in the full range model. They were (a) visionary leadership, (b) a strong conceptual and systems thinker, (c) involving others and empowering, and (d) personal qualities (risk taker, high energy, open, and good communicator).

Hicks (1990) conducted a small sample study of 11 leaders in a missionary organization and found that unstable conditions were not necessarily required for transformational leaders to be effective. In addition, a stable environment was not a prerequisite for leaders to lead who were more transactional.

So, thus far the results are not consistent on how crises affect the emergence of transformational leadership. In some cases, and perhaps it depends on the nature of the crisis, transformational/charismatic leadership will *not* emerge.

---

taking capacity. Then we can discuss the relationship of experience to leadership development.

Certain life experiences, including family upbringing, significant engagements with role models, education and training, dramatic life events and crises, and work experiences, are accumulated and take the shape of what a colleague of mine called a "life biography" or "life script." Let's take a moment to look at this life script from the perspective of people entering a leadership training program.

Instructors often come to realize that all people enter training at some point in their *stream of life events.* (By the way, you can also apply this logic to being a leader or manager responsible for training others on the job.) Not all people have followed the same life course or have had the same life difficulties or opportunities, but they all end up there that first day of training with some anticipation of learning something about leadership. Not all believe that much can be done about this, however, and some are simply not developmentally ready

---

BOX 5.4. Born to Lead?

Johnson, Vernon, Molson, Harris, and Jang (1998) conducted the first ever study linking genetic predispositions to leadership ratings. Their results indicated that leadership was, in part, heritable when comparing results for 247 monozygotic twins. Each twin rated his or her own leadership style by using the MLQ. A great deal of shared variance in higher-level leadership, such as transformational, was seen as being linked to the twins' common genes (average genetic correlations of .5).

---

for the experience. Some are there on their own accord, and some are forced to be present.

What is important to consider here, as well as in your own situation where you are in a leadership role, is that you need to understand as much as you can about each member's "developmental readiness" to help him or her achieve full leadership potential. This is, in part, at the heart of what I referred to in Chapter 4 as *individualized consideration* in action. It also came in Chapter 2 when I said that if you are not ready to sacrifice 5 minutes each day, then perhaps you are not developmentally ready to learn more about building your own leadership potential. Some people are ready, some people can be prepared to be ready or motivated to action, some require direction, and some should be left alone for a while, until such time that it makes sense to intervene in their life courses or streams.

The developmental readiness of people relates to the perspectives they have built about how best to influence others and themselves. Each form of influence is related to the experiences they have accumulated or their life biographies or both. Some people who have a "young biography" may think the world is mostly driven by self-interests and that, to influence others, one must align each person's self-interest around what needs to be accomplished. This can be labeled the *pure transactional approach,* or what Karl Kuhnert referred to as the "operators." Give them the rewards they desire, and they will work to maximize their self-interests.[49]

Other people believe that although self-interest is important to motivation and achievement, it is not the only driver in influencing others to either develop or perform. Their perspective is different, and this is likely a result of differences in their life scripts versus the first group of transactional types. It is quite possible that they have seen others sacrifice their own interests, even lives, for the good of a group, organization, or community, if not for its very survival. For example, in the Israeli military, nearly twice the number of platoon officers die in combat, relative to their percentage in the military, because they literally take the lead in battle with a "follow me" charge to others. Many soldiers have seen their officers give their lives for the good or survival of the squad. I suspect this has a tremendous impact on one's perspective about human motivation, particularly if one is looking to lead others.

Recall Stacey, the teacher described in Chapter 3. She sacrificed her potential to win the most prestigious award in teaching for the good of a group of students she hadn't yet met. Recall the stream of fifth graders coming to her classroom to say good-bye. Do you think this was based on self-interest? When Stacey takes her own time to meet with students over the summer, those students come to understand that she is doing it because she believes in them and that her satisfaction is derived from their achievements. Many of them come back to say good-bye out of respect for the sacrifices Stacey continually makes for her students. In the classroom, when she emphasizes the need for *mutual dependence* to help each student achieve his or her full potential, she is developing a perspective in students that they must give back to others for everyone to succeed fully. She is also teaching them the importance of internal controls. Perhaps most important to transformational leadership development is that one should measure how well leaders are doing, not simply by one's own accomplishments but also by the accomplishments and achievements of others. Again, we are back to the legacy of leaders.

Interestingly enough, Andy Grove, the current CEO of Intel, and Bill Gates of Microsoft recently stated that the key to their respective financial and developmental success is, in large part, the fact that their companies have a higher mutual dependence on each other in terms of investment, learning, and development than probably any other two companies in modern history. I say "companies" because we believe that the military in countries like the United States has long understood the importance of mutual dependence to achieve missions successfully. I'll have more to say about this as we look at what some have referred to as *shared leadership* in teams. It suffices to say that this book began by highlighting the importance of our mutual dependence in helping each other achieve one's full potential, or "vital force," and we will see much more of this when we discuss teams and shared leadership. The notion of mutual dependence is probably best captured in a quote by John Gardner:

> *The achievements of Greece in the 15th century* B.C. *were not the*
> *performances of isolated people, but of individuals acting in an*
> *age of shared excellence.* (John Gardner)

Consider the following questions: *How can you strategically shape your life biography to maximize your full leadership potential? Is it possible to do so? How much range do you think you have to make a difference right now?* Consider that some of your chapters are obviously already fixed but that some of them remain to be created. Every day, portions of a new chapter can be created, ones over which you have some degree of control in terms of your own development. So, what choices you make each day will determine your life biography at later points in your life. What's your business plan for personal leadership development?

In a general sense, exploring new experiences itself is an important facet of developing one's leadership perspective. For example, engaging in how other disciplines diagnose problems, collect data, and evaluate solutions can be helpful in terms of challenging your own assumptions about what is right versus wrong.

Perhaps Albert Einstein captured it best by saying, "The true value of a human being is determined primarily by how he [or she] has attached liberation from the self. . . . Everything that is really great and inspiring is created by the individual who can labor in freedom." Often, the liberation allows us to consider widely different ideas and perspectives, which can lead to breakthrough innovations.

Several research projects point to some areas you should consider, as you begin to take hold of what your life biography should be like, in developing your full leadership potential, as well as the potential of others. I present a profile here, based on what has been found, that characterizes high-potential leaders. I present information you can use in choosing alternative life courses, as opposed to picking a different set of parents, which could also have affected your potential to lead, given the results reviewed above for identical twins.

Leaders who have been evaluated by their followers as more transformational were shown to exhibit a broader range of learning interests. This broader range stimulated a willingness in others to come to these leaders with ideas that were on the boundaries of acceptability or sometimes even beyond those boundaries. They demonstrated a passion for learning new and different things, which often was diffused in the culture of their work unit. They followed an accepted principle that says answers to one's problems can be found by consulting other fields that have not addressed one's particular problem directly but that nevertheless have generated some interesting and potential solutions. This occurs in science all the time when a drug or herb discovered for one purpose appears to have the potential for curing a disease for which it was not initially developed.[50]

Another facet of human development that comes through strongly in prior research is that of gaining experience in situations where one has to influence others without the authority of a position. These situations can be both formal and informal with respect to influencing others. So, those individuals in high school who took on a broader range of responsibilities for which they had to influence others but perhaps had no formal position power were people who engaged the full range of leadership more effectively later in life. These same people also have been shown to develop a more mature "thought" or "implicit" model of leadership that helps guide them in effectively developing others. They are freer from inner problems to focus on dealing with the problems of others.[51,52]

Individuals who have been extremely challenged, sometimes way beyond what they thought possible, but received support in their failures and constructive advice from parents were often the ones who grew up to be the best developers of people. They learned early on what could be derived from both failures and successes (I've put them in this order for emphasis). As they passed through life, they continually sought to work with a mentor who would not simply make life easy by championing all of their cherished causes but rather encourage them to dig down deeply to provide their best efforts. And when their best efforts resulted in a failure, they were encouraged to reflect on aspects of the process that could be improved for another try at the goal. They debriefed failures along with successes![53]

Because we are on reflections, another finding from this work was that those leaders who were most effective went through life crises pursuing one of two learning options. The first option was to not examine deeply what happened and to feel good about the fact that the crisis and stresses were over. The second option was to derive as much meaning from what could be learned by going through the crisis, perhaps via some postmortem analysis of events. These two approaches represent very different perspectives in terms of learning styles and affect how willing the leader is seen by others to want to learn from mistakes, even those one might consider the worst possible mistakes that should have been avoided. Stated another way, even in the worst situations, such leaders turned or transformed the threats of a crisis into a learning opportunity.

A most poignant example of leading under duress is the three learning objectives that Victor Frankel set for himself while in a German concentration camp. Imagine trying to use such an experience as an opportunity to learn, and you can appreciate more fully the title of his book on the subject, *Man's Search for Meaning,* or what we have called one's perspective on life and leadership.[54]

In the last 5 years, I have worked with two companies that went through major ethical violations that almost bankrupted each company. I found in both cases that many people there did not want to talk about "the event." In both cases, strict compliance standards were put in place that ensured such deviations in business practices would never occur again. As a consequence, both companies suffered from a "control"-dominated culture that had lost its ability to innovate. When I asked people what they had learned from these "events," by and large they simply said, "Not to do *that* again!" Unfortunately, in not doing *that* again, most other deviations that would lead to innovation were also not being done. And, by and large, little, if any, debriefing of the event was done to separate out *recoverable* and *unrecoverable* mistakes in their businesses.

Let me point out something that might be very obvious at this point in our discussion. The life experiences that you accumulate both strategically and beyond your control (you always have the control to revisit and reexamine) shape your perspective on how to influence others. The way you go about developing yourself as a role model can also have a significant impact on the way others choose to develop around you or as a *direct* and/or *indirect* consequence of your efforts. If you are in a formal leadership role, then your choices regarding your own development can become a set of choices for others to consider to the extent that they role-model your style and behavior over time.

With respect to whether leaders are born versus made, I have attempted to approach this issue from several angles. First, in terms of your own development, I have argued that you have some choices over the experiences you accumulate and that those experiences, within some limits, can affect the leader you are, the leader you will become, and how you are ultimately perceived by others. They can also affect your perspective of the roles you think are appropriate for followers and, of course, the roles they choose to adopt. Second, what you select to expose yourself to in terms of life experiences signals to others the type of experiences they can engage in if they choose to model your behavior. Also, what they choose to expose you to is part of how your life biography will unfold. For example, if you had a group of followers who absolutely feared to challenge your ideas when they came across new developments in other fields, you are, in effect, shaping the types of experiences that people bring to you and, in turn, your own life biography's development. Did you have a visual image of a stream bypassing a very important location? Good.

Returning to the issue of self-interest, with perhaps a sort of ironic twist, when you stifle the development potential of those who follow you, you are, in effect, stifling your own development by the types of ideas and experiences people are unwilling to present to you. So, it's in your own self-interest to engage other people's ideas and challenges. We return to this issue later, for those autocratic types that just threw the book down and said, Are you yanking my chain? No kidding . . . really.

In this chapter, my intent was to convey to you that although limits are set by genetic predispositions, a tremendous range also exists in which we can work to develop your leadership potential to the highest points along the full range of leadership. Realizing that these boundaries exist is an important basis for you to be an individually considerate leader with others. Using the excuse that leaders are born and not made to avoid developing followers, however, is a rather lame excuse, which no doubt will limit your own full potential as a leader and your followers' leadership potential as well.

I want you to reflect on a set of questions, or perhaps one in particular, if you choose. These questions look at your earlier life biography and how it has shaped your perspective over time in terms of leading others up to this very moment. Use 5 minutes of your reflection time to consider these questions and then consider how you are going to create the next chapter in your life biography. Keep in mind that what gets included in your life biography is not completely in your control but that, on a good day, we would say at least 50% is. Well, what a coincidence.

Coach Bear Bryant shared a story involving the enigmatic dynamics of a love-hate relationship between a coach and a player. Bryant's former player, Bob Gain, was a discipline problem. Bryant remembered being harder on him than on any other player he had ever coached. Years later, Gain was serving in Korea, and on the night before his platoon's first battle, he wrote a letter to his "old damn coach." Bryant was amazed. In the letter, Gain admitted his disdain for Bryant but ended with, "I love you tonight for what I used to hate you for."

- *What type of learning style would best characterize your parents' interactions with you?*
- *What is the worst life crisis you have had to deal with, and what positive things did you learn from it through self-reflection?*

- *How would others describe your range of learning interests?*
- *What is your most important assumption, and what would your reaction be if someone questioned it?*
- *During the next 3 months, what would you like to include in your next life biography chapter?*

Some Things Worth Repeating

- One's leadership development is affected by the life experiences accumulated.
- Specific life experiences appear to be linked to the development of transformational leadership.
- What you model as a leader can determine what you receive in return from your followers that can either enhance or inhibit your development as a leader.

6

Viewing Leadership at Its Many Levels

The fundamental movement over the next 25 years will be in the dispersing of power in organizations.
(Bill O'Brian, CEO of Hanover Insurance)

It is quite common for people to think of leadership as being associated with a particular individual. Yet, in many organizations today, the level at which we observe and discuss leadership has changed quite significantly. What do I mean? Leadership in many organizations today is often not just vested in a single individual, but in a larger collective, such as "teams" or team systems. It has become more common to discuss "shared" or "distributed" leadership practices and even the leadership system(s) in an organization.

I now discuss leadership at three levels—the *individual* leader, the *group,* and the overall *organization,* which I refer to as a system of leadership practices.

At each level, we could discuss the life history of the individual, the team's life history, and the organization, and such a discussion would be equally relevant to the perspective that would be observed at each of those levels in terms of the type of leadership observed. People learn. Teams learn. Organizations learn. (By the way, all three can also fail to learn.)

At the Individual Level

Much of our discussion up to this point has focused on individual-level leadership as exemplified by people such as Sam and Stacey (see Chapter 3). Yet, in perhaps a subtle way, I was discussing more than just individual-level leadership. This leads to a very basic question: If there is just a leader, with no followers to follow, can one observe leadership? Some of my colleagues might argue yes, there is "self-leadership," but beyond that I would argue that a very important ingredient is missing—the "other" person in the leadership process, the person being influenced. This can be a follower, a peer, a customer, a supervisor, or some combination of these people. Most discussions of leadership deal with, at minimum, an interaction between two individuals. Here, our observations center on the treatment of an individual by the leader. Is the leader inspiring? Is the leader demonstrating individualized consideration? Like the cells in the human body, this is clearly a very important building block for the leadership system of the organization, and that is exactly how I want you to think about the beginning of building a leadership system. It starts one cell at a time, and here the cell is the leader and someone else, and then another, and another, and the context, and then the future, and . . . well, let's stop here for the moment. And like cells in the human body, we can say that each of these cells has a cultural footprint that affects the type of interactions we will observe within and between cells. The footprint can be the values of each individual, as well as the values of the organization.

Taking a step backward to move forward (I am trying to practice what I have been preaching here), we must first understand the leader's perspective on how she believes others should be treated; this forms a broad or, in some autocratic cases, narrow basis for interactions with others. If the leader sees the world as a series of transactions, then the basis for her interactions is to satisfy the self-interests of those who work with her; if the self-interests are satisfied, then she fully expects to achieve desired targets. If the leader changes the incentives, she can enhance motivation and performance.

Let's assume that some hypothetical organization is composed of five people, including the leader. Thus, in each interaction the leader has with each of her five followers, the goals and expectations set the basis for transactional relationship. The compact of understanding is then composed of a series of "if you do this, then in return you get that" statements. At an optimum level, all understand what they need to do to be rewarded for their efforts (individual or collective) and contributions to the organization. One transactional relationship leads into another, forming a set of norms in the organization that help guide what is expected of each of the members and what they will get in return for meeting those expectations. The culture itself becomes more transactional over time.

In this rather simple organization, what has begun at an individual level of interaction between the leader and a follower can eventually become part of a larger leadership system characterizing the organization. We have the first evidence of a leadership system. How? The system is promoting a set of expectations that everyone knows about and that guide the interactions of members in that organization, whether they be with the leader or with other members. What occurs over time is quite interesting. What started as an interaction between a leader and her followers grew into a leadership system and culture. And if developed carefully and strategically, a leader will have more than the 5 minutes we've required to be a reflective leader (see Box 6.1). This occurs where the system can substitute for the specific interactions between leader and follower that, at earlier points in the relationship, required greater levels of monitoring and vigilance.

Perhaps you are wondering what actually is going on here. We just moved leadership to the next level of analysis, where it is systemic and can substitute for some lower-level interactions required at the beginning of a relationship. The same may be true of our relationship. If you extend what you've learned from reading this book to the next level of analysis, which is the people you work with and whom you are interested in developing to their full potential, then you substitute for what you've learned in this book. And I anxiously await your substitution!

A local entrepreneur recently started an organization to build the next generation of laser tools for industrial application. He said at the groundbreaking ceremony for this new company that he wanted to build an organization based on the principle that employees of his organization would always be comfortable challenging each other's ideas and his own. He suggested that to survive in this new business required that employees ask difficult questions before their com-

---

BOX 6.1. How Transformational Leadership Relates to Reputation, Cooperation, Friendliness, and Warmth

---

In a study conducted with government councils with first-line supervisors and their work groups, Weierter (1994) found that transformational leadership positively related to perceptions of work group reputation, cooperation, friendliness, and warmth. These factors were later described as potentially substituting for transactional leadership behavior. In other words, they had become part of the leadership system.

---

petitors do. Too many organizations train their employees to leave their brains "at the door." The leadership system requires that this be so. If the founding CEO has his way, it will not be so in this new organization.

A few years ago, I attended a "recognition day" ceremony at a large sunglasses factory in the northeastern United States. At that meeting, an operations worker was describing how he had made a suggestion to the chemist in his area and how his suggestion had led to a change in the chemical processes used to bond gold to sunglass frames. In the first several months, his unit had saved the company more than $700,000 by increasing the level of bonding to the metal, thus reducing the amount of gold going down the drain. He was then asked when he had discovered the alternative way of processing the gold. His reply was, "Several years back." I asked him why it took several years to get his idea implemented. He said, "It took me several years to learn that I should not leave my brain at the door when I come to work. The previous plant manager didn't care to hear our ideas. Phil [the current plant manager] cares, and I bring my brain to work every day now. Once I made the recommendation to our chemist, it was implemented within a few days."

Let's step back and take a look at what this entrepreneur was trying to establish in his new organization. It is quite common in organizations for people not to tell their "leaders" what they really think or, worse yet, what they have known for some time. If you are going to embrace the full range of leadership, you will quickly realize the shortcomings of this approach. Leaders who *control* their organizations with an iron hand think they are less vulnerable. History would suggest otherwise (see Box 6.2). Humankind has never created any better control system than what comes with *internal control based on commitment.* No walls, contracts, punishment systems, regulations, or laws have ever been able

---

BOX 6.2. Transactional Leadership and Participation

Cheverton and Thompson (1996) examined the relationship among follower ratings of leadership, organizational context, and level of "psychological participation." The sample of leaders included middle- to senior-level managers in business and nonbusiness settings. The authors indicated that nonbusiness leaders displayed transformational leadership more often and that higher levels of "psychological participation" were noted among followers of transformational leaders. Transformational leadership created a "climate" for greater levels of participation.

---

to control people's behavior, especially how they think, any better than when those individuals have internalized the control. In other words, they believe, and therefore they do whatever needs to be done willingly, even in the extreme where they sacrifice their own lives for a cause. That's one incredible control mechanism!

The entrepreneur described above fully understood that, by building at the foundation of his organization the norm that ideas were welcome, over time the system of leadership that would evolve should be more receptive to, if not demand, divergent ideas. No brain hooks will appear at the door where employees can leave their thoughts on the way into work. By the way, Apple's new/old corporate motto is "think different." This appears to have been chosen to develop a foundation for intellectual stimulation in every interaction. If properly nurtured, it becomes part of the cultural fabric of the organization and its leadership system.

Something else is going on in this example of a start-up organization that is perhaps not so apparent. Not only is the leader attempting to establish a framework for future interactions he desires in the organization, but he is also recognizing that the people he selects may come from organizations that did not appreciate challenging the ideas of one's superiors. And the "habits of the past" are easily imported into the present unless a conscious effort is made to address those habits, and such habits are quite common in organizations and many cultures throughout the world. For example, in a workshop I conducted in Mexico where we were discussing dependent followership, one participant said that it's common for Mexicans to say, in Spanish, "How may I serve you?" as opposed to "Excuse me, how may I *assist* you?" Similarly, on a trip to Korea this past year, I learned firsthand how difficult it is for people from a "shame culture" to question authority. It is so ingrained not to question managers that one has to change the societal leadership system to effect change at the organizational level, a challenge many Korean Chaebols (Korean conglomerates like Samsung) are now confronting as they attempt to globalize their organizations and workforces, as well as deal with the economic meltdown in their Pacific Rim region.

As an individual leader, you are often forced to assume what has been developed or not developed in those you are attempting to influence. So, even though this local entrepreneur is starting a new organization, this in no way guarantees that old habits may not come through the door. In fact, without a clear statement of his preference, reiterated in many different ways, it is likely that new employees will not come in naturally questioning the ideas of others, particularly those they consider their "bosses." They have typically been trained very differently in schools and in work organizations to "respect" authority, which is fine as long as the people in authority know what they are doing and, more important, are doing the right thing (see Box 6.3). Why challenge is seen as being anathema to having respect for leaders remains a central problem in the *least* innovative organizations. Unfortunately, this is not always the case, and to protect the democracy of a country and any organization requires that people question the "unquestionable," "undiscussables," or "unmentionables." Our system of democracy very much depends on having conflict to help maintain its viability. It lends credence to the need for executive and legislative branches of a government often at odds with itself. I guess I should say "very often," but even so, the United States is still the most vibrant, productive nation on earth.

To build a leadership system requires that we understand two very basic points. First, we can determine what the system will be by stating up front what our ideals are and then behaving in a way that is absolutely congruent with those ideals. Maybe you thought we are now building a life script for the organization. That's a pretty accurate statement.

Second, people come into an organization with preconceived notions or models in their heads, not blank slates. So, consistency is crucial to overcome the habits imported from past experiences with other groups and organizations. That is why I said earlier that consistency or, better yet, predictability around trust building will be one of your greatest challenges and accomplishments if eventually achieved. It is also why companies like Nordstrom, Disney, Cooper Tires, and Southwest Airlines are a "pain in the butt to get into." These organizations expend a great deal of energy on selecting and socializing employees to the desired cultures.

BOX 6.3. Transformational Leadership and Ethnicity

Jung and Avolio (in press-a, in press-b) set out to demonstrate that Asian American college students would react more favorably to transformational versus transactional leadership. They also compared these different styles of leadership with a sample of Caucasian Americans, with each participating in an experimental study in which participants were asked to generate ideas for improving a business school's chance of getting reaccredited. Leadership styles (transactional vs. transformational) and task type (individual vs. group) were both successfully manipulated. Transformational leadership improved the performance at both individual and group levels, especially among collectivistic Asian Americans. Transformational leadership was shown to have direct effects on performance, as well as indirect effects via the trust participants had in the leader and how well they identified with the leader's values. Overall, transactional leadership had a more positive impact on the quantity of ideas generated for Caucasian Americans, whereas transformational leadership had a more positive impact on the generation of long-term ideas requiring fundamental change for Asian American and Caucasian participants. More important, the Asian Americans generated more divergent ideas working alone versus in groups because they did not have to confront each other when working alone.

For some people at the groundbreaking ceremony, what appeared as a simple statement was quite profound in terms of its implications for building a leadership system. This crucial point of initiation can be a very effective start in building a system that will take on its own life. How so? If the leader is consistent with his espoused ideals, those who work at the organization will come to realize "this is the way we do business here . . . it's our perspective on how we treat others." Relationships with customers and suppliers will take on the characteristics of the relationships that are observed first internal to the organization, but eventually they will migrate to external relationships with suppliers and customers as well if they are properly nurtured and reinforced. And at some point, the founder could actually step back and see that the system, once created, is in line with his espoused beliefs and desires. Yet, consistency and continuous reinforcement are necessary for it to evolve to a systemic cultural level. Many forces are against this entrepreneur's espoused beliefs, not least of which are the managers who don't have the confidence to be vulnerable and questioned by followers. Also, some people at that groundbreaking ceremony may be cynical

---

BOX 6.4. Transformational Leadership in India

Pereira (1986) set out to generalize the model of transformational and transactional leadership within the India context. The company in which data were collected is Larsen and Toubro Limited (Ltd), and at the time of the study it was the fifth largest private-sector firm in terms of assets. Self- and other ratings were collected from 58 managers. Pereira confirmed the hierarchical ordering of constructs in the full range model, reporting that transformational leadership accounted for a significantly greater share of the variance in ratings of satisfaction with the leader, job effectiveness, relating the needs of followers to senior leaders, and organizational effectiveness.

In a recent study of 50 Indian firms, the pattern of relationships shown in Figure 6.1 was observed between the type of culture in those organizations and financial performance.

Indicators:	Inducement (Transactional)	Investment (Paternalistic)	Involvement (Transformational)
• Roles :	Narrow	Broad	Flexible
• Supervision:	Direct	Developmental	Facilitative
• Competitive:	Price	Product Differentiation	Innovation
Outcomes			
• ROI %:	7.03	9.64	11.02
• ROA %:	16.37	15.98	20.89

Figure 6.1. Organizational Culture and Performance
SOURCE: Sivasubramaniam, Murry, Avolio, & Jung (1997)
NOTE: Productivity compared to closest competitors.

---

about such words and think it is just "management-by-magazine." Specifically, these are the right "buzz words" to say, now really show me! But the benefits (and here I mean financial) can be profound for the leader who can move on to other activities as the system takes over reinforcing ideas values and principles that were initiated by the leader (see Box 6.4).

Let's take a moment here to capture what is going on in the organization's development cycle; it has implications for understanding leadership at a systemic level, particularly systems that are quite commonly in use today, such as project teams.

Core Attributes

- The basis for the system began with an idea or a perspective of what the leader desired and articulated.

- The leader not only is responsible for clearly articulating what is desired but also must develop a script that people come to understand and believe in over time: "This is the way we do business." All organizations are theater, and therefore we define what the scripts should be, which specify roles, expectations, and the interactions we observe over time.

- Consistency is generally crucial to embedding what one wants to establish in the system and is proportionately more crucial to the extent that the beliefs one is trying to change are heavily ingrained in the way people already think (e.g., "My boss never asked me before what I thought," "Is this person for real?").

- The leader initiates what later she or he will also become part of, or embedded in, so choose carefully the system you are trying to build. The system can become a main support system for your agenda or a terrible obstacle. What script do you want to write? What line do you intend to add each day? The play can also unfold with and without any direction.

- Paradoxically, by not choosing to develop scripts and a leadership system, you are, in effect, creating a system, albeit loosely coupled. People import habits from the past; thus, if you do not decide what the system should be, it will be something it has been because people, like nature, abhor a vacuum. People will create a system to frame their interactions; this is deeply rooted in human nature. So, if you are laissez-faire in your design of an organizational system, it will be created for you without your input; some might even call this a "self-organizing" system. If good people are involved, it may end up being a good system; if not, then it's all left up to chance.

- A reasonable question for you to ask is, "Okay, so what is the bottom line here?" The bottom line is that you can select and develop over time the system *you* choose to be embedded in at some future point. And, you create what eventually exists as a basis for each interaction. It takes discipline and determination to create a system that goes against the habits of the past, and you can rest assured that people will look for any slight deviation from what you espoused, retreating to methods they are familiar with and have used in other organizations. *Be absolutely consistent and build trust. Be inconsistent and let others build the system. It is really your choice.*

> *The difference is knowing what you want and knowing what the end is*
> *supposed to look like. If a coach does not know what the end is*
> *supposed to look like, he won't know it when he sees it.*
> (Coach Vince Lombardi)

And Now, the Team Leadership System

We now have a foundation for discussing team leadership/organizational system development. The development of a team leadership system is introduced here, and we get into more detail about what constitutes shared leadership in teams in Chapter 7.

How do you start building a team leadership system? The first thing to realize is that each member comes to the team with a conception of "how a team works." A mental model of sorts or perspective that forms the basis for interactions regardless of whether one states them explicitly or not, each will have an impact on behavior.[55] As a team leader, it is important to realize that each member has a perspective that, over time, the goal of the leader or leaders on the team should be to bring these mental models into some sort of alignment. Some authors call this process creating a "shared mental model" for guiding team development and performance.[56] One point is clear: Any system out of alignment, human or otherwise, is not able to optimize its performance. Such systems are also inherently unreliable. So, at its foundation, the leader needs to appreciate and understand the diversity of perspectives brought to the group and, through that understanding, to find a way to align each member around certain principles that can guide the team system's development over time. In a self-directed team context, we should substitute the word *leaders* for *leader* in the previous sentence.

Place yourself in the role of team leader. One of the first steps is for you to understand the perspective of each member and, of course, for each member to understand yours. As with the entrepreneur above, he made it clear what his starting point was in terms of the nature of interactions he desired in the new organization and that it was important for him to understand the habits and perspectives brought into the group. The goal is to integrate the diversity of the group around a common purpose; the integration comes about, in part, through the goal created and the principles for how members treat each other in the group. In the discussion of team leadership, we revisit how to use a compact of understanding as a means of building the basis for future interactions, commitment, and trust.

Several points that parallel those mentioned above are worth reiterating. First, think of a team composed of individuals as having the potential to develop into a full range leadership system. Second, one basic responsibility of a leader is to help define a system in which she or he will eventually operate over time. Third, a system composed of human beings is, in large part, based on the integration of each member's mental model into a cohesive or collective model that comes to guide the group or team's behavior as a leader's behavior does at the outset of a team's development.

The "shared" in highly effective teams represents a collective understanding of how members want to relate to each other and the purpose of the relationships or the goal often "idealized" in the way we described this term at the individual level. It also determines, to a very large extent, the methods and styles of relationships with other individuals and groups, both within the organization as well as outside.

As organizations move toward a team system structure, they typically need to rebuild the system of leadership that has existed in their organizations in the past or in what you expect to embed this team system over time. I say "rebuild" here because we are assuming that one system existed prior to moving to teams, a system that was more hierarchically based and tied to superior-subordinate relationships. This is an awesome challenge for many organizations today because the habits are so ingrained in terms of the old system of leadership that it will take tremendous consistency to convince people we are truly trying to move to a team leadership system-based organization.[57] Placing a heavy emphasis on rewarding individual over collective performance is no way to convince people that you are serious about going to teams. Yet, many organizations that have tried to make the transition to teams often lament it's not working very well. I'm not surprised. People are very aware of discrepant signals in organizations and inconsistencies, particularly when one is trying to initiate a radical shift in one's way of thinking and operating. It's one basis for widespread cynicism. Thus, when you say you want to go to a team system and the principles are in place but the behavior is not, what type of conclusions do you expect others to draw over time? Of course, we typically find that what people said is not what they are doing, so the system is being created but it's not the one desired. Reflect on a situation where a gap existed between what was espoused and what you observed in practice. How did the gap affect your perspective, your motivation, and ultimately your performance? By the way, I am assuming here that you are still there and that I have not been shelved away prematurely. Hello. Is anyone out there?

To start building a team system, you should have in mind the system features you want to end up with over time. In other words, envision the type of processes you would want to occur if all your ideals were achieved. What would the interactions look like between you and the other members and among the other members of the team? If you have clearly envisioned the process and have acted consistently with the principles that support that process, you have a good chance of achieving your desired ideals over time. Are you wondering, "What does he mean by *chance?* It seems as if we did everything he said." This is all true, but selection also plays a role in what people do. It is really like every other system in that it is not only in the procedures or processes you attempt to implement but also in the quality of resources and materials you input into building the system. In the human system, the quality of the resources is based on how you select people into the system. In the example that began this chapter, we saw that the leader had an enviable situation in that he had the chance to pick a new workforce from scratch. Consequently, he should begin to put the basic principles into action to form an organizational system while selecting new people into the organization, which is an advantage many organizational leaders do not have, let alone many project leaders, who have to build the team with what they are given or have, versus some ideal selection process. Yet, if you have the ideal, then consider the nature of the resources that will best fit your system and select the best of the group.

If you are currently working, consider how difficult it would be for a team in your organization to self-organize with respect to picking the challenges and resources needed to accomplish that challenge. What institutional habits and systems would prevent this initiative from being successful? How might you change the context so that it is receptive to self-organizing teams? At Motorola, employees have been working on transforming the context for the last 15 to 20 years in order for it to produce 4,000+ self-organized teams. And today, they are having to go through yet another radical change as markets in Asia fall and rival competitors eat away at Motorola's hold on its cellular phone market. Stay tuned.

Teams Embedded in Organizational Cultures

Today, the culture of an organization has never been more relevant to building an optimal leadership system. Why today? The more organizations have decoupled their structures, deleveled, and built networks, the less structure is available to provide guidance to what are and are not appropriate standards and norms for behavior. In replacing managerial structures, the specific need is to establish the type of culture the leadership of an organization wants in place to guide the development of relationships throughout the organization's phases of development.

Another way of looking at what has been described here is that organizations are not of the same form as they were even 10 or 20 years ago. Leadership is migrating to the lowest levels, and more and more people have direct influence in shaping an organization's destiny. With these changes comes a need to reengineer relationships in the organization to take into consideration that, increasingly, the formal structures are blurred and the informal structures have more influence on bottom-line performance.

Back in the late 1970s, a CEO by the name of Bill O'Brian took over the lead at Hanover Insurance. Bill envisioned the changes on the horizon in the insurance business and decided that big corporate headquarters with a large staff would soon be outdated and that the largest concentration of staff should be where it can be most useful—with a company's customers. So, he began a campaign to "localize" decisions at the point of contact with the external customer. In his initial attempt, he failed, in part, because of the ingrained beliefs of "who was in charge." For months, people kept sending the same requests to headquarters for decisions to be made that they were repeatedly told were their prerogative. Bill had to transfer the corporate staff to the field to get the decisions to be "local." He also began a weekly letter to all 10,000+ employees, describing examples that fit with a "localization philosophy." He found through the use of strategic redundancy and consistency of action that he could shift the perspective from a top-down decision-making structure to one based more on lateral integration and distribution of shared power. It took much more time than he thought initially to attack and change past habits that had been imported into the present situation he and Hanover were confronting (see Box 6.5).

In some organizations in which teams have really taken hold, like Xerox and Motorola, the need to examine how peers lead each other in ever-changing team compositions, as well as participate in multiple teams at the same point in time, has become a prominent issue for people in the field of leadership development.[58] Part of the change that is underway is technology driven. More people are connected to each other, and information is accessible in ways it never has been before in organizations.

In traditional organizational structures, the manager was the central unit of information dissemination and retention; this is no longer true in many organizations today. This condition is forcing organizational leaders to rethink their

---

BOX 6.5. Transformational Leadership and Computer Mediation

Sosik, Avolio, and Kahai (in press) conducted a laboratory experiment to examine the impact of different leadership styles delivered via computer mediation. Confederate leaders were employed to deliver the leadership styles consistently across groups/conditions. Participants were undergraduate students involved in an idea-generation task. Results indicated that leadership can have an impact on group processes and outcomes when delivered through computer mediation. Both directive and participative leadership had a positive and significant impact on the number of ideas generated within the experimental sessions, satisfaction with participation, and levels of participation. Directive leadership increased participation in the task versus decreased. Anonymity built into the system used for computer mediation moderated the effects of leadership on group processes and performance.

The use of anonymity in computer-mediated interactions can also be a powerful tool for integrating the diverse opinions of group members in that it is a mechanism to get participants to focus on what was said versus who said it. With early instructions between leader and follower, this may be a useful strategy for developing more open and effective communication.

Kahai, Avolio, and Sosik (1998) examined 58 four-member groups consisting of either graduate or undergraduate students taking part in three tasks. In the first, they made a private decision about an issue and then discussed that issue via computer mediation, followed by a second opportunity to decide on the issue privately. The authors reported that different forms of anonymity increased participation/discussion in these groups. Anonymity also increased satisfaction with the process. Large differences were also found in the pattern of results if the groups started with initial differences of opinions. Being more anonymous was a positive predictor of group interactions with larger differences in initial opinions. These results have significant implications for the development of teams and for dealing with conflict and/or difficult issues in team processes over time. Using computer mediation can help in addressing the polarization that often goes along with groups composed of diverse membership.

Sosik, Avolio, and Kahai (1997) examined the effects of anonymity on groups interacting via computer mediation, assessing the impact of leadership on potency and performance. In a longitudinal experiment to compare the effectiveness of groups interacting on creativity tasks, the authors showed that anonymity amplified the positive effects of transformational leadership on levels of group potency and performance. Performance in this investigation was measured in terms of the level of creative output produced by these groups.

---

structures and processes, the roles of managers, and the roles of those who still report to those managers. Organizational leaders who have recognized these changes and dramatic shifts in structures and technology, as well as in worker needs, have been reconceptualizing how their business structures should be designed. This can be witnessed in almost every sector of the economy in terms of the reengineering tidal wave, the dialogue on the knowledge criterion and "re"learning organization, and all the things being "reinvented." Yes, we are into the age of "re." It's a worldwide housecleaning project to prepare for life in the next century. Yet, to date, we are still exploring how we should lead in the "new age" organizations.

An essential ingredient to business success seems to be the development of a culture that is highly adaptive and prone to re-creation. By "adaptive," I mean a willingness that pervades the culture to get rid of or abandon something that doesn't serve the needs of the business in order to move onto something that is more effective. Someone recently said, "You have to be willing to drown a puppy to be successful in business." (I apologize for the image to all dog lovers out there.) Okay, business doesn't have to be that ruthless. At Microsoft, the culture is highly adaptive in an industry that is under constant change. On average, employees move in and out of jobs every 18 months. The ongoing joke is, "What job are you coming from to go to?" Also, Microsoft employees understand the importance of maintaining high performance in that the bottom 5% each year are released from the company. At Levi Strauss, people have to reapply for their own jobs periodically to ensure they are still relevant to the organization.[59] John Kotter indicated that "only cultures that can help organizations anticipate and adapt to change will be associated with superior performance over long periods of time" (p. 44)[60] Bass and Avolio have designated the adaptive culture as one that is more transformational.[61]

Firms must avoid being seduced by their own success, or what Danny Miller called the "Icarus paradox."[62] I have called it the "failure of success." When we become too comfortable with our successful products or programs, we fail to kill them to move on to better products and programs.

> *Unless you learn to manage the aftereffects of winning, the forces that led*
> *your team to the top will turn around and destroy you.*
> (Pat Riley, former Head Coach of the New York Knicks)

At an organizational level, we are witnessing a dramatic transformation that has been stimulated by events, some of which were discussed above. Taken

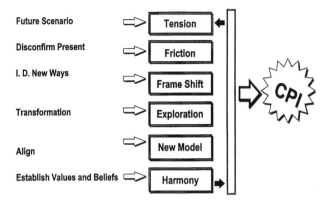

Figure 6.2. Organizational Development at Any Level Requires Change

together and referring to Figure 6.2, a "future scenario" has been emerging that has caused enough *tension* in organizations for the leadership to rethink its total *leadership system.* Whether at an individual, group, or organizational level, as the future scenario becomes more evident and the extent to which this new state is dramatically different from the present or past, some accommodation must be made. (Accommodation is a soft way of saying adaptation or transformation.) Tension, like *adaptive conflict,* is a good thing if it leads to a productive dialogue and a constructive change in the way one operates, a group functions, or an organization transacts its business. Transformational leaders focus the tension into positive energy to create the desired future scenario.

For many leading organizations around the world, changes in technology, the globalization of markets, and the changing nature of the workforce, which is more educated and seeking more involvement in decisions and free agent status, have collectively contributed to a need to reconsider the nature of the current leadership system's design, which affects what is considered a "relevant" organizational culture. Some leaders have seen a cliff on the horizon, it has caused *tension* to make changes, and they have explored ways to make the changes needed in their organizations. Others just don't see the cliff coming, where significant and even fundamental change is required, and because they don't see it, they eventually fall into the abyss. The ones who see the cliff and see it in time will make the necessary adjustments, accommodations, and, ultimately, transformations. Those who don't—well, let's hope for a readily available parachute!

The future state and tension can also be observed at the individual level and is fundamentally the basis for development. For example, many people realize today that, after repeated downsizing and layoffs, guaranteed life span employment no longer exists. This has caused them to rethink career options and also to take advantage of opportunities some organizations are providing that will help them be more "employable" in the event things go downhill at their organization. Other people have become free agents working on their own—about 30% of the U.S. working population.[63] This is a real cliff affecting many people today and into the foreseeable future. It is also a cliff for organizations that now must develop the full potential of their workforces—unfortunately, often for someone else. And of course, everyone wants it done yesterday! You might consider the irony of this situation and of the opportunity and necessity for forming alliances where you only lose your best people temporarily. In Korea in 1997, this could be seen in the movements among the very large Chaebols to slowly consider transforming their management systems and, amid the current economic crisis, what they must address regarding institutional changes. These are the large Korean conglomerates like Samsung, LG, Hyundai, and Daewoo. Leaders of these large Korean organizations, often the founders, who are now reaching their mid-60s to 70s, saw on the horizon a huge cliff. The more Korea's efficient/high-quality manufacturing strategies became successful, which brought them in less than 40 years to the top rungs of the economic ladder in the world, the faster they approached the cliff. Also, the rapid globalization and expansion of their companies required a different type of manager, one more comfortable working in a broad range of cultures spanning large distances. And the more successful the nation became overall, the more its workforce wanted to benefit from its success, driving up salaries and, in turn, the cost of labor. This made the cheap labor in Korea a thing of the past and affected the country's ability to compete on price with other emerging economies.

Korea's success has moved these Korean organizations into the higher service arena, along with other companies that must compete on price and innovation. These changes required more people to be involved in the decision-making processes if innovation was to be nurtured and enhanced. It meant, for many Koreans, that they had become too expensive to manufacture products as cheaply as their neighbors, such as Vietnam and China. On a recent tour of the videotape production facilities at SKC, I asked the reason for so much open space on the production floor. My guide indicated that the jobs were heading to China because labor costs in Korea were nearly 10 times the cost in China. They are somewhat less then that now because of the dramatic drop in the won (the currency of Korea).

Many Koreans admitted to me that, as a culture, they do not have one of the fundamental elements to be innovative: to question the person in charge. Being a "shame type" culture, the second in command is far too deferential to authority to question ideas or directions, although the generation of students coming through the system today may be more prone to questioning than previous generations.[64] This condition obviously must change for Korea to be successful in the new arena of competition that many Korean companies are now entering and that other developed nations entered in the past as they went from performance based on cost/price competition to competition based on innovation. When you are competing on innovation, everyone's ideas can potentially count; where knowledge creation is not nice to have, it is a business necessity.[65] When you are competing on cost, the most structured system that doesn't allow for any deviations may be the most cost efficient. Such systems will eventually cost you, however, by inhibiting innovative thinking.

At the center of transforming from a control culture to a challenging one is the ongoing battle between balancing *control* and *flexibility.* You can imagine which side usually wins out, can't you? An amusing reference to what takes place in an organization's structure where control rules is what Gordon Mac-kenzie called "Orbiting the Giant Hairball." Too often, organizations rely on past policies, decisions, and processes for determining future direction; this creates a "tie up" that inhibits people from breaking out of their old orbits. Gordon described his former job at Hallmark Cards as operating in the role of "loyally subversive." Here again, we return to conflict as one generator of the "vital forces" in an organization.[66] Now, let's see what happened in Korea during 1997 and up until January 1998.

Sometimes the future arrives unexpectedly, as we witnessed in the economic crash of the Pacific Rim countries in 1997 and on into 1998 as a cliff that appeared "suddenly" on their horizon. About a year ago, I visited Korea and addressed some executives on the need to identify and adapt to domestic changes in world markets that were already on their horizon. As is true in all Asian cultures, the members of my audience politely listened to my call to develop more transformational leaders and followers at all levels of their organizations. Many Chaebols appeared flush with resources. They also appeared to have a high degree of complacency with success. About 6 months later, I attended a national conference in the United States at which the top three Chaebols were present; each of the presenters basked in the glory of success, reporting the billions of dollars generated by each of their groups that year. Interestingly enough, in 1997, even while I was in Korea, a call came for the huge Chaebols to restructure, to empower their workforces, and to help smaller and nimbler firms get off the ground.

As I am writing this chapter, I am flying back from Seoul after a very interesting trip to Korea. Guess what. The value of the Korean won dropped nearly 50% in the last few months of 1997, making Korea a paradise for American shoppers but a disaster for the Korean population. Today, in nearly every Korean newspaper article and conversation, one hears over and over again the three letters *IMF.* They stand for International Monetary Fund, which recently attempted to bail Korea out of near financial ruin. It's amazing what a year can bring to a "seemingly" prosperous nation.

I started my presentations in Korea during my second trip by asking whether IMF stood for what the chairman of the Chaebols said when asked about the crisis in Korea: "It's My Fault!" I also offered the following thought: Maybe it will come to mean *It's My Future.* Which one will each leader choose for her or his respective organization? How will these leaders turn this economic tension into an opportunity for significant transformation? Unfortunately, control of the change process is now largely in the hands of the IMF and the new government. Korean president Kim Dae-Jung is urging the leaders of Korea's largest organizations to take drastic corporate restructuring measures—unfortunately, a message that has become urgent on the "wrong" side of the cliff. The situation is so severe that the chairman of Samsung agreed on January 22, 1998, to sell off 128 billion won worth of real estate from his group and pledged 90% of his salary to support employee welfare funds following layoffs. When you don't see the cliff coming, it tends to restrict your options the closer it gets to you. I hope his actions will motivate dramatic changes throughout the Korean economy and serve as a role model for other leaders. Yes, I think Lee Iaccoca just shrugged his shoulders.

In my opinion, the changes required in Korea, largely based on where it has been in its "collective development trajectory," are nothing short of a radical transformation in the way leaders think about their organizations and followers. The "future state" is a global world market that has created enormous "tension" in the way many Korean managers traditionally have been trained to lead and follow. This will lead to a vast exploration in how to develop their managers into global leaders, resulting in a rapid increase in alliances with the learning institutions of other countries, in executives traveling around the world to learn

---

BOX 6.6. Vision and Firm Growth

Baum, Locke, and Kirkpatrick (1998) examined the relationship among vision attributes, vision content, vision communication, and venture growth over a 2-year period. This was the first study to examine the effects of vision on the overall performance of an organization. Vision attributes (e.g., clarity, challenge, future orientation, ability to inspire), vision content (growth image), and vision communication each positively predicted the venture growth of the firm. Vision content and vision attributes were also indirectly related to growth performance through vision communication.

---

the latest in management technology, and a reconsideration of how the culture of Korean society and organizations must be changed to inspire Koreans to succeed in the "new world order." This story is obviously still unfolding, and still not all the leaders have accepted that the cliff is upon them in Korea. I say this because of my own personal observations and the fact that the president of Korea, on January 22, 1998, criticized the Chaebol leaders for only making token adjustments in restructuring their organizations. At this writing, they have not yet fully addressed the issue of complete leadership and followership development.

Many executives said to me while I was in Korea, "Once we address the financial crisis, we will work on the 'leadership problem.'" Why business leaders insist on separating leadership from the "business of business" still amazes me each time I hear such comments. It's like the Israeli bank human resources director who told me recently that her CEO was delaying any type of leadership development effort until their new business strategy was fully deployed. Leadership should drive strategy deployment, and it is much more effective to do it at the front end than to recover it at the back end.

Five or 6 years ago, the former president of Korea set a national goal called *Inwa,* which means to globalize Korea. He appears to have seen a cliff in advance of many others in his society, but unfortunately it has taken an economic catastrophe to get his people's attention (see Box 6.6). In leadership, a crisis is often very handy to refocus people's efforts around a new vision. It may be handy, but too often it is very painful.

As organizations (or countries) enter periods of fundamental change and transformation, some will likely question whether it's for real or not. This is a reasonable thing to ask amid change and confusion. If we step back and reflect on what's happened during the last 25 years or more, we do see patterns that suggest the transformation collectively is very real. The turbulent 1960s and 1970s saw a great deal of discussion about the role of participative management in the design of leadership systems.[67] One at least had to consider being more participative in a period when both leadership and authority were being questioned throughout the United States and in many other countries. The credibility of the entire leadership system was in question, and many of these questions were creating tension in how organizations conceived and designed their leadership systems. With more of former President Nixon's tapes now being released, one can only appreciate in retrospect how important the process of questioning authority truly was at that point in U.S. history.

Interestingly, the push toward building total quality systems has made it essential that management question their roles as directors and/or controllers. Deming and others assured that these questions would be asked, and thus the tension was created for change.[68] As Title VII in the United States and EEOC started to change the composition of the workforce, more and more questions were asked about who should lead and how they can best represent the needs of a new emerging, diverse workforce.[69] Service quality entered the picture, demanding that employees at the point of contact with customers need to be able to make decisions more rapidly. It was a business necessity, not something nice to have. And then the information technology explosion descended on organizations, and many of the pieces that were difficult to pull together started to fall into place, albeit not so easily in some organizations that resisted changing their leadership systems. You might say they had a high level of tolerance for tension.[70]

As we've now entered the final years of this millennium, speed of reaction time became a competitive advantage, the ability to change product lines rapidly became more essential to survival, maximum service quality is what differentiated companies like Gateway in a market flooded with PC competitors, and producing products to the specifications of each individual was now seen as the mass production strategy for entering the next millennium. Even the U.S. Army, in its discussion of the "Army After Next," projecting past the first two decades of the next millennium, has identified the need to master its use of information and speed of reaction to yet unanticipated threats. These are seen as two essential ingredients to the U.S. military's future success in battle. No doubt, the changes occurring in information systems today will create enormous tensions in the military to deal with its very steep hierarchical structure as it blocks many advantages the new information age can provide to the military's speed of response. This level of tension and its effects on the military are worth watching.[71]

Bass, in referring to the challenges facing the Army After Next, stated, "[I]t is expected to be an Army which will deploy extremely quickly, be logistically self-sufficient, be intelligence-rich and facile with instant information its own and enemy forces and conditions" (p. 47).[72] How could one think that, with all these elements changing, the leadership system and cultures in organizations didn't need to change and transform radically? Well, those leaders who saw the cliff emerging started to explore and put into place systems that would prepare their organizations for the new realities of the new global marketplace. The U.S. Navy labeled its new approach to leadership as it moved to an emphasis on maximum quality "total quality leadership." A very nice integration indeed.

Many companies have gone through the early phases of exploration and transformation and are leading the change in the way organizations are defined today. I'll use one example, perhaps not immediately considered by most people and referred to above: the U.S. Armed Services. As in other organizations, technology has had a profound impact on the way the armed services conduct their business. Also, with the ending of the cold war and a single comment made by then Soviet President Gorbachev, many things changed in the way the services did and currently do business.

> *When a man [or woman] ceases to wonder, he [or she] will cease to ascend on the scale of being.* (Alfred North Whitehead)

When President Gorbachev first met General Colin Powell, he leaned across the table and said, "General, find yourself another enemy." Powell said in a recent speech I attended that he was taken aback with the president's comment. Okay, he said he was shocked. The former Soviet Union had been a great enemy for the United States to prepare for during the past 28 years of Powell's career. In some ways, Powell thought we were losing "the good old days," when the lines were clear as symbolically represented by the Berlin Wall. Powell indicated that, during the first two thirds of his career, he learned to near perfection how to "contain" the communist threat. And now, 2 years from retirement, everything in his business had changed. The containment strategy was no longer relevant, and he realized that the world was moving into a much more unpredictable period. The former Soviet Union and its allies needed to be *included, not contained,* to maintain security. This has led to a radical reinventing of our military strategic operations and thinking.

A cliff had quickly emerged and the question became, Do we have the right armed forces strategy and operations for the next millennium? What type of hairball had we created since World War II in the military? And like any other organization, this new future state and the tension it created led to a vast search for new ways of conducting business in the armed services. To be successful now, the U.S. armed services would have to be more responsive to rapidly changing conditions, smaller and more highly trained, able to use the most advanced information technology, more open systems that could win communities rather than simply defeat militaries, and able to maximize their use of a smaller and more restricted pool of talent. Sounds a bit like General Electric, IBM, Xerox, 3M, HP, Intel, and/or ABB, doesn't it? Things had changed for the U.S. Army in the way it had to do its business, requiring a serious "re"consideration of its leadership system. This serious reconsideration is an ongoing exercise today.

Like many CEOs, General Powell had to learn how to question his old assumptions and systems. He humorously remarked that he "only wished Gorbachev had waited until after he had retired to change the world." Because it happened on his watch, however, Powell did what needed to be done to begin the transformation process in the U.S. military.

During the phases of exploration described above, as organizational systems begin to move toward transforming the way people relate to each other, there is a need to bring some consistency and alignment to the new ways of working together. Generally, in most organizations, alignment occurs at its most fundamental level around or on the culture that emerges and, of course, is based, in part, on the national culture(s) in which an organization is embedded. For example, as information becomes more readily accessible to everyone and as everyone's involvement becomes more crucial to success, there is a need to support, if not initiate, collaboration. Thus, in many organizational systems, we see the emergence of collaboration as a central feature or value that leaders are trying to develop in the organization's culture. Valuing the individual and her or his ideas also becomes an important core value in the transformed culture, along with greater respect for differences of opinion or "loyal subversiveness." These all become business necessities, not kinder and gentler ways of doing business. Collaboration is required just as in any other form of interaction or directive that accomplishes what must be achieved by the organization.

It is now common to hear organizational leaders say they've moved from being the manager of a control system to a coach and facilitator who is now viewed as the keeper of the value system in the organization. Mort Meyerson, the former CEO of EDS and now the CEO of Perot Systems mentioned earlier, remarked recently that, at EDS, everything in his job was about some form of control. When he was asked by Ross Perot to come out of retirement to lead Perot Systems, he discovered that most of the "control" processes he had learned and practiced as a former CEO at EDS had to be abandoned in the "new" work environment. Apparently, he did mean "abandoned."

In a more open system, leaders now have the advantage to reach out and reinforce open communication as a fundamental value in the organization, but not without risk. For example, one senior executive got so excited about valuing open communication in his organization that, at the annual meeting of his division, he committed to responding personally to all e-mail messages he received from his division's members. By the next morning, he had received 900 messages! He had to reconfigure "the compact" he made on the fly to make it possible to reach the goal he sincerely wanted to achieve in shaping the culture in his organization. You can be open and accessible without being deluged and abused. One could also interpret the rush of 900 messages as advance warning of a cliff on the horizon. A colleague said to him, "Now look how many people have been waiting to talk to you." Better open the lines of communication . . . carefully.

Recently, the new CEO at Fiat came into his position and set as one of his first challenges working with the top 500 managers around the world to develop a core set of values for Fiat. Fiat employs nearly 400,000 people in hundreds of companies and business lines. Setting this strategic goal was no easy feat in a company that had been led by its founding family for two generations. Many managers were asking, Is this guy for real? Are we entering an exercise, or are we entertaining a truly "transformative" change in the way we function as an organization?

Stay tuned, because at this writing, the core values have just been approved after 2 years of building consensus among the top 500 managers at Fiat. Now, the really difficult part comes in the transformation of any leadership system. The difficult part is educating everyone on what the values really mean in action, how they are to be reinforced and modeled by the leadership of the organization in a consistent and "noticeable" manner. This leadership also includes union leaders. To be absolutely consistent, the values must become what people adopt and believe in.

Of course, many at Fiat are looking quite skeptically at whether this is a "real" change in culture. As in the Fiat example, many CEOs are saying that most of their time is now spent on being the generator and keeper of the values in their organizations. Some have even suggested a change in title to chief learning officer versus executive to capture the transformation occurring in the prioritization of activities associated with their leadership roles.

Let's take a moment to reflect on what has been said in this chapter. The confluence of emerging forces will continue to affect the nature of how organizations develop themselves. In fact, one question you can ask yourself is very simple: *What is organization? What does it mean to you now, what did it mean, and what will it mean in the future, considering the types of changes mentioned above?* Perhaps your answer may be like that of Lee Ward Hock, the founder of VISA International, when he said, "The less obvious organization is, the better!" For many organizations, this statement has a greater ring of truth to it than in even the recent past . . . like yesterday.

Amid tension and change, many will continue to ask, "Is all of this for real, or is it simply some program or 'flavor of the month'?" Some ask this question because they are afraid something is happening they might miss out on. Some ask because they are afraid of the impending changes and would like to hear that the answer is really NO. They may say inside, "But I really like telling people what to do." Others ask because they are perhaps already living the role of the chief learning officer, and such questions bring into focus the next cliff on the horizon before it's upon them.

To answer such a question and to lead, you must step out of the current context in which you are embedded and examine what the next potential context will look like for your organization. This statement sounds a bit word-dense to me, so I am wondering what your inner voice just said. Another way to put it is to use "what if" scenarios to see what will happen if certain things really do change in the environment we intend to operate in over time. In 1955, most, if not all, managers in companies like IBM, EDS, GE, AT&T, and Honeywell were men. This hit me straight on when I walked into a local restaurant that had a picture of *all* the IBM employees standing outside the main and foundation plant in Endicott, New York. IBM started in our town. Two things struck me about the picture: One, virtually no women were in it, except what appeared to be a few employees' wives with their children. Two, every face in the crowd of several thousand was white.

Now, let's ask the questions that one of those managers may have asked himself while that picture was being taken on that day: "If women became managers, what implications would that mean for human resources polices? If everyone could talk to the CEO simultaneously, how might that affect the organization's culture? If each consumer had different preferences that we could meet almost immediately, how would that affect how we market and produce goods and services in our organizations? These seem like obvious questions today, but they would not have been within their time period and context. Yet, they should have been asked by the leadership of the organization. Now, we are taking a picture of you and your organization's employees. Any thoughts about the future? Did you say something?

Sometimes predicting the future is very simple. How? Because the elements of the future are often in the present. It just takes some reflection on the various patterns to see how things can emerge. I know, I should probably have made the word *just* boldface. However, the elements are typically there to suggest that world markets in the future will all appear local; that all women will receive parity in terms of leadership positions in organizations; that by 2020, diversity will be normative, as opposed to programmatic; and that future markets will certainly be raging in Africa and the Middle East. (That's my prediction. Any reflections on alternatives?)

When Ameritech was undergoing a dramatic transformation from a regulated telephone company to an innovative telecommunications organization, one consultant asked the senior managers to write a *Fortune* article on what Ameritech would become 3 years hence. Why don't you consider this an exercise for your unit and/or organization?

Speaking of seeing the future in the present, a few years ago I was sitting in a meeting at a large European conglomerate with a top executive who had traveled extensively around the world. Looking around the "all male" room in 1992, he said, "Let's start to aggressively hire women for our high potential management positions." He then exclaimed, "So far, the best ones are still in the market!" One can see the future in the present if one takes the time to look, to reflect, and to get feedback.

Recently, I visited Israel and gave a presentation to the top 200 managers of a large high-tech company that made telephone systems. I arrived at the tail end of the CEO's presentation to see on his last overhead three words in English. The rest was in Hebrew. The three words, which had no good translation in Hebrew, were "time to market." He was expounding on the importance of diversifying the company's customer base and of getting the best products to market as quickly as possible. The audience listened politely. I came to learn, however, that not all had aligned around his message. Perhaps, this is not so surprising because several years ago this company basically had one major customer: the telephone company for Israel. As the telephone market deregulated in Israel, however, its ripple effect was profound throughout organizations that worked in the telecommunications industry. The market changed, and within a short time a huge cliff emerged, resulting in 1,000 employees being fired in late 1998.

It appears that the dramatic changes going on within organizations and the contexts in which they operate are very real and are driven by many complex, dynamic forces. One need simply witness the transformations occurring in the leading companies around the world, and one can see that the future is already emerging and requiring a very significant change in the configuration of the leadership systems and cultures in which they are embedded. The relevant questions now seem to be, What systems must we retire? (and this includes ways of thinking), What systems must we transform? and How will this affect the people we select and develop for the new leadership positions in our emerging organizations? Many organizational leaders and I are sure that their seconds in command, if they are being heard, are asking themselves these same questions; to be fair, many still are not. My challenge is to get you to ask these questions, reflect on your answers, and decide which directions you will explore . . . sooner or later.

Now, I would like to comment on the future. The emergence of alliances, the need to be fully aligned with your customers, faster reaction time to market, advances in network technology, and a Generation X and soon Y workforce coming in all point to the fact that "collective" or "collaborative" leadership is an area we must seriously explore and develop for organizations into the next millennium. One needs to imagine in her or his organization a situation where 80% of the units formed are self-organizing. This is incredible even to conceive of in current organizations where the organizational structure is "very obviously" bureaucratic. You might say that such an organization doesn't yet exist, but it is possible. If you said that, then you didn't see the number of teams that self-organized last year in Motorola to compete on a global basis in their "Total Customer Satisfaction" program. Yes, the numbers there surprised me as well.

One direction for sure that must now be explored is the topic of our next chapter: *shared leadership* in teams. People will want to share more in the leadership system, to be full stakeholders. They are already being asked to be more involved with customers because it is doable with advanced information technology and because it is actually the right thing to do. They do know more about customer needs. For all of these reasons, we must now consider how the new leadership system will look in our future organizations.

Okay, the camera is ready to snap a picture, which, by the way, is digital, and you can check out the picture on your PC and discard it if it's blurred and try again. Let's see, was it Kodak that recently laid off 10,000 employees? Any thoughts about some cliffs on the horizons?

Some Things Worth Repeating

- A migration of leadership responsibilities is occurring in organizations that is fundamentally changing the leadership systems of those organizations.
- Creating "loyally subversive" followers is an essential ingredient for fundamental and transformative change in organizational systems.
- The future is in the present for those who take the time to uncover it for themselves.
- If we fail to predict the future, we have to live in it nonetheless.

Let me leave you with one question to reflect on: *How have you reinforced your "loyally subversive" followers lately for questioning the "current state" in your organization and/or work unit?*

7

If We Really Need to Do It, Then What Is Shared Leadership?

I decided to step down when employees agreed with me 70% of the time!
(Kawashima, President of Honda Corporation)

Riding back one day from a weekend in Kruger National Park, where I had witnessed my first giraffe in the wild, among many other interesting species (I often emphasize the giraffe because I tell my friends that giraffes have the *best perspective* in the wild, they really have an opportunity to see the forest before the trees . . . and cliffs too!), I came across the concept of *vital forces*. Driving through the northern Transvaal to a management development seminar with a group of senior managers who worked in the South African defense industry, I read a thesis written by a South African woman on leadership and

African humanistic thinking. The author referred to sayings like "A person is not a person unless connected with others" and "We are all together on the inside." In contrast with this expression, I thought of the American cliches "She's a rising star" and "That's quite an individual."

People have their own identities, and it is those identities we are trying to align when we say that all followers now identify with a leader's vision and each other's efforts. Indeed, each person's contribution can be unique and at the same time enhanced through his or her relationships with others. This appears to be the essence of the vital force of a group or team. It's not a trade-off between being individualistic or collectivistic thinking; rather, their integration creates the vital force in highly developed teams, as well as in larger organizational systems.

I finished the thesis and said to my friend and colleague Danie Maritz, who was driving at the time, that maybe *teams* means *t*ogether *e*ach *a*ccomplishes *m*ore *s*uccesses. We had fun playing with the idea that together "each" accomplishes more. I thought I had finally invented my "One Minute Manager," my "Seven Habits," my "In Search of Excellence," until I went through the Pittsburgh airport on my way home and saw this pneumonic on one of those posters, "Teams Are Like a Flock of Eagles" and that sort of thing. Not to be deterred, I am still considering *Five Stretches of Giraffe Leadership* for my next book.

Coming from the most individualistic nation on earth, I've always struggled with the notion of how we can blend the uniqueness of each individual with the specific need to collaborate and coordinate, which is commonly associated with highly developed teams. Vital force became a *stimulus* concept for me to think how this could be accomplished without losing the benefits of the individual, the group, and/or the team.

Have you observed how companies typically treat the *team* concept? Generally, they want people to identify with something, often a trivial representation of what really constitutes "teamness," such as wearing all the same T-shirts or hats. Call it a team, label everyone an equal contributor, do some hokey ceremonies, and put a large sign over the door saying something like Welcome to Team Torino. These same companies also usually provide a day or two of training to jump-start the team. And interestingly enough, this type of team training is usually done with people from different teams, not the team they are trying to develop.

My general impression, and I am interested in yours, is that such approaches often generate more cynicism than teamness. Stated another way, what happens when you tell a group of people they are a team and, by and large, they don't trust each other? They are saying, "Help me with this picture," or if they are 13 years old, they say, "Whatever." There is something much more profound to be discovered in the vital forces in teams and organizations. It starts with an individual who is a full contributor and willing to sacrifice for the team's goals, mission, and/or vision. Such individuals *are* all together on the inside as one unit, so to speak. Being together on the inside is at the core of what I mean by building the vital forces in organizations. Its closest cousin in the leadership literature is being identified with a cause, belief, mission, or vision. This, too, represents being together on the inside.

Several months have past (I love writing this in a book). Back to another game reserve in South Africa, this time with Nic Maritz. (I could just hear Nic saying above, "Hey, what about Nic?" Just when you thought one Maritz was enough, they have two in South Africa! Well, actually there are a lot more, but you may have to wait for the sequel to this book to hear about the rest of the Trekkers in this family.) We were spending a weekend at Mala Mala, a beautiful, rustic lodge on the border of Kruger National Park. When we first arrived at the airport, the guide informed us that a malaria alert was declared at the camp. Fortunately, we had picked up malaria medicine about 4 hours before landing! Unfortunately, this does not provide nearly the lead time to become resistant to malaria, but like children, we downed the four pills for the 4 days that we should have taken for a week prior to coming to Mala Mala. Although I am a trained research scientist, not every action I take is based on science, logic, or rational thought. I guess that's why we all use the term "bounded rationality," which Herb Simon coined. Anyhow, on the drive to the camp, I said something about not being able to afford getting malaria, that my father had gotten it as a young man, and that each year he had a recurrence of malaria when he was down with a serious cold. (I often used the existence of this malaria bug as part of my theory to explain my father's unrelenting autocratic style.) Because I knew I did not want to become an autocratic leader, I really had no desire to pick up this exotic disease.

After we arrived at the base camp, we all went to our cabins to unpack and prepare for lunch. Before coming out to lunch, I took the first of many mosquito spray showers. I arrived at lunch, and our guide quickly went into a long harangue about Americans and their fears of these little friendly mosquitoes. As in most organizations, the rumor mill was alive and well in Mala Mala. Being born in New York City, I can be a bit sarcastic, obnoxious, and assertive when needed. New Yorkers are also prone to understatement. I responded to his attack on my character as to an affliction . . . I am not speaking malaria here! We bantered awhile to the enjoyment of the group, and then we had to wait several hours before the evening ride. If one is going to see the "big five" in the wild (by the way, this could also include personality, but in this case it's game), one usually goes out in open trucks toward dusk, when the animals are "active," so to speak . . . looking for "slow" food!

We arrived at the Jeep that evening with a substitute guide present. Of course, I asked where my "friend" had gone. The new guide's answer was very curt; he said that our original guide was a bit incapacitated in that he had come down with . . . you got it, malaria. I ran back to my cabin and shortly thereafter emerged in a cloud of mosquito spray, my hair all slicked back with ample shots of spray. I must admit that I did have a "New Yorker's Swaggering Rule" running through my head, but I didn't want to rub it in with the group. Even though it may be funny, that wouldn't be exemplary leadership. The mosquito shower became the standard routine activity around the camp. "Hey, Man, got's some good mosquito stuff. Yeah, Man, just scored and it's the bomb!" Sorry, I couldn't resist.

We headed out into the game reserve, and I noticed something that has become the "high bar" I use to judge effective organizational communication networks. All the guides in a 60-mile radius had on headsets, and as they moved around through several thousand acres of game reserve, they were constantly in communication with each other, citing interesting places to go, how to approach areas, and what *not* to approach, frequently communicating whatever support was needed by fellow guides. It was an amazing display of shared leadership and communication. If one guide didn't know the answer to a question, it was quickly found out through the network. A virtual networked company with distributed leadership at a distance. If something happened to your Jeep, you had backup immediately, which for me was quite reassuring. I must admit that it is quite an amazing feeling to have a guide stop the Jeep, which has no doors and top, within 2 feet of a resting lion. I don't care how hot it is or the fact that lions don't run in mid-afternoon; when a lion is sitting there looking at you, and it is his context, and things get very quiet when the guide turns off the engine, only one thought goes through your head: "For God's sake, is the battery in this Jeep beyond its 3-year limit!" I realize you expected me to say, "Do I trust this guide?" Well, at that point the answer was NO! The conditions for trust had not been established, especially having lost one confident guide to malaria.

My other thought was about the Indian sitting next to me who smelled quite a bit like curry. I was racing through my memory to see whether I had ever read anything about lions liking curry. I guess I was being a bit individualistic in my thoughts at that moment. The phrase "We are all together on the inside" took on new meaning as we sat across from that very skinny lion. Well, in all fairness, we really hadn't had enough time to form a team, and in this context, the expression "eating one's lunch" had profound life span implications for all of us.

Although we had a highly sophisticated system of shared communication and leadership, like all organizations, even with the most sophisticated groupware systems, it was not flawless. The second guide on the back of the Jeep, who was Zulu, could see for at least 2 miles through very thick bush. He and the guide driving were a very tightly knit dyad within a larger team system structure. Toward dusk, the guide on the back spotted an elephant, which in the thick bush is not so easy to pick out because of the animal's grayish color. I know, this sounds even strange to me! We headed right up to this young elephant, realizing soon afterward that we had come between a mother and her calf. I discovered two things at that moment. First, that Disney's creation of Dumbo really portrayed the character true to form; the mother elephant could dance and spin, and before we knew it she was charging our Jeep. The guy sitting next to me, still smelling like curry, was of no help, although I made a very gross assumption that he must know something about elephants. Second, an old Jeep *was* capable of going 40 mph in reverse up a steep hill through heavy bush. I am still reminded of that evening in the bush when I eat at one of my favorite restaurants in Florida—The Elephant Walk. This mother, however, wasn't walking!

Another thought also went through my mind. My wife, Beth, who was pregnant with our third child, to be named Sydney, asked me before I left not to take any unnecessary risks. Here I am in this Jeep, being chased by an elephant, surrounded by malaria, and thinking that maybe some men are from Pluto. Oh, yeah, to add insult to injury, the day before going to Mala Mala, I flew for the first time in a microlite plane 500 feet above a game reserve. Well, I, too, am still working on the individualized consideration thing along with logic, common sense, and transitions through mid-adulthood.

Big deviation, I know, but hey, I thought we were getting to know each other. More seriously, to understand fully the profound effect that South Africa has had on me and on those who have visited it since the ending of apartheid, you *must* get some sense of its context. And the bush is to South Africa what the Grand Canyon is to the United States. It's a national treasure and a reasonably good metaphor for *the work is a jungle out there* concept. Sorry, I promise not to do that again.

What we saw in the bush that weekend represented the power vested in networked relationships, distributed leadership, and how each member's vital force was enhanced through his or her connection with others. It also brought into full focus for me the philosophy of Ubuntu, which I mention here and add more detail to later on. For the moment, if you think of African humanistic thinking as the body, then Ubuntu would be its soul.

I have had many late-night discussions in South Africa about the philosophy of Ubuntu, and it requires a book to explain its full meaning. For our purposes here, in terms of discussing shared leadership, I can say that if I translated *Ubuntu,* it would mean for me "unity through diversity." These three words have dominated my thinking about teams and shared leadership since I first came across them in my travels around South Africa. They are at the essence of what President Nelson Mandela has set as a national goal for South Africa, or what really could be called a moral imperative for his nation. He says often that there is "one" South Africa, or "one" nation. Yet, like the former Yugoslavia, it has a highly diverse population with groups that have very little in common in terms of an indigenous culture. The difference in South Africa, however, is that they have Mandela as president, and he is by far one of the most reflective, transformational leaders in modern times and, I might say, throughout history. (Of course, many of my colleagues say that I am extreme in my opinion about President Mandela, almost to the point of hero worship. I would disagree vehemently with this position in that I do hero-worship this idealized leader, so take out the "almost.")

President Mandela battles the historical tendency to create an equation of "blood over brains" and reversed the thinking on this to be "brains over blood" by using "unity through diversity" as a mantra for change. This is truly a remarkable vision, given that apartheid was fundamentally based on *separation* versus *integration* and that although the laws have changed, it will take time for the implicit models in people's minds to change to even come close to the new laws. Maybe a generation or two worth of time . . . I hope, less.

I believe that South Africa represents what many organizations and teams struggle with over time but perhaps with much greater risk. South Africa has had to move from a control-dominated society under apartheid to a society where the controls are within people operating within a democratic collaborative system. In taking this direction, many have had to change their fundamental perspectives about different groups to appreciate their diversity and how together each can accomplish more successes. Of course, the way has been strewn with many difficulties. As controls for compliance have been removed, crime has risen in South African society. Commitment and trust are still not in place to replace the controls that guarded behavior, and now the guards must be in the way people think, or be internalized in everyone. As a nation, South Africans are in a period of extreme vulnerability, but in this period there is certainly greater openness to change, if not inspiration. Let me explain, because this has relevance for all organizations trying to make radical transformations.

Most South Africans I met only knew the system they grew up with, and many, I believe, didn't know what they didn't know about the outside world. Again, as R. D. Laing (1981) said, "The range of what we think and do is limited by what we fail to notice." In the United States, I grew up believing fundamentally in individual liberties and heard this all the time from teachers, lawyers, parents, and presidents. We protect this liberty as a nation, often in the very extreme sense. In South Africa, apartheid was what people were taught to believe in, and it was endorsed not only by the government but also by the church. I must say here that I am not excusing any past mistakes in this country, and they are huge ones. By the way, I find the same is true for most South Africans I meet; they don't offer excuses. I am merely trying to explain the context in which the people of this nation were embedded or grew up over time. Framing this context for you is crucial to put into perspective the challenge of creating unity through diversity that faces this nation. I must add that, in a much less extreme sense, the challenge is not much different for a team that must work with discrepant models in people's heads about how best to work together to become a high-performing system.

> *If you treat a man as he is, he will remain as he is. But if you treat him as*
> *if he were what he ought to be, and could be, he will become what*
> *he ought to be, and could be.* (Johann Wolfgang von Goethe)

The "embeddedness" of people in their past came out very poignantly for me in a workshop I conducted for a large South African bank. Midway through the retreat, I kept trying to get a young black woman to contribute to our discussion. She would contribute with me at the breaks but not in the larger group. She was the only black person in the room and the only female. At the end of the second day, I approached her and said that I thought she had enormous potential and that it was a challenge for me and this organization to unleash her full potential. I wanted her to confront the opinions of these other managers to benefit them as well as her. She looked at me with a lot of emotion in her eyes and said that, for her whole life, she was taught never to confront a white man. Now everything is different; she fully understood the need to, but her automatic response was to question whether it was appropriate each time she attempted to

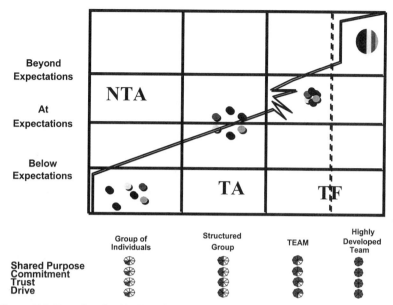

Figure 7.1. Team Leadership Development

question any of her colleagues. She knew intellectually that she must do it. Yet, these implicit models are very difficult "thinking" systems to retire. In South Africa, people have to retire their systems in parallel with creating entirely new ones, making this nation one of the most interesting cases for studying transformational leadership in this century.

The collective experiences and thinking from the work on African humanistic thinking and Ubuntu led to the creation of a figure designed to represent the development of groups to teams and then to highly developed ones. At the far left of Figure 7.1 is a group of people who happen to find themselves together for some reason; this is usually a prerequisite for being a team in that they share some common purpose. You may be surprised at how many organizations try to go to teams without this basic rule in place. I, however, am personally no longer surprised.

Notice the different patterns that are used to represent "each" individual as being different perhaps in perspective, talent, performance potential, and desire. As one moves from left to right in Figure 7.1, the group structures itself by members laying out expectations for "each" other. Again, the patterns are different, and in the structuring process, we don't lose the individuality in the group, although some compromises have to be made on the basis of whatever expectations are set for the group. In working with teams, this is the point that parallels the building of what we've called a compact of understanding. By the way, it is similar to the one we began to develop at the outset of this book.

I have had the opportunity to interview many teams over the last 4 years, teams that had become quite successful in developing to their full potential. One question I've asked at the end of a 2-hour interview was always answered in the same way by all of these respective teams. Members of the most "highly developed" teams said that if they could go back and do it all over again, they would have set clearer expectations early on for themselves. "Thinking we were all adults, we short-circuited this process, and it led to very bad, destructive conflicts."

I now believe that the *storming* that groups supposedly go through naturally is actually a consequence of poorly articulated expectations. It may also be a result of what Hackman described as insufficient direction being given to the group.[73] In my opinion, if we can get the compact of understanding correct up front, we can move from early formation to adaptive conflict, which becomes the basis for building a highly developed team leadership system, where leadership is fully shared among members (see Box 7.1). And by saying "shared," I mean disproportionately influencing each other to do something at any one point in time. Stated differently, it is rare that each member is influencing another equally at any one point in time. Jehn has also come up with a useful framework for classifying the effects of different forms of conflict.[74] For example, Jehn identified both *relational conflict* and *process conflict* as being detrimental to performance and satisfaction. *Task conflict,* which focuses on the content in a group's work and goals, was identified as being situational in its impact and showed positive effects under certain conditions. Moderate to high levels of task conflict were positively related to group performance. Group development and performance can be largely affected either positively or negatively by the type of conflict. Resolving relationship and process conflicts quickly was seen as being key to effective group performance.

Included in Figure 7.1 is a squiggly line that appears before a structured group (structured around expectations of each other) becomes a team. In any development process, there is a need for tension to create exploration, change, and ultimately a transformation. This is as true in individual development as it is in group or organizational development. Groups must "test their system" to know how well they are working together. The components of their system can be seen in their relationships, tasks, process, and common goals.

BOX 7.1.　The Nature of Different Styles of Conflict

Lehnen, Ayman, and Korabik (1995) examined the types of conflict styles used by male and female leaders. The sample included managers and vice principals in Canada, rated by their followers. Results indicated that self-rated transformational leadership was more strongly associated with using an integrative conflict management style. The relationship between transformational leadership and satisfaction was shown to be mediated by the conflict management style used by the leader. Leaders who described themselves as more transformational used integrative conflict management styles and had followers with greater levels of satisfaction. This relationship was stronger for the female versus male managers in the sample. Self-described male transformational leaders described themselves as using more of a compromising style of conflict management.

The occurrence of events testing a group's system was labeled by Gersick "punctuated equilibrium."[75] Some will have more dramatic tests than others, but in the end a test must occur where the basic expectations and principles of the group are examined by the group and changed, if needed, to address new challenges and opportunities. If members come away from challenges saying, "We all did what we expected of each other," or, "We even exceeded each other's expectations," then a higher level of trust and cohesion will result. This is reflected in a closing of the circle in Figure 7.1. Members have learned that placing confidence in their team members is fully justified. They have also learned how each member performed under stress or extreme duress, so they are much closer to understanding fully each other's strength and weaknesses. It is a clear transition point in time that many teams need some outside input and coaching in order to pass to achieve a full-blown transformation in perspectives. The process represented in Ubuntu philosophy suggests that members have gone from the *I* to the *me* to the *we* or *us*. *I* is in reference to oneself only. *Me* is in reference to others. And *we* represents myself within a larger collective, or a highly developed team unit.

The transition or transformation that occurs in going from *I* to *me* to *we* is a crucial point in time where reflection on what is happening to oneself and the group is essential for further transformational leadership development. Reflective learning provides each member the opportunity to examine where he or she is with respect to the group's development, as well as where other members are in their respective development trajectories. Indeed, it is perhaps a more difficult type of reflective learning than occurs in individual leader-follower interactions in that each member is reflecting on an entity he or she is more a central part of than in more traditional leader-follower interactions. It is also analogous to asking someone to step out of his or her culture—and don't think so individualistically, "Okay, now what do you see?" It is difficult to step out of what we are fundamentally embedded in over time and what gets "hard wired" in each of us. The process of decoding is also quite a challenge.

Let's return to the transition or transformation point depicted in Figure 7.1. If the group successfully addresses its challenges and members have come away generally satisfied with each other, we can start to describe them as a team. Indeed, by working together, each member does accomplish more, and the team accomplishes more over time. As a leadership system, we expect to see the four I's of transformational leadership. Members care about each other's development. They are willing and even eager to challenge each other's perspectives without thinking that someone is being attacked. Often, they have inspired each other to get through the difficult times together. Ultimately, they have a higher identification and confidence in the team's ideals, central purpose, and, one might even say, vision in some cases.

Comparing the team to the group, the group operates collectively on a more transactional level. Members can be highly corrective or even avoidant where no structure for expectations of members exists. So, what we often see at the lowest end of development is members avoiding taking responsibility or some taking it and others not. We see people correcting each other, and this often leads to arguments over who said what and, in the extreme, to out-of-control "storming." Relationships within the group are in conflict, and the process feels out of control. We see attempts to set agreements and contracts as the basis for developing trust and commitment. Self-interest usually is more dominant than collective at the beginning, although some members may feel conflicted because they would like to work as a team but are having problems with members who seem to be "in things for themselves." This clearly indicates a lack of trust.

At the far right of Figure 7.1 is a "highly developed team." We chose "highly developed" because we were interested in the membership's perspective and thought that performance would follow perspective and development. In terms of perspective, we thought that members of highly developed teams, just like highly developed leaders, were willing to sacrifice that which they most desired for the good of the team. Their perspective is more highly developed because no longer does self-interest rule the day. This does not mean that self-interests

**"An entity of extraordinary
ability and energy"**

Figure 7.2. To Join Forces

are ignored, just that when it is important to do so, members will delay without reservation their self-interest to move closer to the idealized goal of the team. Why? Because, at the highly developed stage, they have complete identification with the team and its goals, yet as represented in the figure, they each retain their own individual identities. The retention of each member's identity linked together in a common purpose forms the basis of a team unit's vital force. We show in Figure 7.2 what we started with to build the team. Individual identities are pulled together through leadership and a common purpose into an extraordinary force. By the way, "to join forces" is a dictionary definition of the verb *team.*

The retention of individual identities paradoxically provides the basis for shared leadership and often constructive, adaptive conflict. Members have to share each of their unique contributions. If more than one person can do the same thing, we might say we have one too many people in the room. By bringing together the diversity resident in a team, we typically provide the synergistic value associated with teams that are described as high performing by numerous authors, including Kazenbach and Smith in *The Wisdom of Teams.*[76]

The symbol chosen to represent the highly developed team is that of a circle that retains the shadings but shows them in harmony, or blending together. One manager remarked, on first seeing Figure 7.1 and hearing of the different phases of development, that he agreed up to the last phase. He thought the symbol we chose should have been a square, not a circle. Interesting. I asked him why. He said that, in a team, everyone makes equal contributions. He was from the United States and has what I have come to witness many times—a very typical

U.S.A.-centric view about teams. A team means we are all going to move toward making more similar contributions. I disagreed with his point and said that, with the circle, at any one point in time contributions to the team are likely never equal. Sharing usually means someone has more than someone else to give, and in highly developed teams the same is true. The allowance of unequal contribution makes great teams truly great.

The circle symbolically represents that, in highly developed teams, some members lead when it is their opportunity to lead, and some members follow in an exemplary fashion; this can change again and again over time. So, whoever is central or more in control at one point in time will move to the periphery as others who have the knowledge, expertise, or persistence need to move to the center of a challenge, threat, or opportunity. Only by combining the unequal contributions of members in the team, or distinct competencies, can we have shared leadership and a highly developed team. Of course, over a long period of time and with the right selection strategy, we can say that the team, theoretically, will approximate a box versus a circle. However, as people always say to me, "In the real world" (and my response is typically, "Now which one are we referring to this time?"), things just don't happen that way. So, let's stick with the circle for now.

We have also looked at attributes of the group and team that coincide with stage of development. A listing or description of these attributes is presented in Figure 7.3. We placed the attributes into the phases of team development where they are most likely to be prominent. This should not suggest to you that they could not emerge earlier or later in the process of development. Most evidence suggests they typically overlap phases.

Seltzer, Numerof, and Bass reported that when other factors were held constant, transactional leaders who focused on corrections and mistakes increased the stress and "burnout" among their followers (see also Box 7.2).[77] Seltzer and his colleagues concluded that stress was more highly correlated with the excessive use of active management-by-exception and the absence of transformational leadership. In times of stress, team members need to know what they are doing wrong, but they also need to know that they have each other's support, a full willingness to challenge members' ideas, the drive to attain their goals, and the ideals to do so in a fair and principled manner. Team leaders and members must balance the drive for new ideas and performance with consideration for the varying needs of each individual. Burgess, Salas, Cannon-Bowers, and Hall have recommended that the type of leadership required for teams

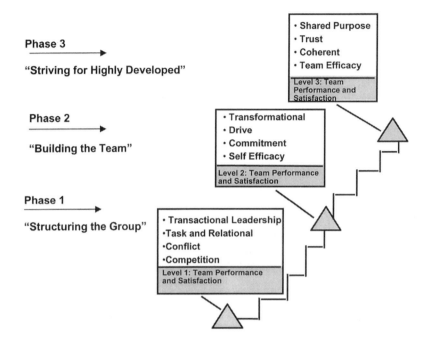

Figure 7.3. Summary of Team Development Phases

BOX 7.2. Stress, Burnout, Turnover, and Transformational Leadership

---

Densten and Sarros (1995) examined the relationship among leadership, stress, and burnout in police service organizations in Australia. Earlier research by Selzer, Numerof, and Bass (1989) demonstrated an inverse relationship among burnout, effectiveness, and satisfaction. The study involved a sample of 480 police personnel evaluating middle- to senior-level ranks. Higher levels of idealized leadership and transactional contingent reward were related to less emotional exhaustion and, to a lesser degree, personal accomplishment burnout. Leadership accounted for 14% of the variance in emotional burnout.

Bryant (1990) reported that nursing supervisors who were rated by their followers as more transformational had lower turnover rates in their units.

---

working under stress is very much in line with the full range model of leadership.[78] Strategies they recommended include checking team member performance, providing feedback, monitoring performance, and troubleshooting to locate and correct errors, which would all fall within the transactional range of leadership. Transformational strategies recommended for handling stress included developing individual member competence to handle uncertain events, to build a thorough understanding of the mission, to establish an alignment of members' goals with those of the team, and probably more important, establishing trust to provide each other support when it is most needed.

Viewing Leadership From at Least Two Levels

I have now introduced a parallel version of the full range model at two levels. The first was at the individual leader and follower level, and we spent the first several chapters describing the model and perspectives associated with each level along the full range. In this chapter and the previous one, we began to discuss the same model of leadership as part of building a team leadership system. Yet, the only thing that has changed is what we applied leadership to, not the concepts along the full range of leadership. Members of teams are inspiring, and so can be an individual leader. Leaders can show individualized consideration, and so can team members with each other. Teams operate at the highest levels on the basis of trust, integrity, and identification. All these characteristics apply to what we have associated with exemplary leadership at the individual level. Indeed, transformational leaders and transformational leadership are associated with teams, especially those that are highly developed.[79]

My colleagues and I believe that using the same full range model for examining both individual and team leadership has a distinct advantage. The model and its components can be said to represent a "cross-level" theory. The advantage is that the more we move to networked and team-based organizations, the more we must move back and forth between individual and team leadership systems. There is no reason to suspect that the concepts at one level do not apply to another. In fact, we have now found in two separate investigations—one with platoons in the U.S. Army and a second with students working in self-directed groups over the course of a semester—that the hierarchical pattern of relationships observed with individual leadership and performance paralleled findings with teams. Specifically, platoons that were seen as more transformational by

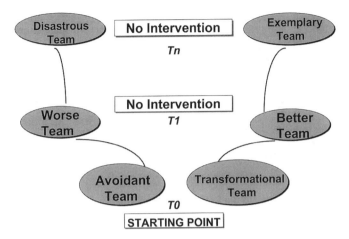

Figure 7.4. Performance Patterns Over Time for Avoidant Versus Transformational Team Leadership

members rating their leadership had higher levels of objective and subjective performance.[80] The same was true for student groups when comparing their measures of performance in terms of grades for semester-long projects.[81]

In Figure 7.4, I am attempting to show how teams that were more transformational performed over time versus those that were avoidant and corrective. Interestingly, the good teams became even better at an accelerated rate, whereas the bad teams became disastrous. Figure 7.5 presents the actual values or path coefficients, which demonstrate that the leadership "in" a team was formed relatively early on (Month 1), and it predicted both the subsequent leadership in the team and its level of potency and performance.

Going back to the concept of *vital forces,* I believe that one main element in team development that has often caused teams to fail when it has not been properly developed is its leadership system. Many other authors now agree with this opinion.

Through proper transactions and the use of transformational leadership, each individual's contribution to development and performance is maximized. It is the mechanism or process that facilitates the ideal of creating unity through diversity.

The sharing of leadership becomes feasible when commitment has been built into the team, along with members' identification with each other, the mission, and the vision (see Box 7.3). A Zulu expression called *Umphakati*

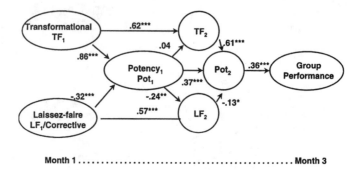

Figure 7.5. A Time-Based Model of Team Leadership, Potency, and Performance
SOURCE: Sivasubramaniam et al. (1997).
NOTE: Model Fit Indices: GFI = .98; AFGI = .91; RMSR = .04.
*$p < .05$; ** $p < .01$; *** $p < .001$.

perhaps captures this best: Within the best teams, "We are all together on the inside." This would represent a very pure definition of identification and would provide a firm basis for members being willing to share in their leadership and followership responsibilities, as well as to sacrifice as needed for the good of the group. Stated another way, if we all identify with what's important, who cares who is leading, as long as it's the best person or people for the task at that particular moment in time. Such levels of trust and identification are not easy to build, but once built, they can have dramatic, positive effects on a team's effort, performance, and perhaps most important, sustainability (see Box 7.4).

BOX 7.3. The Role of Leadership in Building Teams

One common factor often identified with failure to implement a team system successfully has been lack of emphasis on the role leadership plays in building effective teams (Sinclair, 1992; Stewart & Manz, 1994). Yet, only a few models of team effectiveness (Gladstein, 1984; Kozlowski, Gully, Salas, & Canon-Bowers, 1996) have explicitly considered leadership to be one determinant of team effectiveness. This, too, will change as more authors realize the central role leadership plays in team development.

BOX 7.4. Connecting Between Team Transformational Leadership and Performance

---

Bass and Avolio (1997) examined the leadership in U.S. Army platoons, focusing on both individual and team leadership. In the initial pilot study, 18 platoons participated. Three months prior to attending a 2-week training camp, the platoon officers and the platoon itself were rated in terms of the full range of leadership. Leadership ratings of the platoon commander, the sergeant, and the platoon itself predicted performance in Joint Readiness Training Camp (JRTC). Specifically, transformational and active transactional leadership predicted more effective performance in JRTC. Passive leadership and laissez-faire leadership were negatively related to performance.

Avolio, Jung, Murry, and Sivasubramaniam (1996) provided initial results by using a newly designed instrument of team leadership behavior called the Team Multifactor Leadership Questionnaire (TMLQ). Initial results with this sample, as well as with the platoon samples from the U.S. military, produced six interpretable factors. These six factors primarily replicate the full range model, including the following scales: Inspiring, Intellectual Stimulating, Individualized Consideration, Transactional Contingent Reward, Active Management-by-Exception, and Passive Management-by-Exception/Laissez-Faire Leadership.

Sivasubramaniam, Murry, Avolio, and Jung (1997) contrasted the higher-order factor of transformational leadership and corrective transactional leadership in teams to predict how potent the teams perceived themselves to be over time, as well as to predict performance over a 3-month interval. Student teams participating in this study rated themselves at Month 1 and Month 3 on how they perceived the collective leadership of their respective teams. Leadership ratings taken early on were highly predictive of subsequent leadership ratings for both transformational leadership and corrective/passive management-by-exception. Transformational leadership directly predicted the performance of these groups while also predicting performance indirectly through levels of group potency. A similar pattern emerged for active management-by-exception leadership (see Figure 7.4).

Some Things Worth Repeating

- The early foundation for building an effective team leadership system is clarifying expectations.
- Teams must go through adaptive conflict and tension to develop themselves fully.

- Task conflict can contribute positively to group performance and satisfaction, whereas relational and process conflict contributes negatively and should be eliminated as soon as possible.
- Shared leadership rarely, if ever, means equal.
- A direct parallel exists between leadership at the individual level and leadership in teams.
- Never forget your mosquito spray when going to Mala Mala. Kidding! I think.

Let me leave you with a few core questions to reflect on:

Have you ever been on a team where all of you were truly together on the inside? Your family perhaps? Do you know of a team that has fully achieved "unity through diversity"?

Building the Context to Embed a Transformational Leadership System

An Eastern monarch once charged his wise men to invent him a sentence to be ever in view, and which should be true and appropriate in all times and situations. They presented him the words: "And this, too, shall pass away." How much it expresses! How chastening in the hour of pride! How consoling in the depths of affliction.
(Abraham Lincoln)

Are you familiar with the NIMBY acronym? It means *not in my b*ack yard. I use it here because often people will say to me in workshops, "You know, what you are teaching us sounds great. In fact, you should teach my boss these concepts. But in our organization, its chances of success are nil." *Not* o*ur* o*r*ganization, or NOO! My speech after hearing this is typically along the following lines: "Do you want to lead, or do you want to continue to manage in the same way as in the past? Innovation in organizations often comes from the line, the second in command or followers, so why do we need to wait for them, meaning the bosses, to be enlightened? What can *you* do now?" Then, I usually tell them how many leaders died for what they believed in and how the forces against them were so awesome that no one ever thought one individual could really make a difference. I then drop a few names for emphasis: Gandhi, Mandela, Christ, Churchill, King, Cartwright, Carmichael. . . . Usually, when I get to Cartwright and Carmichael, the light bulbs turn on a bit.

Madeline Cartwright was a principal at Blaine Elementary School in Philadelphia, Pennsylvania. Blaine Elementary School was in one of the worst sections of inner-city Philadelphia. At that time, 60% to 70% of the parents of students attending Blaine were drug addicts. The school was a horrible building, filthy and dirty, with few redeeming qualities.

When Madeline took over, she was appalled at the conditions in the school. It came to a head one day when she had a group of students simply talk about what happened to them on the way to school that morning. It was an innocent question, but what she heard was so disheartening that her resolve to make a difference was firmly rooted. One student talked of the gunfire on the streets that he avoided on the way to school. Another talked about his fears in having to go by one of the many crack houses on her street. A third mentioned the sound of the cracking glass beneath her sneakers from the shot-out store windows and cars. Another mentioned her father being taken by an ambulance to the hospital for a drug overdose and wondered aloud whether he would be there when she returned home; often, they brought him back the same day. Her description was so matter-of-fact that this obviously was a common occurrence in her home.

Exhausted by the morning's events, Madeline and another teacher left the building to go to lunch at a local McDonald's. Halfway through their lunch, Madeline remarked on how clean the restaurant was, compared to the school. "Here we sit in a McDonald's, and compared to our school building, it's like paradise. How can we expect children in our school to feel good about themselves when the hallways are so filthy, the bathrooms stink of urine, and windows are taped from being broken time after time?" Again, Madeline's resolve to make a difference in the school was growing.

When she returned to the school that afternoon, she asked the head of the maintenance department to take another shot at getting the bathrooms and school in shape and asked what he needed to achieve her request. He responded politely that the maintenance staff were doing the very best they could and that they couldn't do much better, given their resources. For some who simply follow in a dependent way, that may have been as far as things went. For Madeline, however, it was the beginning of a very interesting and transformational journey.

On a Friday afternoon, she went down to the maintenance department to ask the custodians to leave her some supplies for a few cleanup jobs she wanted to do over the weekend. Although reluctant, the head of maintenance complied with her request. She was the principal of the school, after all, giving him a specific order. Belonging to a "hairball" organization has some advantages.

Over the weekend, Madeline went into the worst part of the school—its bathrooms—and hyper-cleaned them. When the maintenance staff returned on Monday, she indicated that, from now on, those bathrooms were expected to be *this clean. Questions? None. Good.*

Interestingly, when some of the parents heard this story, they were amazed that some bureaucrat would get down on her hands and knees to scrub bathrooms for their children (see Box 8.1). Not too long afterward, more parents began to volunteer to help in the school. Sometimes guilt is the first stage of change; sometimes it is at a higher level, like vision; and sometimes guilt and vision have to go together to get dramatic things accomplished. Either way, her actions created some positive tension, and things changed.

In the spirit of making the children feel good about themselves, Madeline instituted a rule for the children that was directly against district policy—most districts', I'm sure. She sent a letter to parents, indicating that if their children came to school in dirty clothes, she would ask them to change and would wash their clothes on the spot. Fortunately for Madeline, her husband was quite handy and was able to buy and fix up a washer that was placed in the school's gymnasium. And if students came to school in dirty clothes, they were washed! *Questions? None. Good.*

To increase attendance in school, which on a bad day was 30%, Madeline took charge of calling each parent to see why her or his child was absent from school. If there was no answer at home, she got in her car and went straight to the home. If the child was home and not sick, she took the child in her car to school. Attendance quickly soared to 80% to 90% on a good day. The superintendent, who was extremely supportive of Madeline's efforts at Blaine, was getting heat from other administrators and politicians for the "radical" steps Madeline was taking. He knew that Madeline would do what needed to be done for the sake of the children, even if it meant violating district policies. He identified with her efforts but also had to work within the system he was heading, and at times he had to pull in the reigns on her efforts. It was never easy. In the

---

BOX 8.1. Transformational Leadership and Innovation

Following the work cited in Box 4.4, Keller (1992) studied 66 project groups containing professional employees from three industrial R&D organizations. Keller assessed intellectual stimulation of the project leaders as evaluated by followers. Level of intellectual stimulation predicted the quality of projects completed. Keller also reported that transformational leadership had a greater impact on project quality for R&D project teams engaged in research versus teams engaged in product development. Transformational leadership was more impactful when the products were being conceptualized, as opposed to what might appear to be a more transactional process of getting product developed and shipped out the door.

Similarly, Howell and Shea (1998) studied the impact of "champions of innovation" on 40 radical product innovations in 13 organizations. More effective champions were described as engaging in more "ambassadorial" and "scout" activities, whereas less effective ones operated as guards. The former characteristics contributed to teams that had a greater sense of potency and new product innovation success. Teams that were "guarded" created less penetrable boundaries that resulted in less optimal environmental scanning and isolation. In terms of the context, the authors also reported that support for innovation in the organizational culture was an important factor in enhancing a champion's success.

---

end, he became the needed champion, which helped Madeline in the transformation of her school system (see Box 8.2).[82]

Again, in the spirit of making the students feel good, Madeline knew that most of these children continually heard from their parents and others in their neighborhoods what they *couldn't* do and what they *couldn't* accomplish. Madeline instituted the policy that anytime a child in the school came across the word *can't,* she or he should cross it out! At a school assembly where this new rule was announced, she picked up an old book, took a red pen, and crossed out the word *can't* each time it appeared on a page. She told the students that *can't* was no longer part of the English language in this school. *Questions? None. Good.*

> *In most organizations, most really new things get accomplished by subterfuge and cunning.*
> (Ted Levitt, Editor of *Harvard Business Review*)

BOX 8.2. School Administrators, Transformational Leadership, and Performance

---

Leithwood, Jantzi, Silins, and Dart (1990) concluded that transformational leadership practices were more strongly related to school restructuring outcomes than was transactional leadership. Management-by-exception had a strong negative correlation with school conditions and processes. Developing a shared vision and consensus about group goals and providing intellectual stimulation contributed most positively to the conditions and processes associated with school restructuring and performance.

Leithwood and Jantzi (1990) examined the leadership practices of administrators in each of 12 schools. These schools had been identified as having highly collaborative environments. The driver developing this collaborative culture was the top school administrator, who displayed transformational leadership. Specifically, "principals have access to strategies which are transformational in effect and, hence assist in the development of collaborative school cultures" (p. 276).

Leithwood and Steinbach (1991) examined the "everyday" problem-solving strategies promoted by school principals. Nine elementary school principals were designated as "expert" problem solvers versus "typical" principals of less effective schools. Expert and typical "type" principals varied substantially in how they approached dealing with problems. Comparisons of expert versus typical principals is provided in Box 8.3.

There is much more to tell about Madeline's efforts back then at the school, but I think it suffices to say that no one thought she could accomplish what she initially accomplished. Her secret to being successful was that she saw possibilities first and then dealt with obstacles. Her perspective was different from that of the average transactional bureaucrat, who feels compelled to work always within the system, no matter how flawed it might be (see Box 8.3). She saw threats as an opportunity to inspire others. She had something essential to leading under duress: She had the courage to follow what she believed and to do something about her beliefs. She was only one person, but what an amazing vital force she created once she got the staff, parents, and teachers working along with her and fully identifying with her efforts.

We can learn many things from Madeline Cartwright's example. When I first read about her story in the *Wall Street Journal* early one morning, I was inspired and also distraught. At that time, I had two children (a third was added, whom you met in Chapter 7, in Mala Mala, named Sydney) who were both in elementary school. My children left that morning on a shiny yellow bus, with their new school bags and colorful lunch boxes. The school they went to was bright, cheery, and clean. Nothing about the context suggested the word *can't*. I was sorry that other children, all children, didn't have the same opportunity. But I was inspired by Madeline's example and invited her to speak at an annual event for our Center for Leadership Studies. She agreed and was as inspiring in person as she was in the article I read. We learned, that evening in her address, that she was dirt poor and grew up in a situation where most black children never finished elementary school. And now, here she was, presenting at our university in the role of the principal of a school some thought she would never graduate from in her lifetime. As the announcer said when the U.S. hockey team beat the awesome and "unbeatable" Soviet team in the 1980 Olympics, "You gotta believe!"

In sum, transformational leaders often believe that they face a challenging problem rather than a crisis. Viewing it as a challenge versus a crisis leads them to open channels for input, as opposed to close sources of information, like the "guards" who curtail innovation described above, as often occurs in crises—personal or otherwise. They become more open to incorporating ideas and suggestions from their followers, peers, or bosses into final decisions even when the opinions differ from their own. Transformational leaders express their desire to hear more arguments before coming to a conclusion. They are not the types of leaders who seek consensus when the building is on fire. And, like Madeline Cartwright, when they have to take a stand out ahead of others, and often alone, they do. *Questions? None. Good.*

It's the Context, Really!

Although I still tell this story, most recently to a group of Israeli Defense Force consultants who had used the word *can't* once too often in a workshop where they were learning about the full range leadership program, I started to realize that sometimes what people are trying to say is correct about the context. In many situations, the context is not at all receptive to the changes we would like to institute—even very beneficial ones.[83] And, as noted above, support for innovation within an organization's culture was a key factor in championing the development of successful/innovative products. As much as I try to challenge people to action, some things in the context still must be addressed before one can begin to move forward. It has led me to advise many organizations to look to the context before working on changing specific leadership styles and

BOX 8.3. Different Principal Leadership Styles

Expert	*Typical*
Interpretation	
Seeks out and takes into consideration other views	Assumes that others share interpretation
Looks at problems in relation to the larger whole or mission	Has tendency to view problems in isolation
Goals	
Works to get staff agreement	Is more concerned with achieving own goals
Has less of a personal stake in her or his solution	Is strongly committed to preconceived notions
Principals/Values	
Places highest value on respect for others	Impact of decisions on clients
Constraints	
Anticipates obstacles	Does not anticipate obstacles
Adapts flexibly to unanticipated obstacles	Rarely responds effectively to obstacles
Views obstacles as opportunities	Views obstacles as obstacles
Solutions	
Outlines clearly the process for problem solving and expectations of others	Is unstructured
Checks collaborators' interpretations of problems	Assumes that others have same interpretation
Remains open to new and challenging views	Stubbornly sticks to her or his own views
Ensures that follow-up is planned	Rarely plans
Affect	
Uses humor to diffuse tension and to clarify perspectives	

behaviors (see Box 8.4). The reality is simple: The context is often the people, and if not directly people, it was built by people. So, to change in some radical or significant way, we must first change the context and then get more specific with altering and adapting styles and behaviors to the new context. Shake it up and dazzle them when everyone is confused. It works for both good and bad charismatic leaders, who are well known for rising to power in the "worst of times."[84] It is not so surprising, given what we described above.

I now firmly believe that many training programs have little, if any, positive impact because often we are attempting to insert a foreign body into an inhospitable host. My realization of this led to the creation of the training cycle presented in Figure 8.1. When I work with "leaders and followers" in organizations or with team interventions, I present this figure in our preliminary planning session. In presenting the figure here, I am attempting to reinforce several important points about developing a full range of leadership potential. Let me highlight these points for your consideration by referring to Figure 8.1.

- Leadership development is a time-based process and cannot be accomplished at one point in time.
- The context must be considered in planning the leadership development intervention to anticipate obstacles in order to reinforce what has been learned to help transfer what was learned in the workshop back to the job.
- Boosters are needed to reinforce what has been learned and to provide support during crucial transition periods. In the follow-up, change typically occurs after people have had a chance to reflect on what they were taught in foundation training.
- The more training interventions are "seamless" with respect to transferring what was learned back to the job, the more impact training effects will have over time. Stated another way, if we use unrealistic cases or role modeling exercises, we should not expect a positive transfer of training. We should always incorporate issues of relevance to our target audience.
- Training should not be conceived of as a discrete program, but rather as an organizational intervention supported by other interventions over time. Training must have a clear, central purpose that will affect how people perform in their roles. Ideally, the best training programs create a sense of identification with the core values and beliefs they are attempting to transfer to participants.

The training cycle begins with an appreciation or *awareness* of each trainer's ideal/implicit model of leadership. From there, it works through building an understanding of the full range model, applying that model in terms of feedback on the trainee's leadership style, followed by the development of a plan for intervention and mechanisms to follow up on the plan.

After a series of applications and substantial practice, the intent over time is to encourage the trainee to *adopt* new ways of leading and following in order to *achieve* a higher level of development and performance. The cycle is continuous and iterative in the sense that it repeats itself at each new level of awareness and application.

In Chapter 3, I introduced the idea of the "life stream" in terms of explaining individual development. In the context of the model presented in Figure 8.1, we

Leadership Development Cycle

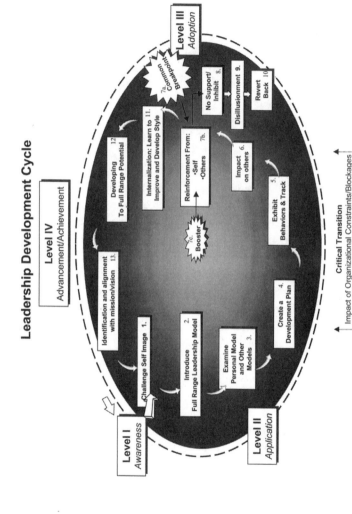

Figure 8.1. Leadership Development Cycle

SOURCE: Adapted from Quinn's empowerment cycle (Quinn, Anderson, & Finklestein, 1996).
NOTES: Most leadership development efforts involve I and II. Development impact depends on critical transition/booster.
Change in internal perspective must eventually align with external opportunities/constraints/perspectives.

131

are converging several life streams into an event I call a "leadership training workshop." By converging, we of course are typically overshadowing individual differences. This is typically by economic necessity because we can't afford to have separate training interventions for each person, catered to her or his personal development cycle. Or can we? Well, we can at least set this as our high bar for expectations and then design our training interventions to try to attain this ideal. Recall that the full range model has at its highest point a leader who models ideals we all strive to achieve. So, to be a consistent role model for the model, we should also set ideals that may seem unrealistic or unattainable. My hopes are that you will take the opportunity to do the same after some reflection.

One way to approach the problem of individualizing training programs is to assume it is important and to find mechanisms before, during, and after the intervention to address each individual's needs and potential. This often requires a significant change in many trainers' thinking about training (see Box 8.4). For example, we here at the Center for Leadership Studies have found that one main obstacle to transferring what is learned from leadership training back to the job is one's peers. So, in the design of workshops, we create peer learning partners, who are often connected after the workshop to facilitate and support the transfer of learning back to the work context. The learning partnerships can be set up on the basis of their mutual goals for themselves, proximity to each other, willingness to work together, need to work together, or some combination. The main point here is that we use peers to facilitate the process of training beyond the formal context of the training program. Moreover, we are attempting to enlist peers in sharing the responsibility for maximizing each other's development by supporting it where it counts—back on the job.

In addition to using peers in face-to-face interactions following a formal training intervention, we are exploring the use of various forms of information technology to see how we can enhance training effects on learning and performance.[85] For example, we are developing a Web site where participants can continue to interact in large and small learning groups after the close of a training session. This Web site is also now used to collect 360° feedback via e-mail. The interactions can be set up to be anonymous, depending on the needs of the group and its members. We can also send out to each individual some developmental tips based on feedback they've received on our leadership surveys and the goals they set prior to or within the workshop. This system has been designed to link to any organization's e-mail system so that every few days or on a weekly basis the person receives a tip on what she or he might consider incorporating into a leadership planning response. We are linking to this leadership learning Web site

---

BOX 8.4. More on Stability and Transformational Leadership

Bass (1998) reported on research comparing stable versus unstable environments. Findings were in line with expectations about transformational leaders. Specifically, transformational leadership mean ratings of leaders were higher in unstable environments, whereas transactional management-by-exception was slightly higher in stable conditions.

Similarly, House (1995) indicated that commitment levels of followers of 24 charismatic entrepreneurial CEOs was positively related to the uncertainty of the environments in which they operated. A significant positive relationship was found between CEO leadership and commitment when the environments were more unstable and uncertain.

In contrast, Hicks (1990) conducted a small sample study of 11 leaders in a missionary organization and reported that unstable conditions were not necessarily required for transformational leaders to be effective. In addition, a stable environment was not a prerequisite for leaders to lead who were more transactional.

---

additional support in the form of groupware technology to allow for activities such as electronic brainstorming. As this system matures, we will try to tie it into the development and appraisal process within the organization and, if possible, the reward system. In a very direct way, we are trying to tie the program into all fabrics of the context and in so doing accomplish two things. First, we fully intend to transform the context because a leadership intervention, if seen as a systemic or strategic one, will be successful if it changes the context. Second, it is our goal to root the program intervention deeply into the context that we want to take to the next phase of development, and by changing the context we are also attacking the culture of the organization's "back yard." By the way, you have already been invited to visit the Web site. It's like what Yogi Berra once said, "It's déjà vu all over again."

Our second point above was that the context must be considered in any leadership intervention. For instance, if we are training people to be more individually considerate, what mechanisms exist to support this type or style of leadership in the context? Are people rewarded for taking the time to develop people and/or to take on the role of a learning partner? Where is the recognition for such behavior?

Typically, in the preplanning sessions for a workshop, I try to find something the senior leadership would like to change in the context and to make that an overarching goal for the workshop. In doing so, I am attempting to integrate the fabric of the context into the workshop, or, I guess, vice versa. For example, in a bank in the Midwest, the workshop was used as a means of bringing together branch managers who had previously worked at another bank prior to merging with the bank for whom we were designing the training program. Each workshop took on very specific issues that were arising from the mergers and acquisitions, 11 or so in the last several years. With two health care associations that were considering co-locating their facilities, the advantages of co-location became one major thrust for the workshop.

In my experience, when a senior executive says that she just wants a leadership training workshop and that she would prefer not to include the contextual stuff mentioned above, my advice is DON'T DO IT! It will certainly help some individual managers or project leaders at work, at home, or with a board they work with in their community. But, it will likely not have the full impact the organization's leadership expects from the "program." It may simply mean that they or their context or both are not developmentally ready for the type of intervention we are planning. Here, a lack of developmental readiness may be seen at the organizational level, and it is one's own judgment how far trainees can currently be pulled. Readiness is not yes or no; it is a diagnostic judgment that should lead to a question in your mind: *What can I do now to prepare for what I really want to accomplish later?* It is leadership, by the way, based on a heavy dose of reflection.

The *booster* concept in the leadership development cycle is rooted in several principles. First, what individuals learn about leadership development may take some time to take root in thought, intentions, and behaviors. The booster is a mechanism for getting people to revisit what they've learned after they have had some specific experiences to tie to the model and workshop intervention. If we assume that the first workshop intervention provides participants with a frame of reference against which to catalog experiences, the first booster can be used to reflect on how the person could have changed to modify the events that were cataloged. Recall I indicated that one can create, to some degree, one's own "life biography" or stream. This is all part of that larger change process being undertaken.

Second, the booster provides people an opportunity to hear how others are applying the model in practice. This can be done in a learning group that periodically meets with or without a facilitator or by bringing back the entire group for a follow-up workshop. It can also be accomplished via the Web site discussed above. The booster is an opportunity to revisit one's plan for personal development, to revise it, and to estimate progress toward achieving its goals and objectives.

Third, the booster is a symbolic representation that leadership development is CPI. Recall that we used the acronym CPI to represent continuous *personal, people,* and *process* improvement. The booster is a mechanism to help continuously revise what one has been doing to improve on her or his plan. It can be a corrective intervention or simply a reinforcer to continue with the plan that at present seems to be hitting all its targets.

> *Developing people as fast as possible is the way to have a vibrant and*
> *exciting organization.*
> (Roy Vagelos, Former Chairman of Merck)

In many ways, the booster session and/or follow-up sends a signal to everyone that the organization is serious about the change process and that we are going to work on it until we get it right. It is a serious statement for any trainer to make because she or he is saying, "I'll be back. If I taught you things that were bullshit, I'll hear it. If I taught you things that were worthwhile, I hope to hear it, but perhaps not as loud as the items in the bullshit category." It says to participants, "Let me be honest with you. I am coming back to learn whether what we set out to accomplish was accomplished. If so, what else can we do to come closer to achieving our highest goals and expectations? If not, then my question is, Who the hell screwed up?" (I'm kidding. Just wanted to grab your attention.) "If not, then what do we need to do to revise our plans or to get back on track, whatever the track may be at the present time?"

I believe that leadership training should be seamless with respect to the context in which it is intended to be embedded. I mean here that it should be tied to something real that someone wants to transform. I call many of the workshop activities in which I have trainees participate "real play" versus "role play." What issues must the leadership system address in the organization? Why not make these issues target points for change in the leadership intervention? Of course, some people are more or less ready to deal with "real issues," so the ones you pick can be "low hanging fruit" to start off, and then you can move incrementally to more significant challenges. By using this strategy, we can build the collective efficacy and potency of the group we are working with to take on even more significant challenges. By building collective efficacy in a group, we can effect a transformation both in the context as well as in performance.

At some point in the process, you should recognize that you have moved from being a trainer to an organizational development (OD) consultant in the trainees' eyes, but in your mind, I hope these are always completely intertwined. If you have recognized this already, then you can see that my philosophy of training leadership is to build it into an OD/strategic intervention. In so doing, we are training, but we are also cognizant of the context in which we are attempting to effect change. To reiterate a basic principle: Leadership must be viewed as a *process* and *system;* it is difficult to conceive of training leadership in any way that does not include the context in which leaders, peers, and followers must operate over time.

In some ways, I have already covered the last point from above when I discussed how leadership development must be viewed as an organizational intervention, but let me add in a few examples for clarity. During the last several years, I have been involved in situations where an organization totally reengineered its system/processes only to find out afterward that it had totally destroyed trust and loyalty and was successful in making the "old" leadership system even more dysfunctional. As a consequence of its destruction through such interventions, I have become more convinced of the importance of viewing leadership as a system. Let me use an example to clarify this point.

In one extreme instance, I attended a meeting with a group of reengineering experts at which the presenter kept saying proudly to the senior execs in the room that, in their work they don't use the "f" word. He didn't mean the one you might be thinking of, or at least the one I initially thought of, to be perfectly honest. He meant *facilitator.* Reengineering was a technical process, a hard process that was not going to be muddied by those soft interventions that used facilitators and talked about group processes such as leadership. This group of senior managers who were engineers themselves met his comments with smiles and nods of approval. We're men, and men don't need facilitators. We can very well screw things up on our own! Of course, that was before all hell broke loose in the organization following this radical reengineering intervention. By the way, I am usually brought back to many of those organizations because someone finally recognized that it was the soft or relational processes, stupid, that really seemed to matter in the end. Pay me later, I guess.

I have come to learn how to talk in system-level terms and to use technical jargon to help senior executives understand that any training intervention we undertake will affect multiple systems with each embedded in the other. Not all of them understand; therefore, in my opinion, not all are quite ready for leadership training as a strategic intervention. Certainly, there is always a technical system, no matter how complex, that we can put our hands around. But there is also a human system, much more complex, that must also be considered when planning to reengineer technical processes. Stated another way, in most instances it is virtually impossible to separate out the technical from the human system's processes. Any change in one will often have a very significant impact on the other. I guess that is why many reengineering gurus write a second book, entitled something like *Uh, Sorry We Left Out the People Thing.*

In another example, an organization was investing millions of dollars in a new Enterprise Resource Program (ERP) information system. The culture of the organization was very resistant to change, and after 6 months of false starts the senior management asked the consultants implementing ERP to rewrite the code to "fit" their organization. Although the consultants were against doing this, they finally agreed. What did they agree to do? They agreed to take an information processing system designed for business functions of 2005 and retrofit it to an organizational culture, structure, and system designed for the 1950s. The context won! The consultants made a lot more money than expected, and the new system still didn't work. Help! Of course, the more transformational approach is to decide where your business should be in the future and then develop the technology infrastructure to support your vision. You can look in the rearview mirror for ideas, but focusing there too long usually results in a crash.

Also, in the medical field as an example, many practitioners have come to the realization that the physician must treat the "whole" person. One cannot simply solve the physical aspects of a disease and expect a full and expedient recovery. Often, very severe emotional issues must be addressed in parallel that, traditionally, the average physician was not prepared or trained to handle in school. The same is true of many reengineering firms I have seen in operation— that, despite the problems caused by reengineering, resistance to recognizing the role of the "soft" processes in organizational transformations still appears to be strong. It leads me to ask the question again that I asked in Chapter 6: What is organization? My answer is that it includes *people, context,* and *processes,* technical or otherwise. It is all about *relationships.*

Let me summarize the main thrust of this chapter so far. Our focus has been on examining the context at various levels and over time as we plan and subsequently implement a leadership development intervention. I have argued that it is difficult, if not impossible, to achieve the goals of a leadership intervention without considering the context. Yet, one cannot be overwhelmed by the context either, and sometimes a leader such as Madeline Cartwright must first attack the context to ignite a significant transformation in the way people think and behave. Change the context first, create positive tension, and then worry about changing people's perspectives later on. I have attempted in a very direct way in this chapter to reverse the figure (usually leaders and followers or team) with the background or context in which they operate. I gave examples to show that, by attending to the context, we have a chance at also changing the individuals who operate within that context. At the very least, if you change the context, you gain people's attention, which is a prerequisite for development.[86]

Perhaps many questions can be asked now, including, Doesn't the context raise the level of abstraction of our intervention? Yes, but not beyond where it must be, in my opinion. You might also ask yourself, *What characteristics of my context would be the biggest enhancer (inhibitor) to an intervention based on the full range model of leadership?* For instance, if your organization had a traditional organizational design and hierarchy of authority, what would help and hinder your organization going to teams? (I had a feeling you were waiting for the team discussion.) How inconsistent is the reward system for reinforcing collaborative efforts? How willing are your managers to distribute decision-making authority to teams? How much discretion will these managers provide to support the team in achieving its own decisions? If these questions don't get asked in the planning phase, I can tell you from years of experience that they will get asked in the training intervention, if not afterward in the "recovery" phase. Maybe that's what the "re" means in *reengineering.*

Okay, here comes teams. In one situation, I worked with a Wall Street firm that decided to "go to teams." A visionary leader kicked off the process, supported by an energized OD staff that put every ounce of effort into moving the support and technical operations to a team-based environment. People in New York put up enormous resistance to the change. Some said, "It's damn socialism, and in the extreme, communistic." The resistance was so fervent that the firm decided to move the operational staff 1,200 miles away from New York City. This was considered far enough away to allow the *team* concept to grow but near enough to shuttle back and forth as needed. The location was also in the same time zone, which remains an advantage when calling someone on the telephone.

The *team* concept was introduced in a new facility in the South. This was a pure green field operation, except that many of the managers who were transferred to the new facilities came from the old hierarchical, authoritative system. They became, for the next 3 years, the "relos," or those who relocated, which should suggest how quickly they assimilated into the new "emerging" culture.

In New York, one responded to a request by first asking, "*Who* requested it?" Based on this query, the priorities were set on how fast it got done, if at all.

The former New Yorkers in this firm were highly suspicious of this "socialistic system" emerging in the South. They were extremely concerned that this was the management board's attempt at leveling bonuses. Some New Yorkers found the *team* concept intriguing; however, most were either annoyed by it or simply angry about it and were not reserved about expressing their dissatisfaction, often LOUDLY.

The difficulties this organization had in going to teams is a testament to preparing the context for such radical change. The "relos" had a difficult time dealing with the change in roles from being a manager and having all the technical knowledge and power to being a coach—a term that was actually used for their position. They now were supposed to facilitate more than manage. Yet, the immediate image I had after meeting the relos was a 300-pound football player being asked to ballet dance. Even if he can do it, it still looks a little funny.

It was typical for managers in New York to call down to their support staff in the South and ask for "who" is in charge of this or that. When the response came back that a team was in charge, often the person in New York went ballistic. For the entire 3 years I worked with this organization, there was a constant struggle between the "team people" from the South and the "individualists" from the North. I often say that humans have not necessarily evolved so far from monkeys in their development when it comes to wanting to know who is in charge, how power is exercised, how aberrant behavior is dealt with, and of course, who ultimately gets the banana. So, we had two very different primate colonies that simply didn't understand each other's rules at the outset. Taking some literary freedom with Marlin Perkins, this is not unique in the humankind kingdom.

Indeed, even though many people "in the firm" were pleased that their firm was doing something ahead of other Wall Street firms, when it came down to the practical day-to-day operations, they exerted constant resistance to going to a team-based system—especially one professing to be what I now would call "collective individualism." For all intents and purposes, the *team* concept was evolving in a very hostile context and over time had achieved certain aspects of Ubuntu (see Chapter 7).

One humorous example of the resistance was relayed to me by the head of the OD team. Mike had asked to have his business card redone to label his position as "senior coach," rather than something like "vice president" for blah, blah, blah. Every time he sent in his corrected card to New York City, it came back the same old way. It took an intervention from the worldwide head of the firm's support operation to get the corrected card sent to him, after 6 months of trying! Certain cultures are sown deep. Also, if you are a card-carrying monkey of one colony, you just aren't allowed to change it overnight.

The *team* concept really came to a head in the firm when a task force was put together to discuss how the compensation system might be revised to take into consideration that the organization was moving to teams. I immediately heard in my mind, "MELTDOWN! DIVE, DIVE, DIVE." Messing around with the compensation system in a Wall Street firm can be likened to telling the American Civil Liberties Union that the protections for freedom of speech and individual liberties were no longer "in vogue" within the United States. Or telling the Catholic Church that it was time to add an 11th commandment that would alter or revise the previous 10. Hey, no problem. The reaction in the firm, particularly by the star earners, was like an affliction to a horrible disease. It led to a "bring out your dead" mentality. Body count soared. Too much "friendly fire" for any one firm to endure.

Along with other events, the visionary who began the team process left the firm, along with the OD consultants who had championed the *team* concept. Also, some key coaches who had become converts subsequently left. Of course, they set up a consulting group (I mean team) to do with other companies what they attempted to do in this firm. I must add that it is unfair simply to say that the *team* concept no longer exists in "the firm" (I can't resist); it does, but in a much more limited way than it was initially envisioned. It has now become sort of a 2-day training program. The prior context had won over the new intervention.

My experience now with several organizations indicates that, at an organizational level, the organization must go through a crucial transition (squiggly line) to go from a *team* concept being driven by its founder to a belief that is fully identified by the workforce and its collective leadership. Also, on the basis of my experience, the move to alter the performance appraisal and reward system has been one of the significant turning points where the proverbial "do do" hits the fan! When a *team* concept becomes a team leadership system, we must change how people are evaluated, developed, and rewarded. At this point in the development of the new system, we go from it being a good basis for personal relations and for building cooperation to being a system that is more integrated into other facets of the organization's system, such as compensation and evaluation. By linking it to compensation and evaluation, the leadership of the organization is saying, "This is a fundamental change or accommodation involving an alteration in our ways of thinking and operating." You may have surmised on your own that preparing for this point of tension requires leadership that helps show the way an entire system must change, why it must change, and how things will be affected subsequently.

Let me summarize several key points raised above. First, the context is so crucial to the transformation process that often the context must be changed first or challenged if any real change is to take place. Second, individuals we would evaluate as transformational don't accept the context as given. Indeed, they see opportunities in the context that others see as overwhelming obstacles that cannot be overcome. Transformational leaders see the elements of the future in the current context and move to capitalize on what they see, before others do, which puts them ahead of the competition. Third, we used an example here of going to teams because, in discussing leadership systems, my colleagues and I see team or shared leadership as being one very important and distinct level of leadership in organizations. I also said earlier that, in many organizations today and into the foreseeable future, one key challenge will be to understand what constitutes the full potential of shared leadership processes in teams. This challenge is on the doorstep of all the organizations that have in the recent past and are currently deleveling operations and moving toward a truly networked organization.

I have summarized in Figure 8.2 the team system process whereby people develop their perspective of going from the *I* to the *me,* to the *we* and *us.* Going from left to right, we start with a diverse set of inputs, establish our expectations, develop our unit through adaptive conflict, which, if properly led, results in higher levels of integration and coherence. Elements of the team system such as "Power Sharing" and "Shared Leadership" reflect what we end up observing in highly developed teams.

Following our tradition, let me leave you with one question to consider for further reflection. Take a look at the context in which you currently lead and follow. *What would you challenge or change to effect a "true" transformation in the way your organizational unit develops the full potential of its members?*

Some Things Worth Repeating

- The context includes the people; thus, it must be changed if a full and successful transformation is expected.
- If you take the context as a given, then you are limiting your ability to transform the organization.
- One of the greatest challenges that leaders have is attacking the habits of the past to replace them with the assumptions on which the future needs to be based.
- Know the part toward which you are directing the transformation of the people and context. *Don't* ask the programmers to rewrite the code to make things as they were, because you are avoiding what they can and should be.

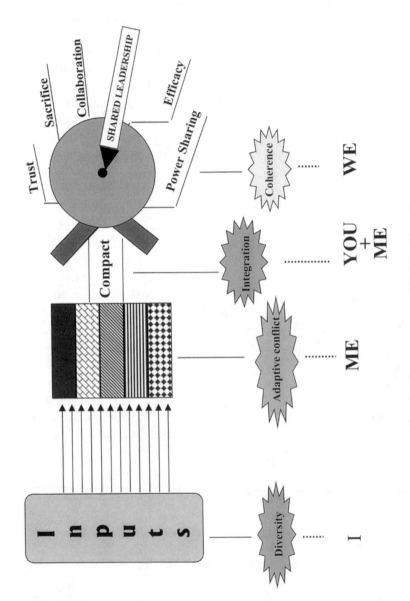

Figure 8.2. Summary View of Building Team System

9

Four Principles at the Base of the Full Range Model—Which Rose to the Top Over and Over Again

Even if you're on the right track, you'll get run over if you just sit there.
   (Will Rogers)

I am willing to admit that I may not always be right, but I am never wrong.
   (Samuel Golden Mayer)

My context changed during the week I was writing this chapter, along with that of many others around the world. In 1 week, two great women who had a fundamental impact on their countries and the world passed away. The first was Princess Diana, who died in a car accident in Paris. The other was Mother Teresa, whose fragile but huge heart gave out at age 87. Both were

143

friends of each other, and both were united in helping those who couldn't help themselves. They each represented something very special about the highest ends of humanity, as well as the core of what the high end of leadership is based on. A third, somewhat different, leader also died during the same week—Mobutu Sese Seko—whom many will forget quickly. He was the president of the former Zaire for 32 years. He died a man without a country and likely a leader who left behind a very shallow shadow, along with a large bank account of stolen assets.

I'll begin with the four principles that I have interwoven throughout my discussions about leadership in this book. Each of these principles can be applied to understanding individual-, team-, and organizational-level leadership.

The first principle pertains to managing one's vulnerabilities:

> Principle 1: The most exemplary leaders, teams, and organizations are balanced in how they manage their vulnerabilities. Vulnerabilities are embraced, understood, dealt with, and certainly not avoided.

The immediate reaction to this statement by many people in leadership positions is usually, "Can you just repeat what you said, and then please explain your point again?" The reaction is so consistent that it appears to represent an archetype across many cultures. Many people are afraid to discuss openly their vulnerabilities, especially when those people are "leaders." Ironically, our individual and collective strengths are intricately tied to understanding our core collective vulnerabilities.

Many seem to believe that leaders are closer to invulnerable; however, in many instances this has been proven false. Indeed, the best ones typically come along in the worst situations when they and their followers feel most vulnerable and make a difference, resulting in people following them to victory! Well, it is sometimes not always a victory in the "real world." Of course, many examples are cited in the leadership literature to support this conclusion, going back to Weber's foundation work on the emergence of charismatic leadership.[87] Weber argued that one precondition for charisma to emerge in organizations is a crisis. Charisma is "crisis-induced," and some evidence supports Weber's position, although other evidence indicates it is not always necessary to have a crisis for a charismatic leader to emerge, as noted earlier (in Box 5.2) in the work I cited by Pillai and Rivera.

Weber's basic argument is that a leader comes along in crisis and shows those in desperate need the way out of their mess. Through the leader's direction comes hope and a promise of a better future. Examples such as Hitler are often used, depicting how he brought the German people out of economic ruin and despair created after World War I into . . . well, you have heard that story before. The same can be said, but for vastly different reasons, for Franklin D. Roosevelt around the Depression, for Winston Churchill in World War II, and perhaps most recently in the events surrounding Apple Computer with Steven Jobs, who returned to the board to save Apple from further financial ruin, if not total extinction. And in 1998, Apple surprised Wall Street with its first quarterly profits in years, after Jobs stepped in as interim CEO. By late-1998, Apple's stock had risen by 10 points, and the company was introducing an exciting new line of Mac equipment.

We can speak of countries, companies, teams, and individuals, and to a large extent our conclusions would likely be the same. Being cognizant of one's vulnerabilities and allowing for a sufficient level is one basis for sustaining effective leadership over long periods of time. Lose touch with your vulnerabilities, and you run the risk of them overwhelming you. Simply face them head-on, and you may still fail. No guarantees. Facing them is necessary but not sufficient for success. This only provides the basis for the remaining three principles.

In the time the world knew of Mother Teresa, she always appeared so vulnerable. She was frail and typically ill, to some extent because of the lifestyle she chose and because of the very sick people she helped throughout her lifetime. Her vulnerability didn't just attract the world to her, but created awe and reverence for her deeds. Her beliefs, compassion, courage, and inner strength also helped, in case you were thinking vulnerability is it! It is not. Being vulnerable made her all the more credible and trustworthy. This was also very true for a leader in a very different context described in Chapter 4. This was the platoon leader who led "with them" and "ahead of them." And I said that, in the Israeli Defense Forces, such leaders have the highest rate of fatalities—a rather extreme index of vulnerability. In fact, as I am writing this portion of the book, a young platoon commander who was taking part in a leadership training experiment that Taly Dvir, Dov Eden, Boas Shamir, and I were conducting was subsequently killed in Lebanon. He was killed running back and forth between bunkers to make sure his soldiers were safe. He became too vulnerable, and he was killed. This is real stuff, and maybe it could have been avoided. Unfortunately, it wasn't, and his country, family, and friends now mourn his sacrifice. I will have more to say about the remarkable team I worked with in Israel on this project, and the student leader by the name of Taly, who in everyone's estimation engineered what will no doubt be the definitive study on training leadership conducted during the last 20 to 30 years. She will likely attribute these extra-

---

BOX 9.1. More on Visionary Leadership and Its Impact

Martin (1996) reported a strong positive relationship between visionary leadership, trust building, and follower attitudinal reactions with 4,454 executives. Setting the vision and building the context of trust were two crucial elements in achieving positive and supportive reactions from followers.

Berson, Shamir, Avolio, and Popper (1998) examined the relationships between vision content and ratings of transformational leadership for 229 leaders. They reported a positive relationship between vision content that was optimistic and ratings of transformational leadership. Also, they reported that this relationship was moderated by organizational (e.g., size) and personal (e.g., experience as a manager, tenure) attributes. Specifically, transformational managers with high amounts of experience and low tenure produced the most optimistic visionary speeches. (Also refer to den Hartog, Van Muijen, & Koopman, 1996, for additional discussion on content analysis of visionary statements.)

---

ordinary accomplishments to being a lion, Leo being her astrological sign. As a Gemini, I have my doubts—well, at least today, but tomorrow I could view this situation in a completely different way!

Anyone willing to risk what the platoon leader or Mother Teresa did for the good of others? Are these people worth listening to and believing? Wouldn't you be more willing to listen to them? The platoon leader may have acted out of inexperience, but he cared deeply for his platoon. Many would do the same. Wouldn't you listen to him if he was willing to sacrifice his own safety for your safety? It's a hell of way to build credibility and trust. Once established, however, there is no higher form of control over people than control based on commitment to a cause, mission, and/or vision (see Box 9.1).

Mother Teresa's case is probably the clearest example of how one's vulnerabilities represent the core of anyone's inner and outer strengths. She said she was never worthy of the attention being given to her and surely not worthy of receiving the Noble Peace Prize. Yet, the world thought she was worthy and granted her the respect and support that world-class leaders command. Several days after her death, the Catholic Church seemed to be searching for ways to expedite her sainthood. Even the Church was concerned about reducing cycle time for a worthy cause!

Another great lady died during that week. You might ask, "How was Princess Diana vulnerable, or even a leader?" She was in so many ways, but let's focus on the most obvious. She struggled from the very start as a young 20-year-old, with the strict demands of the royal family. She and her husband, Prince Charles, struggled from the start with what was supposed to be a fairy-tale marriage. She struggled with the need to expose her sons to a broad range of world experiences versus the lens the royal family chose to use for its kings and princes-in-waiting. Over time, she showed her distress and how vulnerable she had become in the limelight of what many compared to being a Hollywood star.

Diana's willingness to show her vulnerabilities to the world, coupled with her interest in and kindness toward people, made her an awesome force in the House of Windsor for more than 15 years. In his moving eulogy for his sister, Diana's brother, Charles, began by saying,

> We are all united not only in our desire to pay our respects to Diana, but rather in our need to do so . . . that it was her innermost feelings of suffering that made it possible for her to connect with her constituency of the rejected. For all of her status, glamour, and applause, Diana remained a very insecure person at heart. . . . The world sensed this part of her character and cherished her vulnerability, whilst admiring her honesty.

In these heartfelt words of a brother mourning his sister lies a core aspect of the essence of the vital force in exemplary leaders, followers, and teams that willingly work together to accomplish great things. Charles said, "in our need" to pay respect to her. This can only mean what we all felt we owed to her for what she was willing to sacrifice for others. A willingness to sacrifice on her part, to step out of her royal world into the world of AIDS victims, the homeless, and the sick, makes us all owe her something, or at least feel that we do.

In hearing these words on the morning of Princess Diana's funeral, I thought to myself how often I felt her vulnerability as I might feel myself in her situation. She seemed so vulnerable, yet she also seemed so strong to me. In this balance, often the "magic" of leadership is created. She took a stand and dared to be different in a royal world steeped in thousands of years of tradition. She made people feel real and that she was real and touchable in a world that seems to most of us so untouchable. She did it, in her brother's words, through her deep compassion for others and her wonderfully mischievous sense of humor. Interest in and compassion for others is at the base of what we've called *individualized consideration.* It is not a 1-minute style; it is fundamental to who you are and how you treat people all the time, whether they are followers, peers, or your boss. Once discovered in oneself, vulnerability is an awesome force, but as I've said time and time again, certainly a fragile one. It is fragile because the world is not always fair. That is the risk such exemplary leaders take, and I guess one could easily add followers and team members. They, too, are often overly exposed and extremely vulnerable—too vulnerable.

Princess Diana had two characteristics worth restating: (a) She had something inside her that made a difference in how she chose to treat others, which links to her values and perspective about humanity, and (b) what was inside her was often exposed to the outside and manifested itself in terms of her vulnerability and "life spirit" or "vital force."

People like Princess Diana, Mother Teresa, Jesus Christ, Mahatma Gandhi, Nelson Mandela, and Martin Luther King, Jr., seem always so vulnerable on reflection and often have sacrificed the most for others to be free, to live normal lives, to be treated with respect, and to have beliefs that endure throughout life. In each of their cases—some already, and others yet to come—the legacy or "shadow of their institutions" runs deep and long. They have made a difference in the world and are remembered as such for their positive contributions to humankind. These people show what Stacey (see Chapter 3) showed with her students—a willingness to give of themselves, to be vulnerable because they cared and knew who they were as people and what they could offer to others. When recently asked about his father's accomplishments, Martin Luther King Jr.'s son indicated that his father would be pleased with the progress in our nation regarding racial integration and equity, but not fully satisfied at all. Personally, I am tremendously satisfied that we in the United States honor his "shadow" each January for his contribution to creating unity through diversity in our country. I do believe that the key to maintaining the United States as the leader of the free world is how it will maximize its differences. Through our diversity of intellect, values, and culture, we will lead the world in innovation.

We can contrast the individuals described above with Mobutu Sese Seko, Adolph Hitler, Pol Pot, Joseph Stalin, Ferdinand Marcos, Saddam Hussein, Nicolae Ceausescu, Benito Mussolini, and Chairman Mao, who were ruthless in protecting their vulnerabilities, fearing their exposures and the risks they saw to their influence and control of others. Now, look at their institutions and their shadows. Who in the end was most vulnerable? I'm waiting . . .

Also, while writing this chapter, my friend Joe Ebert gave me a videotape to review on the famous Blue Angels flying team. This group of pilots is renowned for their acrobatic stunts in F16 jets, often traveling in excess of 1,000 mph toward each other, flying 25 feet apart, and flying 150 feet from the ground upside down. Frankly, I am getting a bit nauseous just thinking about their accomplishments.

A clear message from the interview with each of the Blue Angel pilots is their keen sense of each other's vulnerability. Two of the pilots said they were just "average" pilots given an extraordinary opportunity to represent their country. They said time and time again that they must know even the smallest weakness of each other in order to be successful. And in their jobs, the redline between success and failure is death. No one can be hesitant to point out either his own or another member's vulnerabilities. Through the examination and understanding of each of their vulnerabilities, the vital force of this team is created and endures over time.

A portion of the videotape discusses the process of debriefing used by the team. If only we could get more management "teams" to go through such debriefs, we would be well along the way to dealing with vulnerabilities that stifle very bright people from securing their team's vital force. Imagine your management team sitting down and *reviewing* each member's weaknesses, mistakes, and hesitancies. Consider now that rank is irrelevant. Are you still with me, or are you saying, "In the real world, Bruce, . . . ?" Well, this is the process the Blue Angels go through every day, and it requires generally twice the amount of time to debrief that it takes to fly the actual mission. By the way, how high and fast does your "team" fly in the real world? How do you debrief events for your team's development? Also, the Blue Angels conduct a predebriefing before they even execute the mission.

I often suggest to teams to pick an event that is a marker event for the team and to go through the process of debriefing that event. It is a wonderful process for reflective learning if you are willing to place your vulnerabilities on the table. It helps groups and individuals explore very deeply where they have traveled in their process of working together. The U.S. Army has institutionalized this process and calls it After Action Reviews.

I came across a quote that symbolized for me the core of this process—"reflective learning"—I keep coming back to in this book: T. S. Eliot once said that the outcome of exploration is "to arrive where we started and know the place for the first time."

The examples provided above had something very closely aligned with vulnerability that we can turn to next. The former dictator of Romania, Nicolae Ceausescu, was so concerned about any threats or challenges to his power that he never allowed any questions to come from the audience. At one rally, a brave individual stood up and began to question his policies. He got so unnerved that he couldn't speak. He finally had to leave the stage to collect himself. Aren't those strong, invulnerable dictators really something? It was clearly evident in the words of the Blue Angel aviators, who saw their mutual or collective role as being the *advance team* for the U.S. Navy air force. One pilot even said, "It's the guys out there on the carriers in the Gulf that make it possible for us to be the kind of representatives we are for them and for our nation." They not only understood their own vulnerabilities, but their understanding extended out to their fellow pilots as well.

Let me now move to a second principle, which is *identification.*

Principle 2: Through identification, the greatest force for control is created between leaders and followers, and that force is called *commitment,* not *compliance.*

Good people who have good core values choose things we can all identify with and come to support fully over time. Passion comes from identification; without identification, there is no passion and little, if any, commitment. Often, a leader must become adept at articulating the message to people in ways they can find to identify with that message. Steven Jobs accomplished this with Apple by conveying to his workforce that Apple, a renegade company, would design and produce computers for "everyone else." Other companies were producing computers for the engineers and techies, whereas Apple would produce computers for "everyone else" without the technical sophistication needed to run a typical computer. This, of course, was opposite to the image in most computer companies that a technical writer wrote code that only a "real man" could read. The company symbolized what Jobs was striving to get others to identify with by flying the skull and crossbones flag above the Macintosh lab. Today, the ads again under Jobs's reenergized leadership simply say, "Think different," like perhaps in an intellectually stimulating way.

Ironically, Apple's fear of being too vulnerable in the market likely created its greatest vulnerability, which was its failure to release its operating system, as the DOS system was released to clone manufacturers of PCs back in the 1980s. The fear of giving up that which was most cherished led to its loss becoming what could have been the standard operating system for the masses. The company, like the individual leader or team, failed to manage its vulnerability and in the end lost its identification in the market. At one time, having a Macintosh in one's home represented an identification or bond among its users. Those people were not going to accept the techno drivel we get in those manuals.

If we wanted to erase a file, then a garbage can icon was easy enough to remember. If you're anything like me, I could walk tall knowing that I could get on this system and use it without reading the manual. It was almost a badge of courage to point out to people, "Reading a manual . . . ah, who needs it!"

Oh, how times have changed. Recently, I was with a colleague from Palo Alto, California, who used to work for Sun Microsystems. He remarked at one point in our conversation, "That would be like going out and buying a Macintosh today." His reference to this product was similar to what Ford must have felt when people said, "That's like buying an Edsel." Owning Apple stock, I grimaced but am still awaiting a turnaround, which shows signs of occurring. Specifically, in *USA Today* on January 7, 1998, the title of an article in the Business section was "Apple Stock Soaring." As I keep saying, you gotta believe, or was that the announcer in the 1980 Olympic games?

All great leaders find a way to get their followers to identify with something that becomes so central to their values and belief systems that they virtually become inseparable. In Princess Diana's case, we can come up with many things in terms of her work and compassion. Yet, I believe that what we identified with in her was her ability to step out of the role that others were so determined to lock her into—to act real, to be herself, and at the same time to do good, if not extraordinary, things with her life for others.

In Mother Teresa, we saw an extreme version of commitment to her beliefs and values. She was the prototype of what people believe should represent service to humankind, or a "servant leader."[88] Amid terrible scandals in which officials of the Catholic Church have been charged with taking advantage of their position and power, here stood this small and frail woman doing what she always believed was within her job description. She didn't deserve the recognition that was placed upon her, because she would say time and time again, I am just doing my job, which is simply an extension of God's work. That's the reward, and people of all faiths identified with her and her beliefs that she showed through her own sacrifices throughout her life for humankind.

Once a leader has his or her followers' identification, most other things are relatively easy to accomplish, except one—getting people to question what is being done, to be sure we don't fail with spiraling successes. I guess we could rephrase a popular aphorism here: "Don't wallow in your own success." People identify with the vision and mission and therefore are willing to put in the extra effort typically needed to accomplish great visions. If you ask members of the team or organization, they would likely say, "There is no question why we are doing this. There is only a question of how we are going to do what is the right thing to do." Teams that can identify with a central purpose can argue all they want because everyone knows in the end that each member is striving to achieve the same end. The Blue Angels do it for survival at the lowest end of motivation, but they also do it for the highest end that we have labeled their identification with the mission they represent in the U.S. Navy. They identify with representing the U.S. Navy and, more important, their country in displaying the best of what we are capable of doing, where we all have a common goal. That is the power of identification, and it can be wonderfully taken advantage of and, in the "real world," horribly misused by what we called "pseudo" transformational leaders.

Leaders such as Marshall "Bo" Applewhite, late of the Heaven's Gate cult, or other cult leaders such as Jim Jones and David Koresh, often horribly misuse the power of identification. People in the Heaven's Gate cult identified with Applewhite's vision of a better life beyond their current one. The Hale-Bopp comet speeding past Earth in 1997 was seen as the sign that it was time to leave this life, according to Applewhite and the 39 out of 40 other cult members who agreed to commit suicide along with him. (Perhaps you are wondering about the last person. Why didn't he go with the group? In an interview following the demise of Applewhite et al., he said that he believed in the vision but was just not ready to go yet.) More than 900 did the same in a Jonestown, Guyana, jungle commune in 1978 for another cult leader, Jim Jones, leader of the Peoples Temple, a California-based religious cult. And then there was the disaster caused by the Branch Davidians and the U.S. government in Waco, Texas. Although we do say in organizations that we want people to go to the wall for our products, it's absolutely crucial that, when appropriate, they question the products before we "hit the wall"—or should we stick with the cliff metaphor?

Many leaders simply have abused the power of identification that people had in them and their vision. They kept everyone from questioning it; unfortunately, in their own minds, they became way too vulnerable. Their sense of invulnerability reduced significantly what they were able to learn from others. And as often is the case, they preyed on the most vulnerable people to gain commitment. God did not want David Koresh to be the only man having sex with very young women in his congregation. There is no gray area here; he used religion to leverage his power over others for his own gain, which was personalized power. So, I don't call it commitment. I think *coercion* and *compliance* are much more appropriate terms. For people who did not have a strong character and who needed continuous, positive recognition, cult leaders often gladly provided followers with what they needed to gain power over others. In the

---

BOX 9.2. Religious Leaders and Transformational Leadership

Transformational charismatic leadership can have a positive impact in religious institutions. Onnen (1987) examined the leadership of clergy in the Methodist Church. Churches led by transformational clergy were better attended and had higher growth rates in terms of membership. Such clergy were generally seen by the laity as more effective and satisfying to work with. Druskat (1994) completed a study of Roman Catholic Brothers and Sisters, reporting that Sisters were seen as more transformational than Brothers in the Catholic Church. (It's no wonder they always get the Chevy Impala station wagon, whereas the Brothers get the Volvo. Oh, I'm just kidding.) Followers were more satisfied with both male and female leaders who were more transformational.

---

extreme case, it was almost always for their gain, but ironically it usually resulted in their demise. That happened in their "real world" too (see Box 9.2).

I said above that crises can induce charismatic leadership because people are looking for those types of leaders who can help them feel safe and well again. We only hope, in these instances, that the right people come along; unfortunately, history shows that this is not always the case.

In one case, a leader appears to have come along that most in the world can identify with: Nelson Mandela. As I noted earlier, he is attempting to lead South Africa to identify with a *"one nation" for all* concept. This may not seem all that remarkable unless one takes into consideration the 400-year practice of "separate but equal," which culminated in legalizing the system of apartheid in South Africa.

Mandela is a symbol getting people to identify with his mission through inclusion in a society that controlled, in the strictest sense, exclusion of one group from another. He has been committed to a vision of "one" South Africa and has sacrificed dearly as a consequence of his beliefs. His sacrifice, confidence, persistence, sense of fairness, and willingness to be vulnerable have made his chance of success all the more possible. Any leader willing to endure the type of treatment he endured in prison for 27 years is worth listening to and arguably identifying with in his efforts—particularly someone who has repeatedly said that together they will build the future, not re-create the past, now with blacks in a superior position over whites. He repeats over and over again that looking back to blame others will never create the "new" South Africa, a difficult thing to say when members of one's family have been grossly discriminated against for generations. One could ask, "What makes South Africa different from the former Yugoslavia?" I am very biased in my response because I believe that Mandela is and will be one of the truly great leaders of our century, but I believe that the answer is simple: It is Mandela and others like him. Now, go back and examine what Mobutu did in a similar situation many years back. He didn't gain identification, he forced compliance in others, and after 32 years he was finally thrown out of power.

I had the good fortune to meet a young Zulu chief on my last trip to South Africa. We were at a conference center outside Johannesburg that focuses on providing an environment where guests and residents can learn to appreciate each other's cultural differences. It is called a "cultural village." This particular location's theme is to immerse visitors into the cultures of different South African tribes. Consequently, many different members of tribes live at the village, and visitors are permitted to live among them if they choose. It is important to point out that often the tribes represented have traditionally been bitter enemies. The night we all danced around the fire, however, it didn't appear that anyone was unhappy with anyone else. The vision of the center is to immerse people in various cultures to explore each other's differences and ultimately find a basis for unity.

I was assigned to stay that evening in the Zulu village. I met this man, who was apparently a very young and respected king of the Zulu tribe. I spent time with him that evening, discussing various differences and similarities in our lives. He was about my age, yet our life streams were very different. I found him to be a very pure, positive force in life. He was so positive and warm to others, always smiling and embracing people with his words and his touch.

I heard from one staff member a story about this positive and optimistic fellow that brought me back again to what T. S. Eliot said: "For the first time to the same place." Apparently, before the end of apartheid, this particular chief was arrested as a young man and put into one of the worst prisons in South Africa. Typically, when one was placed in this prison, one was never heard from again.

For several weeks, this remarkable chief received repeatedly one beating after the other. At the end of this period of time, he realized, lying on the floor of his cell, that he was nearing his own death. Most major bones in his body were broken, including his jaw. He was preparing himself for the last beating, lying there on his cell floor.

One thing he had extreme difficulty with was the realization that his family would not know where he had died and could not prepare him properly for moving on to the next phase of his existence. Lying there on the cell floor, he heard, very faintly, voices coming through the drainpipe in the floor from another cell. He began to say his name, but it was almost inaudible because of his broken jaw. Somehow, however, he was able to be heard by the people in that next cell as he asked again and again for whoever was there to tell his family where he died.

One person who heard his pleas told a visitor what she had heard. When this visitor left the prison, she immediately went to the house of a friend who knew of a sympathetic and very wealthy white woman who had considerable influence in the apartheid-era South African government. On hearing her story, she went immediately to the prison to inquire about the chief's whereabouts. Now having been publicly exposed, the police couldn't take the chance of killing him. So, for weeks they denied that he was in the prison; this gave the chief time to recover to an "acceptable" level to be released. Yet, this lady persisted until finally the chief was healed enough to be allowed visitors.

Through a fortuitous event, a great man's life was saved. And for me, it was a privilege to meet this person who exuded optimism, kindness, and good humor. He shared with me no sense of hatred or vengeance. Amazing being white and at least feeling that symbolically this man could embrace me without any ill will. I have met many black South Africans who, like this chief, move from the past to create the future. One of them is General Mobuto, who spent several years on Robbins Island with Mandela. He, too, is one of the warmest and most gracious persons I have had the good fortune to meet in my life stream, and together they have made me realize how important it is to put the past where it belongs—in the past. Frankly, I still struggle with this one.

General Mobuto was an aspiring mathematician when he was pulled from his university post and placed in prison. He lost everything except his pride and beliefs. I met General Mobuto at one of the first meetings of our Center for Leadership Studies in South Africa. I walked by a room at Stellenbosch University, which is in the cape, and saw an older gentleman sitting alone. It's funny that one never knows when one will stumble across great people. I did that day. Almost from the first time he spoke, it was as if he had etched in his "intellectual chips" pure wisdom. He seemed to have a reflective capacity about life that was simply extraordinary. I remember, after spending that first day with him, thinking that if General Mobuto was representative of the type of quality people in South Africa's leadership, it was difficult for me to think how incredible President Mandela must be as an individual. I mean, he was chosen above all others to lead the new South Africa, but I would take his second in command anytime!

In many ways, like the Zulu chief I mentioned above, General Mobuto embraces life in such a positive way. He is revered by people in the military, not for being a military man; he was not. As I said, he was a college professor, and throughout history professors have made the very best leaders! (I heard that. Okay, I'm a college professor, and I did go overboard a bit. How about if we agree that at least one college professor has turned into an outstanding leader, and I am referring here to General Mobuto?)

The general has told me many interesting stories, but one I want to share is about how he and the other ANC leaders imprisoned on Robbins Island dealt with their incarceration. He said that the group of leaders put on the island were all highly educated men. He had a Ph.D., and Mandela was a lawyer. Their guards were very young men with little formal education. Over time, they came to label the prison "Robbins University" or "Mandela U." They decided that they would teach their captors about the type of quality people they had in their prison, and ultimately the world would also find out about their deeds. They also focused on their own education to prepare themselves for leadership roles in the postapartheid government. They quickly realized that most whites knew little, if anything, about the black culture. So, they set out to educate the guards and did so quite effectively over time. He said to me that these young guards knew little about life and often would consult with him and other ANC leaders in prison on how to deal with the normal life situations that a young man must confront. Over time, the guards became advocates for their prisoners. Once again, General Mobuto had assumed the role of professor, and he and his colleagues did so by questioning a basic assumption. They questioned that a prison could not be a center for learning and ethical conduct. They proved in their situation that this assumption was terribly wrong, and in so doing they gained the identification and trust of their captors (see Box 9.3).

I always enjoy seeing General Mobuto, and I am really proud to walk into a room and have him turn to me and simply say, "Hello, Bruce." I am proud that he knows me and calls me by my first name, not because he remembers it, but because he is someone whom I am "simply proud to be around." Why? He teaches people all the time that the key to creating one's vital force always lies within reach of oneself. It's on the inside. We may go out on wild adventures, but we always return to ourselves a little better if we have developed at all.

BOX 9.3. Transformational Leadership in Correctional Institutions

---

Gillis, Getkate, Robinson, and Porporino (1995) examined the ratings of supervisors given by offenders within correctional service institutions. Those who rated their supervisors as more transformational had more positive work attitudes and greater work motivation. Nonleadership was related to lower work motivation and job involvement. The credibility of the leaders was related to whether they were seen as transformational.

Shirley MacLaine said that same thing about acting at the 1998 Golden Globe Awards. The more she learned who she was, the better she could represent others as an actress. Leadership is learned from the inside out.

Many of these leaders, along with Mandela, have been able to build a very strong sense of identification with the new South Africa. I have never met a white, black, or colored person in South Africa who didn't have a positive feeling for Mandela in general, even if he or she did not agree with the government's specific policies or initiatives. People respect this great man and realize the type of sacrifices he has made to transform South Africa into what could be the most highly diverse and integrated nation on Earth as we turn into the next millennium (see Box 9.4). One hell of a transformation if you simply stop to think where

---

BOX 9.4. Charismatic Leaders and Impression Management

Gardner and Avolio (1998) proposed a model of impression management to help identify the strategies used by charismatic/transformational leaders to influence followers. Specifically, they provided an explanation of the linkages between a leader's motives, values, vision, and desired identity images and the type of impression management strategies used by the leader to create with followers a charismatic relationship.

Charismatic leaders are described as using impression management (IM) strategies such as "framing" to position their vision in ways that their words amplify audience values and stress its importance to followers so that they will come to identify with it over time. "How the vision is communicated thus becomes as important as what is communicated." (Westley & Mintzberg, 1991, pp. 43-44)

---

this nation started. Amazing stuff for any typical country, and South Africa is not any typical country.

By the way, those prison guards from South Africa did grow up. I heard General Colin Powell speak recently in Minneapolis, and he described an experience he had at President Mandela's inauguration. General Powell said that when Mandela ascended onto the stage to give his acceptance speech, he was seen waving enthusiastically at a small group of men sitting in the first row. Powell observed this group of white men smiling with pride as their new president took over the reigns of their country. You may have guessed, they were Mandela's correctional officers on Robbins Island.

Let me move to the third principle, which is *trust* and has been implied in our discussions of vulnerability and identification:

Principle 3: Our highest trust is typically afforded to those we identify with and to those who often appear to be or are vulnerable.

I said "appear to be or are vulnerable" purposefully. And in doing so, I thought I may have heard a reaction from your side. Let me try to explain. Some leaders set up the "common enemy" strategy. They are saying, "I and we" are all vulnerable to these "evil" forces if we don't work together, and of course they mean also, "If you don't follow me." Some such leaders are quite elaborate in their use of impression management techniques that get followers to think that everyone else is out to get them and that only through their "unquestioning" support will the result be favorable. Recall former President Ronald Reagan's call to contain and defeat the "evil empire," referring to the former Soviet Union. Some people come to trust them because often their descriptions of threats contain some validity. Unfortunately, the trust is usually misplaced, and such leaders, depending on how deeply troubled they are, will take advantage of that trust until there are no more credits to offer from followers.

We see this level of misguided trust in the former televangelist Jim Bakker. He continually lied to his congregation and took advantage of their sacrifices to enhance his wealth and sate his extravagant desires, all in the name of God. He was a symbol of the church and, indirectly, of God. Through his affiliation with the church and position, along with his ability to be identified with his constituency, he was able, with then wife Tammy Faye, to steal repeatedly from his congregation. Yet, when he violated a core aspect of what people identified with in the church—Thou shalt not steal—he was summarily thrown out. Another

---

BOX 9.5. Credibility, Trustworthiness, and Leadership

In a 1998 survey conducted by the Society for Human Resource Management ("The Importance of Trust," 1998), a national sample of respondents indicated that the number one attribute they look for in managers is credibility and trustworthiness. Being trusted shows up continuously as the top attribute associated with exemplary leadership.

---

televangelist, Jimmy Swaggert, was thrown out for another sacred violation—Thou shalt not commit adultery.

Time after time, study after study has shown that the most important attribute a leader can have is trust and/or integrity (see Box 9.5).[89] With trust, one can almost rule the world, and unfortunately destroy it as well.

Mother Teresa gained the trust of millions worldwide. Anyone willing to sacrifice for so many people had to be trying to do the right thing. When the choice was to do something for someone else, for herself, or for her own organization, she chose others over herself. The world came to trust her and to identify with her cause.

Many trusted Princess Diana for different reasons. True, she chose to sacrifice for other people, but it was more likely her ability to show us all how "real" she was that ultimately resulted in many trusting her over time. In her situation, many might say, "Look at this stuffy royal family. I would also do just the opposite of what they wanted me to do because I believe it is the right thing to do. I won't take a back seat as others have done for a thousand years, simply because I'm a woman." Many people could identify with her struggles, similar to their own struggles with a conservative and rigid management; or perhaps school administrators unwilling to bend with the times; or community organizations and politicians who never seem to listen or care about us; and so forth. Here is this jet-setting, glamorous woman who stopped to listen, to question, and to care for others. Many could identify with her willingness to question the unquestionable and extended her their trust.

Another example is Sam, whom I referred to in Chapter 3. Sam was a technology supervisor in the Canadian Correctional Services. His unit repaired damaged government cars, among other metal products. He had one of the lowest recidivism rates in the services. I first met him on a tour of a high-security prison in northeastern Canada. I was contracted to train leaders to be more

---

BOX 9.6. Singaporean Principals' Trust and Transformational Leadership

---

Recall that, in Box 3.2, we said that Koh (1990) reported a positive relationship between ratings of Singaporean principals' transformational leadership and levels of trust expressed by teachers, which in turn positively predicted school performance.

---

transformational, with the hopes of translating this "alienated" workforce into productive members of Canadian society. Sam was one of the supervisors who attended this workshop.

It was apparent to me from the start that Sam treated inmates as "real" people: He gave them respect, he was tough on them, and he worked very hard not to have to see them again and again and again. He realized that these people needed no further instruction on how to fail, nor did they need to be reminded they had failed themselves, their families, and society. They were in his shop because they had failed at most everything they did, including crime.

Sam identified with their situation. He worked to build their confidence and self-efficacy, and he treated them as he would expect them to be treated once leaving the institution, with respect and dignity. He was attempting to create their future in the present and showed that, with support, they could make it out there on their own. Years after leaving prison, many wrote Sam, many called, and some even named their children after him. And, unfortunately, some came back to visit for extended periods of time. Even Sam couldn't transform everyone (see Box 9.6).

Sam was trusted, and he put trust in others. In his shop were people guilty of manslaughter and murder, and Sam put his back to them, realizing full well his vulnerabilities. Yet, his controls were probably far greater than in most other supervisors' workshops. His group of inmates demonstrated a commitment to him, along with the controls that existed in the system. I believe that if anyone were to have harmed Sam, and certainly many could have, the reaction would have been swift and uncompromising. That person's future would have been very limited in that society, and for anyone who needed it, appropriate controls as in any organization would have been activated—by one's peers.

Sam was an extraordinary teacher, and like Stacey and Madeline, he got people to do things we'd be amazed any individual could accomplish. Amazing

---

BOX 9.7. More on Mediation: Self-Efficacy and Transformational Leadership

---

Carless, Mann, and Wearing (1995) obtained MLQ ratings of 695 middle-level branch managers employed by a large Australian bank who were rated by their direct reports. The focus of the study was to examine whether self-efficacy predicted transformational leadership and whether, in turn, group cohesion mediated the relationship between transformational leadership and performance. The authors reported that self-efficacy was a significant predictor of transformational leadership and performance. Group cohesion was a significant mediator of leadership and performance.

---

things happen when people are committed. Predictable things happen when people are controlled through compliance.

The perspective of some leaders drives them to see the future in current events. It helps them consider and understand how one crazy idea can make a business innovation, a new medical breakthrough, or provide a completely new direction or cause to pause and reflect (see Box 9.7). The leaders' perspectives can drive the leaders to see the merits of investing in people versus view them as a cost on the balance sheet. It helps some leaders pursue and wonder why someone is not "doing so well today." It provides leaders with the understanding to be empathic toward others. Yet, at another extreme, it influences leaders to say, "That will never work," "I don't get paid to develop people, so just make do," and "Don't you ever do anything right?"

The fourth principle is the most abstract, but I discussed it with you earlier. It pertains to a person's perspective.

Principle 4: The leaders demonstrate a perspective or frame of reference or both that they can put themselves in those situations that others endure that maybe are different from their own and fully appreciate how others feel and react. They work to understand the situation even when they are a part of it emotionally and intellectually. They offer a way out, or at least alternatives to consider for future action.

This perspective, which I have now introduced at several points in this book, represents the lens through which leaders look at the world. Behind the lens is the person's "software" that interprets what is focused on and perceived.

By the way, those second in command and below have lenses and software too, and if they are built like the leaders, then asking them about the organization when the leader is absent should result in the same answer, and often does. A large part of the institution left behind by a leader is the perspective developed in his or her followers. Variations in perspective-taking capacity lead some people to protect themselves from an intrusion into even their slightest vulnerabilities; others will fully expose themselves, knowing that they are doing the right thing. They deeply believe that it's worth the risk for the good of their group.

I introduced Mort Meyerson, the former CEO of Electronic Data Systems (EDS), to you in Chapters 5 and 6. Recall that, after retiring from EDS, Meyerson was called by Ross Perot to run his new organization called Perot Systems. Although hesitant at first to come out of retirement, he took the position and never looked back. In a recent interview, he indicated that nearly everything he did at EDS in his leadership role changed in his new role. He discovered that the needs and requirements of his workforce at Perot Systems were completely different, and at first he felt quite vulnerable. It took time for his perspective to shift, but it apparently did over time.

In the interview, Meyerson described the types of controls EDS placed on its employees. Yet, when he began working at Perot Systems, he could see that the new breed of worker was different from the one he had led at EDS. First, they knew many things that he had no idea how to do. They were technical specialists way beyond his capabilities, as well as those of other managers at Perot Systems. Second, they sought development and were not content simply to receive what the corporation decided to provide them in terms of responsibility and training. Third, he quickly realized that a control mentality completely underestimated the employees' ability to achieve their full potential. He had to change his perspective and style to accommodate a change in their needs, capabilities, and desires. Things changed, and so would his perspective have to change about the needs of employees and his role to be successful. He became the coach versus commander, the facilitator versus foreman, and the teacher versus tormentor . . . sorry, I needed a "t" word that rhymed.

Meyerson's story has been repeated again and again throughout the United States and in other countries that are developing organizations representative of more advanced social systems. Here, I mean that members of the organizational community are well equipped to take more responsibility for the direction it chooses. A tremendous "perspective shift" is occurring in the way managers "control" people and work processes. As organizational transformations have taken hold during the last decade, implications for the way managers lead have been nothing short of dramatic and often very stressful. This is truly deep collective change.

Going back to an interview with Steven Kerr, Vice President for Corporate Leadership Development at GE (see Chapter 3), Kerr described Jack Welch's direct involvement in the development and coaching of leadership in GE. He described Welch's passion for getting his senior managers to "honor the initiatives," not control.[90] He described Welch's intimate knowledge of the career paths of more than 1,000 GE employees in their succession-planning program. He argued in the interview for "critical reflection." Earlier, we discussed a similar process that was labeled "debriefing," and in the U.S. military, After Action Reviews (AARs). To reflect critically requires being comfortable with one's level of exposure and vulnerability. One also has to believe in what one is doing and where an even better idea can make a better contribution to performance. It requires trust to feel safe to offer and receive critical ideas. And, it requires a shift in perspective that coordinated conflict around ideas is a very good process for the acceleration of change and the unearthing of insightful ideas.[91] Thus, we need to build the perspective-taking capacity of leaders in order for them to be adaptive to the changes they will certainly confront throughout their careers and lives.

A deep perspective, once developed in individuals, provides them with a frame of reference that guides their actions to a point where we describe their behavior as self-sacrificing, being solidly committed to others, being trustworthy, and/or having a high level of integrity. James McGregor Burns said that transforming leaders sacrifice their own gain for the gain of others. They are morally uplifting.[92] Paraphrasing Nelson Mandela, let's not look back to right the wrongs, let's look forward and not forget the wrongs but ensure the system that we build won't allow them to ever happen again. And the system he is referring to is based on core values and beliefs to guide exemplary behavior. It's a total leadership system.

A group of black students 2 years ago decided to shut down the Peninsula Technion campus near Cape Town, South Africa. This used to be called the "University of the Bush" because blacks were sent there for schooling to be "out of sight" of the whites. In the new South Africa, the campus has become more integrated. For several days a few years ago, however, a small group of students closed off the campus, arguing that university officials should fully reinstate them after being expelled either for not paying tuition or for poor grades. Some of these students had flunked out, and some had not paid their bills. I thought, prior to my visit to this campus, what the reaction might be in the United States. I had seen such situations before and administrators doing everything in their power to negotiate themselves out of the mess but forgetting basic principals and beliefs that apply to all students, including the ones under scrutiny.

As often happens in South Africa, when a conflict seems to be without obvious solutions, the country's president is implored to come in and resolve it. Mandela has been resistant to do so, but in this case he chose to intervene and comment. In a country that had been legally divided along racial lines, many whites expected a resolution in favor of the black students. Rationally, they had been abused for so many years that a decision in their favor could balance the scales, so to speak. Many right-wing whites have waited for such actions to say, "You see, our worst fears are now finally being realized." Many black leaders wanted Mandela to support the black groups because it would build the needed cohesion in their community. Some moral imperative underlay their view, or should I say "perspective."

Mandela's response was quick and decisive. He said that two things affected his decision. First, he discovered that the university did everything it could have done to collect the tuition it required, following due process. Recall that Mandela is a lawyer. Second, the university had provided every reasonable chance for these students to succeed and to avoid being thrown out. He asked rhetorically, What's the issue here? There is no issue. This is a fair, "color-blind" system, and whether it's black, colored, or white students, these students were treated fairly within the parameters of the system. Color was irrelevant. They were gone.

Many called Mandela a traitor to his people. To Mandela, this was unacceptable because all the people in South Africa were "his" people, and his people were not based on color, but rather on their citizenship. That's his perspective; it is internal, based on core/universal values, and it helps guide such leaders in making the toughest decisions. Interesting, isn't it?

Prior to the 1994 World Cup rugby games held in South Africa, many of Mandela's advisors had asked him not to open the games. Rugby was what many in South Africa identified as a "white man's sport." The national rugby team had never had a black player. If he opened the games, many would say he would be indirectly supporting the legacy of apartheid.

On the day of the opening ceremony, President Mandela opened the games by holding hands with the captain of the rugby team, wearing a jersey with his number on it. Not only that, but the national airline of South Africa flew a 747 jet, painted in the national colors of the new South Africa, several hundred feet above the stadium. Mandela rose and said there was now one South Africa and one national rugby team, and on the field that day was the team representing the new South Africa. If you have traveled in any country that plays rugby, you'll realize the importance of his actions and this statement to the identification that people have with their country. It was a profound, and some said very courageous, step forward to building the new South Africa, which everyone must be a part of for efforts to succeed. Mandela could have read the political winds to decide what his choice should have been that day. Fortunately, he appears to be a leader who demonstrates a deep belief and inner perspective that guides his actions in even the most difficult circumstances.

We, too, here in the United States have had such leaders—in Abraham Lincoln, for example, who abolished slavery, knowing full well that he would throw the nation into civil war. Yet, he did so because he knew, without law or guidance of external rules or procedures, the difference between right and wrong. Leaders who make such difficult decisions take action based on their inner beliefs and values, and over time, people come to trust those leaders to do the right thing. We trust their perspective; it provides us and them with very predictable courses of action and a basis for framing the problems we must eventually confront together. Moreover, their perspective becomes the shadow of their institution, which is left behind. We strive as a nation to provide justice for all. We may fail a lot, but we now know the right thing to do as a consequence of leaders like President Lincoln, Martin Luther King, Jr., Robert Kennedy, and Mrs. Tooker (my third-grade teacher, who taught her students during the dawn of civil rights to treat everyone with dignity and respect).

Having now reviewed these four very important leadership principles, let me conclude this chapter with a question for you to reflect on. *If you have known anyone with the type of perspectives I have described above, what type of influence did that person have on your perspective, and how does he or she still influence the growth of your perspective even today?* Although often one is enough, some people are fortunate enough to have had more then one individual in their lives who had this type of impact on their development. It is my belief that, all other things being equal, those people emerge as our best leaders.

I am rewriting this chapter on Father's Day in the United States. It is a very difficult chapter for me to write because I see the gap between where my perspective is and where it needs to go to fulfill the first leadership role for my three children. I am willing to count on teachers and managers to some extent but feel compelled to make their jobs easier. Before my children wake up today, I've really got a lot of work to do.

Some Things Worth Repeating

- The four principles discussed in the chapter are necessary, but not sufficient, for achieving the full range of leadership.
- Gaining commitment through showing one's vulnerabilities, building identification, and gaining trust is the highest form of control. It is called commitment.
- What may appear at first to be a liability may very well provide the basis for an individual's, team's, or organization's greatest strengths.
- What makes the best leaders predictable is the breadth and depth of their perspective.

Let me break with the past tradition and tell you about one more leader who didn't accept her context and who demonstrated through her actions a deep and profound perspective to care for others. Her name was Amy Beatrice Carmichael. She was born on December 16, 1867, in Belfast, Ireland. Amy's father died when she was quite young. Following his death, she threw herself into serving others. When she was barely 20 years old, Amy took off for missionary work in Japan. Following her work in Japan, she traveled to China and then to Sri Lanka. She returned to Ireland briefly for the funeral of the head of her missionary. Soon afterward, however, she went to Bangalore, India. She remained in India for the next 55 years. In India, Amy created an organization to protect the children of the temple. One tradition among the Hindus was that a girl child was promised to the gods before birth in order to curry their favor. The girl would then be delivered to the temple women and be prepared to be the prostitute of the priests by age 5. Amy created the Dahnavur Fellowship. She was affectionately called "Amma," or mother, in Tamil, and worked to protect thousands of little girls from being sacrificed for the good of the church. Perhaps more remarkable about Amma is that, after a tragic accident, she spent the next 20 years bedridden but still led her missionary organization in an exemplary fashion. When I personally feel that things are getting too difficult in my organization, I am reminded of people like Amma, Stacey, Sam, and Madeline. I hope now that you are also inspired to try again, one more time, when things get tough.

10

It's Not Leadership If It Affects Performance— Directly

Every team that wants to move toward significance and greatness has to decide what truths it will hold to be self-evident and to get those values circulated through the organization.
(Pat Riley, former Head Coach of the New York Knicks)

Here is another one of those statements I make with senior managers that often gets their Human Resources directors to update their résumés: If leadership doesn't affect performance, then why have we flown you in here to run a leadership seminar? Very good question indeed.

A basic principle to keep in mind is that *if a leader has a direct impact on performance, she or he is probably too directly involved in what the other person or group is doing.* This point goes back to some of our earlier discussion of

---

BOX 10.1. Transformational Leadership and Bank Financial Performance

---

Geyer and Steyrer (1998) reported that, in a large-scale study of German banks, transactional leadership was more predictive of short-term performance, whereas transformational leadership was predictive of longer term financial performance of bank branches. We need now ask what mediating factors resulted in these differences in predicting performance.

---

control systems in organizations (see Chapter 6). We can't control commitment; it comes through building trust, identification, and a willingness to support the leader, group members, organization, and so forth. What we really need to explore is exactly how both leaders and leadership can indirectly and positively influence development (see Box 10.1). Some have called these indirect factors "substitutes" or "surrogates" for leadership.[93] I really don't think they are always "substitutes" for the leader, but rather they can be "extensions" of the leader developed over time that have become institutionalized positive aspects of the leader's style and perspective. Once institutionalized, they may seem at some later time to be a substitute for the person—as I guess they should be.

Recall my comments in Chapters 1 and 2 about the importance of focusing on the second in command. What information would you get if you talked with the second in command? I argued that you would get the message from the second that was communicated by the first, but in her or his words, filtered through her or his identification with what the leader had set out to accomplish in the mission or vision. Of course, without a clear mission and vision, you usually get many, many different stories because there is no one script that is evident to follow (see Box 10.2). Often, the indirect influence of leaders is the most profound and the most troublesome to explain. Let me try to explain.

A leader articulates a vision of some desired future state—for example, "All children in this nation will someday grow up in an environment where the full range of opportunities is available to them solely on the basis of ability, and nothing else, meaning things like race, religion, gender, and so forth." The vision creates many examples in people's minds in which this idealized vision becomes concrete and visible with respect to a brother, a sister, or one's child. My children and your children can all compete for the same jobs, for the same colleges, for the same homes, and to live in the same communities. The ideas contained in

---

BOX 10.2. Leading at a Distance

Howell, Neufield, and Avolio (1998) reported that the relationship between charismatic leadership and business unit performance varied, depending on whether followers were "close" to or at a "distance" from their followers. Charismatic leadership had a more positive impact on bank financial performance, where followers were rating the charisma of a leader who was at a distance.

Shamir (1995) reported that distant charismatic leaders were viewed as expressing more ideological positions and visions, showing less fear of being criticized for voicing their opinions. Close charismatics were seen as being more considerate and open with others, setting higher performance standards, using more original and creative thinking, and having a greater impact on task-related motivation.

---

the vision begin to diffuse and affect our willingness and desire to make a difference in our work. This leads Human Resources professionals to design selection systems that are culture-fair. Others develop programs to uplift the disadvantaged through training and special education projects. Still others take a stand in the courts on what constitutes fair treatment of people at work, in education, and in the broader community. Presidents develop and support legislation such as the Civil Rights Act, and now the vision is reinforced by the power of law, in case controls have to substitute for commitment (see Box 10.3).

Ultimately, if it is successful, a leader's vision will have a positive impact on people's identification with the cause or core emphasis in the vision. As we learned from our earlier discussion, identification leads to certain actions that will support the vision and that become aligned around it. Next comes a deeper sense of commitment to actions. New ideas emerge as mistakes are made and then resolved. This type of adjustment occurs again and again over time. The leader has an impact, often years beyond her or his own lifetime in terms of the culture, values, and ultimately the law that resulted as a consequence of the vision.

We have seen in many instances that a vision may be only articulated but not necessarily fully accomplished in the leader's lifetime. Or, the leader "went in advance of others" with a belief and an idea, and everyone else worked to make it happen once its relevance and importance were discerned. Leaders indirectly affect others through the picture of the future they create via a vision.

BOX 10.3. Attributions to Social Close and Distant Leaders

Yagil (1998) reported that the attribution of charisma to "socially" distant leaders was related to the level of acceptance of the leader's ideas and perceptions of the leader's ability to perform the mission. Attribution of charisma to socially close leaders depended on personal modeling and confidence expressed in followers' personal ability.

A young employee comes into an organization. She is not very confident in her abilities, which are considerable, according to everyone else's judgment. Her manager spends the first several months trying to identify the source of this employee's poor self-concept. He diagnoses areas of need and works to fill those areas with support and further developmental opportunities. He provides alternative ways of looking at development. He gives her confidence by saying she is capable of doing more challenging tasks. Through the confidence and support he expresses to her, he builds efficacy, confidence, trust, and identification with the central purposes or mission of the organization. A Pygmalion effect is observed.

In the beginning, this leader must sacrifice a great deal of his time without any apparent short-term impact on bottom-line performance. Over time, the employee's confidence grows, and it ultimately effects a change in her perspective about herself. This is seen in her addressing the same old question with new information and data: "Who am I, and what am I now capable of doing? I have come back to the same place for the first time because my perspective about myself has developed." If fully successful in this transformation, the manager is able to build in his employee some internal controls and standards of what she is now capable of doing or choosing not to do in the event he is not around to coach her in future challenges. Perhaps someday she will do the same for others who eventually report to her. And at this level, we can say that the manager's influence would have cascaded like falling dominoes to new employees with whom he'd never had direct contact.[94] A very effective and proud legacy, or shadow, is now being institutionalized for this leader through his intermediary efforts.

To initiate the developmental process, we can go back to Figure 6.2. The leader depicted a future different from the person's conception of what she was "capable" of fulfilling. This created some tension for her. And as Albert Einstein once said, "A happy man [person] is too satisfied with the present to dwell too much on the past." The leader was able to convey the positive sense of that future to his follower, and over time to get her to believe in it and to believe in herself. The believing in herself represents the transformation in perspective from "he tells me I can do it" to "I know I can do this" to "I know I can help others do this." She takes actions and decisions that stretch her and those around her. She challenges her own thinking and others she would never have questioned. She begins to expand her boundaries of vulnerability and moves to positions of increasing challenges and opportunities. Eventually, she can get others to identify with things that are important and to delay her self-gratification for the good of others when needed.

One day, the manager must leave—Relax, it's just a promotion, not anything horrible. She's alone physically, but she retains the cell of her leader throughout her life in her perspective, and like falling dominoes, his influence has continued to influence her, and she, in turn, has an influence on the next person, and the next one, and so on down the line. Each of their "mental models" or perspectives now overlaps. In large part, the leader can sustain his influence to the extent that the mental model he maintains is transferred to followers and shared. The mental model can contain the leader's philosophy on how to treat others, or it may be specific to a particular initiative or agenda constituting a vision. Then someday in the future, the initial follower is met by another follower, and for all intents and purposes she appears to be the one in charge, yet the cell remains from the prior leader's influence. In some ways, she has become a partial substitute for her mentor. Perhaps, others will see her as a "born" leader.

Recall that, in Box 6.1, we reported that Weierter (1994), in a study of work group leaders from Australia, found that the transformational leadership behaviors associated with individualized consideration and intellectual stimulation had a positive impact on perceptions of reputation, cooperativeness, friendliness, and warmth. Weierter argued that transformational leadership created a work group climate that over time became a substitute for the direct effects of transformational leadership . . . a substitute of sorts, although still rated in the leadership of an individual.

Interestingly, one can see the same process occurring in the evolution of highly developed and/or high-performing teams. When groups get together and are out of alignment, this usually means members having conflicting views or no views at all on who will do what or sometimes even what will be considered for discussion. As group members interact over time, a sharing of perspectives and understanding occurs that, if properly led, can result in an alignment among

---

BOX 10.4. Groups Versus Teams

Current empirical research on teams indicates that exemplary leadership can have a positive impact on group orientation, efficacy, and performance (Hackman, 1990; Kumpfer, Turner, Hopkins, & Librett, 1993). The type of leadership that we believe differentiates groups from teams can be labeled "transformational."

---

group members. This alignment ultimately can be around shared values, the vision or central purpose for the group, how the group will lead itself, and so forth. Many authors now talk about groups building a shared mental model that becomes the basis for a group becoming a team and that team fully sharing in its leadership responsibilities (see Box 10.4). The model provides for developing alignment and cohesion. For groups starting from very diverse points, the achievement of this type of alignment is indeed a great accomplishment.[95]

A few years pass. One day, a young man is working for the woman we described above as "the follower." He appears very capable but lacks the drive and self-concept to succeed fully. She studies him to learn his weaknesses and strengths. She takes the time to build his confidence and efficacy. She cares about him and articulates a future he never would have considered on his own. Over time, he expands his boundaries of vulnerability and takes on increasingly difficult challenges and opportunities. He begins to make a positive difference with others in terms of their development. At one point, he tells a friend that his new manager is a "born leader." We know differently, don't we? Hello?

In the descriptions of both individuals, we have outlined what constitutes the developmental core of transformational leadership—the higher end of the full range. It is represented in the behavior of the leader who works to develop others to their full potential. The foundation for those behaviors is the leader's "deep" perspective, understanding, model of life, what she or he values, and sense of right and wrong. The leader develops her- or himself and, in turn, develops others to exceed current development and performance capacities. This can occur in a leader-follower relationship or in a group or team between one colleague and another. Such transformations may even occur with the follower developing the leader, which is even more common today, given the deleveling going on in organizations and the fact that managers typically do not have the full slate of advanced technical skills of people who report to them.[96]

BOX 10.5. Full Range Leadership and Its Indirect Effects in Higher Education

---

Cowen (1990) examined the relationship between the range of styles contained in the full range model and changes in enrollment patterns at public 4-year institutions of higher education in the United States. In the final sample of presidents and their followers who responded to the surveys, 153 institutions were represented. No relationship was found between presidential leadership and the changes that were occurring in enrollments over the 5-year period prior to the survey administration. A significant and positive relationship was found, however, among follower ratings of satisfaction with the president, the president's tenure with the institution, and percentage of change in enrollments.

The indirect and sustainable effects of leadership are what my colleagues and I are striving for in our work on extending the full range of leadership development (see Box 10.5). We must help leaders understand their indirect effects on others and where their legacies can make a positive difference, albeit indirectly and often with no direct credit given to the leader. This is where we begin to get at the deep processes of leadership that wrap around the four principles discussed in Chapter 9. It is where we go from talking about leadership styles to deep perspectives and philosophy around leadership development. It is not always noticeable or apparent in the second and third in command to even a very discriminating eye, but we can conclude that it is there through the constellation of actions taken by a leader and her or his followers over time.

Now, let's consider a contrasting example. The new CEO of an organization wants to build among his staff a true learning system. He says, "Challenging each other is a great thing, and we must support the initiatives of people. Conflict is okay over ideas; it stimulates reat insights." He conveys his beliefs and principles, which are based on a very high moral character. He gets down to the business of running the organization, and the response is, well, not so good. People don't offer ideas. What he said is okay with all of them, and they are very willing to implement new initiatives. They say in actions and sometimes words, "You're in charge and we're not, so if it's what you want, sure we will be happy to do it." They are *passive* and *dependent* followers. They don't want to take risk, they don't want to feel vulnerable, and they are simply very comfortable taking orders. On the surface, all looks well.

These followers are the ideal match in the extreme with the autocratic leader. Unfortunately, this type of leader is always a heartbeat away from complete system failure. If a major problem is there and noticed by such followers, the chances are less than 50/50 that they will tell the leader. They are risk averse, and such feedback requires some risk, which they are often unwilling to take because they are controlled by the leader to not "rock the boat," as opposed to being committed to challenging things that don't make any sense to them.

One piece missing from the above puzzle is that the former CEO of this group ruled with an arbitrary and capricious hand. Whether you were right or wrong was irrelevant. The leader had a bad mood day, and you suffered. Over time, the group established these elaborate filtering mechanisms, and it became increasingly difficult to learn what the staff truly thought about anything. Impression management in its most extreme negative form was the framework of choice. You only know me by what you see, not by what I feel. If you did know how I felt, you might call the police!

Bad leaders have legacies, too, that often outlast their time "in office." Bad leaders can be defined here as *not* morally uplifting, inspiring, intellectually stimulating, individually considerate, or transactional in the contingent reward sense. These bad leaders may only manage by exception, and one should avoid mistakes at all costs. And perhaps contradicting what I said earlier, the effects can be deep but rarely positive. I say "rarely" because sometimes they do become examples of what you *don't* want people to do, which could also be viewed as a powerful form of training leaders about what not to do as leaders. These leaders indirectly affect the people around them even after they are long gone. Followers have come to doubt themselves, to not take risks. They see a narrow alleyway to the future, one that is dark and threatening. The leader's indirect impact is as palpable as that of the former, more positive leader I described above. Now, we must work them out of the system to go from a state of "learned helplessness" that currently exists to full empowerment. Yeah, right! Just go for it!

The mental models that "difficult leaders" put into place in terms of developing their followers' perspectives must be abandoned and retired for progress to take hold. This is a huge chasm to cross and is often underestimated by new and inexperienced leaders, as well as by some old and more experienced ones. Changing such embedded systems, particularly when you were the original architect, can be extremely challenging, if not sometimes nearly impossible. I said "nearly."

BOX 10.6. Air Force Cadets and Transformational Leadership

Over a 2-year period, nearly 12,000 cadets from the Air Force Academy rated 160 USAF officer leaders by using the MLQ survey. Other survey measures were also collected, tapping into motivation, organizational climate, attitudes toward reward and discipline policies, and performance (Clover, 1988). Positive relationships were reported between transformational leadership and organizational climate in air force squad units.

BOX 10.7. Intellectual Capital and Organizational Transformation

---

Nearly two thirds of managers and hourly workers responding to a national survey of employees reported that they believe their organizations are operating on 50% or less of their intellectual capital. Many workers believe that they are undervalued, that their thinking is unimportant. (*HR News,* 1997). This is quite ironic, given the next statement.

"In the post-industrial era, the success of a corporation lies more in its intellectual system than in its physical assets." (Quinn, Anderson, & Finklestein, 1996, p. 71)

Some Specific Indirect Effects

A lot of attention has been paid lately to looking into the indirect effects of leadership in areas such as innovation and performance (see Box 10.6). Below, I list some of the more important ones that have been uncovered. Taking these effects into consideration should help build in your mind a system-level model of leadership development. This is crucial to your fully understanding the process of leadership, in that at its highest level of analysis, we are trying to develop and embed a full range leadership system into the organization (see Box 10.7). We start with one individual, if need be, and work our way up, as well sideways and then down again.

- Leaders who are more transformational increase the commitment and trust levels of people who work around them. The increase in trust and commitment, in turn, has been shown in several independent studies to affect individual and unit performance. For example, and as noted earlier (Boxes 3.3 and 9.6), the transformational leadership of Singaporean school principals increased their followers' trust, which, in turn, predicted school performance.[97]

- Leaders who are more transformational affect positively the efficacy levels of those people who report to them. Their raised levels of efficacy have led to higher individual performance.[98]

- Leaders who are more intellectually stimulating get followers to generate a wider range of ideas, which, in turn, leads to greater product innovation, designs, and patents.[99,100]

- At a group level, members of teams that exhibited more transformational leadership exhibited higher levels of potency and efficacy, which, in turn, predicted higher levels of group performance.[101]

- A study on communication processes found that leadership affected unit performance indirectly through the style and content of communication. Transformational leadership had a positive impact on communication content and style.

- Managers who used more individualized consideration had more personal interactions with employees, which, in turn, predicted bottom-line unit performance (see Box 10.8).[102]

- In the Avolio et al. paper entitled *A Funny Thing Happened on the Way to the Bottom Line,* cited in Box 10.8, leaders who were seen as more transformational used humor in more constructive ways, which, in turn, predicted bottom-line unit performance.[103]

Many more studies show the merits of transformational leadership having an indirect impact on performance. I reviewed these research findings here to have you consider where you might target your efforts as a leader. We believe that a leader's efforts should be targeted to enhancing the *processes* that directly and indirectly affect performance, thus building over time a full range leadership system. Getting leaders to think in this manner gives them an opportunity to see from a process perspective how they can transform individuals, units, and entire organizations to higher levels of leadership potential. Herein lies the essence of transforming followers into leaders.

The significant trend during the last 10 years has been to examine leadership by using more of a process perspective. Part of this emphasis parallels trends in total quality management (TQM) and reengineering, which have forced us to examine many organizational processes, including human system processes, at a more strategic level.[104] This focus has allowed us to take a much closer look

---

BOX 10.8. Transformational Leadership and the Use of Humor

Avolio, Howell, and Sosik (1999) reported on a study of directors of strategic business units in Canada, indicating that those who were seen by followers as more transformational also used humor in a way to build morale, reduce stress, and enhance creativity, which, in turn, positively affected bottom-line performance. Sense of humor exhibited by the leader moderated the impact of leadership on performance.

Many examples of the use of humor by leaders suggest that it has positive benefits on performance. For example, in 1998, *Fortune* magazine identified Southwest Airlines as the number one company to work for in the United States. Southwest's CEO, Herb Kelleher, is well known for using humor as an integral part of the airline's business strategy. In fact, the use of humor is an area assessed as part of each prospective employee's interview.

CEO Robert Stillman leads Cognex, one of the fastest growing software companies in the United States. A former MIT professor, Dr. Bob, as he is affectionately called by his workers, leads employees in the corporate anthem along with a backup rock band, hands out money bags containing $10,000 from the back of a security truck for merit raises, and goes through Three Stooges routines to welcome new employees to the company. Consider the type of climate these leaders create and the impact it may have indirectly on creativity and performance.

---

at the interaction between leaders and followers and the context in which each is embedded. The context is where we focus our discussion next.

This Situation and Its Moderating Effects

You have certainly heard people ask, "Under what conditions or situation will that work?" In leadership, this is a crucial issue in that almost all styles of leadership can be effective in one context but not in another. Let's take some extreme views on this statement. Punishment that is arbitrary and capricious has been used for years by the military in training basic recruits to help them *adapt* to military discipline and command. By using arbitrary punishment, you can break people down, make them dependent on you, and then gradually put the pieces back together in the way you see them fit. Yet, in most other contexts, it sucks . . . uh, I mean it doesn't work up to the standards we expect and therefore lacks validity.[105]

Being avoidant as a leader is almost always ineffective. Yet, in many instances a leader may choose to be avoidant, and it can be seen by others as a contribution versus shirking in one's responsibilities. A leader may avoid making a decision until the issue has had time to sink into the way of thinking of the group being led. Leaders often avoid engaging in conflict until the time is right and avoid taking responsibility if they have empowered others to do so on their behalf.

In a context where the cost of mistakes is very high, leaders find it very difficult to be intellectually stimulating and creative in their dealings with others. "Why should I think out of the box if it will only get me or us into trouble? We operate in a no-mistakes culture, which means simply stay within the established rules and don't rock the boat."

In a very different context, my colleagues and I measured support for innovation. We found that, in contexts where "support for innovation" was high, the unit's performance was more positively predicted by the leader's level of transformational leadership. Support for innovation was found to be a potent moderator of the relationship between transformational leadership and performance. By moderator, we mean that if support was high versus low, the positive effects of transformational leadership on performance were augmented.[106]

The examples and discussion above point to two very important aspects of understanding the leadership process. First, leadership behavior is mediated or moderated or both in its impact on performance. For example, leaders set up a compact for disciplinary actions; these actions lead to a reduction in aberrant behavior, which over time enhances unit cohesion, morale, and ultimately performance.

Second, the conditions under which leadership is observed has an affect on how that leadership affects the individual or group and their performance. In crisis, a determined and persistent leader may be seen as achieving the difference between success and failure. In a more stable setting, such characteristics might be seen as being too headstrong and inflexible. The context shapes how the leader will actually be described by others. Leadership is therefore never contextually neutral, although in some "weak" contexts the effect the context has on the interpretation of leadership is expected to be minimal.[107]

As I am writing this chapter, I have just returned from an organization that I believe many would say has a very "strong" context. I met with the CEO of a large European organization to discuss a leadership training intervention being planned in conjunction with his Human Resources staff. When I first walked into his office, I realized pretty quickly that he wanted, perhaps needed, to control the next hour-long discussion. He appeared to be very concerned about losing control by allowing his followers to take broader action on their own. One symbol of his concern was his near-violent reaction to the HR officer's suggestion to conduct 360° survey feedback with him and his staff.

This CEO was adamant that the 360° survey should not be used in his organization because it was too much effort for very little payoff. He did not feel the need for such surveys because *he* was sensitive enough to problems that were bothering *his* staff. He could go to a workshop and simply sense what *his* staff was thinking. I found his comments rather curious, in that he showed very little awareness of how the HR staff member and I felt at our first meeting. Yet, I still was very willing to listen to his argument because, in terms of performance, he was a very successful leader.

The gist of the meeting was to have him take my colleagues and me through his vision and how to involve all of us in its implementation. He kept saying that he wanted training that was not "in the clouds." He wanted something that was tangible and would have bottom-line impact, and he was quite afraid of having one of those "process type" sessions that generated more confusion than light. Ironically, we had fully intended to lay out some specific issues to be included in the training workshop that could result in the specification of concrete goals for our work together. He didn't stop to consider, however, that this was the direction we had already set. He kept saying to start with the target or goal you want to achieve and then convince as many people as you can where you want to go. Shoot the rest! (I added the last point on the basis of my own inferences.)

The CEO demonstrated a very clear perspective of his leadership style and philosophy in that first meeting. He wanted to be the focus of everyone's attention. If we could stay away from process and clouds, then, he thought, we would have a chance of getting something tangible accomplished through training. He was a very bright and clever man but didn't get the essence of the situation he was confronting. Let me explain. He tended to exaggerate the need for his control and influence over others to the point of generating high levels of fear among those around him. Everyone seemed to wait to see whether he would blow off steam of some kind. The HR staff over time supported him by reassuring that nothing would get "out of control." One should ask why. What productive end does this serve? Unfortunately, I've had to ask myself this question too many times, and the answers go beyond the objectives for this book.

The company the CEO headed had come through a disastrous 4-year period. It was a 100-year-old company that had gone rapidly downhill before he took command. When he came in, he replaced nearly three fourths of the senior management, many of whom had started their careers with the firm. He and "his" management team then proceeded to destroy the century-old culture, replacing it with a very "hard" and "driven" management system—the type I often hear described as "our culture is to build shareholder wealth." He described his involvement here as being in a war of survival in which he was the general and "they" were the soldiers. Order and then watch them act. In his view, he needed to get the system under complete control before he could again relinquish control. His ideas were probably right for this crisis period, but he was naive about how he was going to change a control-oriented system to an involving and commitment-oriented system with empowered followers. His behavior in our first meeting suggested to me that he was completely unaware of the impact of his style on the ultimate transformation he himself desired. He talked about building an innovative culture, but he also indicated the issues that we should discuss in our retreat. Yet, I saw a ray of hope in that when he was confronted, he often said that it was only one man's opinion and that we would have to get input from others. I'm not sure he always did, but there was a crack in the wall to look through.

I was reminded in our discussion of something another leader had once said. General Colin Powell said that his most important leadership lesson came through his work with his commanding officer when he was a lieutenant. His commander taught him that "leadership was where people were willing to follow you because they were curious." Imagine the trust it takes to follow someone willingly just because you are curious, as opposed to scared.

The other thing this CEO didn't realize was that he had picked a whole new level of direct reports that were not much different from he, and their directive and unrelenting style became part of the "new" culture in this organization. Perhaps without knowing it, he was at a very significant turning point. He and his management team had destroyed the old values and had made no attempt in 4 years to institute a new set of core values—well, maybe one, "shareholder wealth," which I don't consider a value. Other managers at lower levels yearned for a value system that provided clear indicators of what it takes to be successful in this organization. The timing was ripe for change; however, the approach he was taking was highly problematic. He was not yet convinced of the relevance of leadership training, although he appeared to understand it on an intuitive level. His embedded system concerning prior training interventions was not a very positive one. Thus, we needed to get him to relinquish some old assumptions to move forward to develop a new framework and deeper perspective.

Around the world, many managers like the one I described above are successfully leading their organizations. And for all intents and purposes, they are often the drivers of success in those respective organizations. Yet, when they see the need to move their firms toward high-performance systems and teams, they suddenly realize they must change their styles and cultures. Yet, it is most interesting to witness that, although wanting to move toward a more inclusive culture, they are role-modeling again and again that they are still partly stuck in an embedded system they themselves created. And they are typically shocked to realize, well into the change process, that "their" people are not getting "their" change message across to followers. "We are saying change, take responsibility for decisions" . . . and then comes this huge silence, when no one steps up to make a decision. What they must realize is that they have to attack this problem from at least three viewpoints.

First, they must become the "cells" for the type of behavior they want to see in others. If training is important, then they must be the first ones to go to training. Second, they must understand the needs of their followers and try gradually to move those who are most prepared to a position of greater independence. They don't have to convince everyone all at once, just a few strong champions of the change process. Once these are convinced and reinforced to change, then the leader can work on others. Third, the institution in which the people are embedded has to be changed in a very strategic sense. If you are emphasizing more discretion in decision making, then make it as visible as possible by pointing to areas where the people must make decisions. Here is where a little bit of avoidant leadership can go a long way. Specifically, wait long enough, and someone is bound to fill the gap and make a decision.

The leadership training that goes on in autocratically run organizations takes more time to work out. Yet, there are certainly some success stories where this training has occurred, and the changes have been dramatic. Nevertheless, it takes persistent effort, and it has to be done in a very consistent and strategically redundant way until people finally believe that you are serious. It takes this amount of time because you are changing not only behavior but also the rules and regulations that have become embedded in the fabric of the culture and your followers' shared mental models (see Box 10.9).[108] If you spent several years institutionalizing this way of thinking to create a dependent followership, then expect it to take at least half the time to consciously undo what was embedded, to replace it with something new. You might have asked where I got "half the

---

BOX 10.9. Transformational Leadership and TQM

Horine and Bass (1993) reported a positive relationship between the transformational ratings of three top CEOs and the achievement of the Malcolm Baldridge Award in those respective companies. Those who won this prestigious award created continuous improvement cultures and processes in their respective organizations.

---

time." In all honesty, I just made it up because it sounded difficult but reasonable. Attribute it to my attempt at reducing cycle time in their change processes.

What can you take from this chapter, and what should you think about? Many people are under the misconception that leaders directly influence performance. I say "misconception" because often a leader's influence is indirect through the follower, through the context, or through some interaction of the two over time. I would go even further by saying that perhaps the most important aspects of a leader's influence is the impact she or he has over time and indirectly on performance. If I can get you to think in these terms, then I will have shifted your view to more of a process view of leadership, rather then a simple focus on behaviors, styles, and/or outcomes. And this process view starts with your internal perspective, which over time becomes reflected in the organizational system and culture.

I want you to consider a roundabout way to having an impact on those people you are attempting to influence. You can set up the context in a way that will provide people with more degrees of freedom. You can provide them with more autonomy and discretion, along with facilitation and coaching. You can build trust before attempting to build teams. You can gain commitment or loyalty before attempting to discover innovation. In all of these actions, you are attempting to influence others indirectly, and in doing so you can take advantage of the full range of leadership development, including the target individual, the follower, and of course the changes in the context manifested over time.

Now, to some points for reflection. Think about when you have been in a situation where you have had a very indirect and positive influence on someone's performance or development. *What did you do to start the process? What worked and didn't work? How long did it take? How did you know you were successful? How did you feel when the other person got the credit for your indirect influence?*

Now, look at something you went about changing directly and see what you could have done differently in perhaps a more indirect way. This may sound a bit like a personal debriefing process. I do hope so.

Some Things Worth Repeating

- To have a sustainable impact on followers, leaders must consider the system changes required for long-term and deep change.
- A leader can build her or his legacy by developing followers into leaders, who, in turn, have similar effects on their followers over time.
- Most likely, if a leader continuously has a direct effect on performance, she or he is probably not leading very well, nor transformationally.

11

Several Strange Places to Learn About Full Leadership Development

---

Throughout our discussion of leadership, I have from time to time inserted some perhaps strange places where leadership can be observed and developed. This includes Sam's shop in the correctional services system, among others (see Chapter 3). Let me expand the domain of places one can observe leadership, by saying that, in every organization and in every culture, some form of leadership can be observed. In fact, a recent project involving over 60 countries suggests not only that leadership can be observed but also that some "universal" characteristics and attributes likely span all cultures (see Box 11.1).

I'd like to share a few unique places with you where I have observed the type of leadership discussed in this book that underscores some of the key points I've been raising. I use these examples more or less as points for reflective learning—in some cases, my own learning—as I often try to revisit many places

---

BOX 11.1. The GLOBE Project

House (1997) has been leading a multiyear research project to examine in over 60 countries the degree to which leadership perceptions vary across national cultures. Thus far, the Global Leadership and Organizational Behavior Effectiveness (GLOBE) research team indicates that certain leadership factors appear to transcend cultures. The eight global leadership factors identified thus far include styles such as Team Builder, Charismatic, and Nonparticipative Leadership.

I have been and worked to make sure I got everything out that I could learn. I really do mean "try," as I sometimes realize my own limitations.

About 6 years ago, my colleagues and I at the Center for Leadership Studies received a large army grant to study the development of leadership that takes place during one's 4-year college career. Sounds rather straightforward except that the institution was an all-male military academy with a 150-year "deep" tradition and culture. This institution had created a very complex culture for developing its leaders. Even though everyone we met said this was one of the best training programs for leadership, no one had a clue why it worked, and often said so, in so many words.

Our introduction onto the campus was not followed by a round of applause in all quarters. Many faculty members were completely antimilitary (which I always found quite interesting), and having yet another group of competing academics supported by the military study leadership was the last thing they wanted at their institution. To get our project accepted by the faculty required a great deal of individualized consideration on our part.

Our overarching goal for this project was to meet the freshman class at orientation as they were saying good-bye to their parents and then to follow them through to graduation, which we actually accomplished, bloodied but unbowed. In this institution, freshman were treated as the lowest form of human existence, whom upperclassmen affectionately called "rats." For nearly a year, they were treated with complete disrespect by their upperclassmen, who saw as their mission in life to mold these rats into human beings the entire world would be proud of over time. And like many other "bonding" programs, often actions were taken to the extreme. Yet, I hasten to add, the commandant at the time of this study did everything in his power not only to support our research program but also to bring a sense of enlightenment to the leadership development process in the institution. Marty (not his real name) had been a rat many years ago and had served in the military, as well as had worked in a very responsible leadership role in industry before returning to take over the commandant's position in this institution. He saw many positives in the bonding process brought about by having rats walk the "ratline," but he also wanted to raise the cadets higher up on the range of leadership to be more reflective and broader in their views of developing the full potential of their "brother rats." This was an admirable goal, but it was thought to be rather strange by the hard-core military types within the institution. Indeed, in some ways, the resistance to his initiatives cost him his health and his job eventually, although some might say he was modestly successful in changing some ways of this institution. Modestly.

During my first week of observation, which was the freshman orientation session, I thought the processes used by the upperclassmen were often cruel and extreme. Once they found a weak cadet among the group of 400+ rats, they would work on him day and night until he broke down. Alternatively, if someone seemed to emerge as a leader, they went after him with a vengeance, often breaking him down as well over time. The pressure to perform was extreme, and the constant harassing by the upperclassmen made life for the first several months quite unappealing (you might say I have a flair here for the under-statement). This leveling process continued for most of the first year.

On the surface, anyone might ask, "What really can be learned about leadership in this type of institution?" You browbeat them until they submit, and then you build them back up, if they had the tenacity to stick around for a year. And in our first year, more than 150 out of the 400+ cadets left the institution.

As I've recommended to you throughout this book, I had to reflect on what was going on to understand the depth of the leadership system that I was privileged to observe in this setting. I revisited this issue in my mind many times. Let me point to some examples that I think have some universal application and also fit with the concepts I've already mentioned in previous chapters.

As I compared this institution to my own university, I came to realize that what the institution's leaders were doing was gradually giving students more responsibility, although day to day it did not seem as such. Every year, cadets would take a significant jump in the level of responsibility afforded to them, and it began with developing the next generation of followers (new rats) into leaders within the institution. In this role alone, the seriousness by which the upperclass-men approached their task was truly remarkable and quite reflective of high levels of identification with the institution. Of course, some of it was the joy in getting back at the next class, which would lower one's own suffering, in the form of cognitive dissonance reduction with the cruel experiences of the year before. (*Cognitive dissonance reduction* is one of those interesting terms psychologists use to explain how people restore a sense of fairness in their minds after being treated unfairly. In this instance, a cadet may think his entire first year was hell and unfair. Yet, when it's his turn to "lead," a sense of justice regarding the issue of fairness is restored in his mind.)

I believe that, in the United States, there are very few institutions where the students are able to kick out another student. At this institution, if a student violated the "honor code," he was drummed out of the corps. This meant a full review and trial largely run by students in what they called their "honor court." Although the administration had input, the students largely drove the process. I was told that, in the 150 years of the institution's history, only one case was reversed and in that case the administration screwed up, not the students. Being a faculty member, I can say I'm not surprised. Okay, I'm just kidding for all those college administrators who just threw this book in their circular files. Remember, humor is a positive mediator of leadership. I have rarely seen anything comparable to this decision-making authority at other U.S. or foreign institutions of higher education.

The first year was clearly geared toward making the rats feel vulnerable, building a sense of identification in each other (becoming a "brother rat"), developing trust based in part on the honor code and in large part through fear, and developing the deep perspective in the rats that now you know what god awful followership is so that when you are a leader you will be much more aware of your followers' needs and how you choose to address them or not address them. Certainly for some cadets, this was "implosive therapy" for developing confidence and self-discipline. You throw them in the shit and see what floats. (I have a feeling I just had my book banned from public libraries.) For others, it was too much too soon. It was an either-or model, meaning you either take it, assimilate it, and identify with it, or you leave it. Given its extreme focus on building discipline, I am not at all surprised that leaders emerged. Leadership is several parts Darwinian mixed with some compassion, intelligence, energy, and a willingness to be a bit bolder than the crowd alongside you and/or, over time, also behind you.

To address the severe nature of the system, many very interesting facets had "naturally" emerged in the institution's culture and structure during the last 150 years. For example, each rat was assigned an upperclassman who would harass him, but the rat also had a "dyke" (term used for a mentor, which was not my

---

BOX 11.2. A Key to Xerox's Competitiveness

> Xerox Corporation has set up a friendly "battle" between its optical scanning
> and electronic imaging groups. The purpose is to put pressure on the old
> products to be either improved or gotten rid of to make way for new products.
> By creating such internal tension, Xerox hopes to beat its competition to the
> destruction of their best products. Systems based on conflict can produce
> interesting developments.

---

first guess either), whom he could go to for advice and counseling. This was
someone he could choose or who sought him out for help and advice. Over time,
it led to an elaborate array of leadership relationships because one's dyke's dyke
became your uncle dyke and so on and so forth. This form of diagonal mentoring
(a term coined by Micha Popper, a colleague of mine in Israel) provided a
counterbalance to the harsh realities of the ratline. In my view, what seemed to
emerge over time somewhat spontaneously were systems of checks and bal-
ances. The dyke is one such example.

Another interesting feature of the institution was the overlap between the
class and military systems. Each of these systems had different levels and ranks,
so to speak. So, it was possible to find someone who was senior to you in the
class system but perhaps junior with respect to military rank. This required
constant attention by the cadets to potential conflicts of interest between the two
systems. In fact, it built tension or conflict into the system's structure, and now
today we have companies talking about how one team builds the best product
and the other destroys it (see Box 11.2).

It is also possible to view the institution's processes as an elaborate assessment center for leadership development and emergence. Because all cadets lived
on campus within the same housing complex, they were all almost always under
constant review by their peers. The seniors lived on the first floor, the juniors
on the second, and so forth on up to the rats, who received the least desirable
quarters on the top floor. Throughout each year, your classmates got to observe
you dealing with the most difficult stressors, persisting at tasks for which others
accepted defeat, and coming up with quick ideas under duress; and of course
they observed the type of credibility and integrity you exhibited throughout the
entire day. Cadets would often say that they knew very well who the good and
bad cadets were . . . no doubt.

In our study, we were interested in how moral development and "perspective-taking capacity" developed over time, among many other facets of leadership. We used several measures of perspective-taking capacity, including an interview designed by Jerome Kegan (Lahey, Souvaine, Kegan, Goodman, & Felix, 1991). In this projective interview, people are asked to respond in any order they choose to a series of words typed on 10 index cards. The first one might be *fear*. The general idea is that people at different levels of moral development or perspective-taking capacity will have the ability to frame fear in different ways. One expects the individuals at lower levels to frame fear in terms of protecting self-interest, whereas at higher levels it may be fear of what others think of you or, even higher, what you think of yourself in terms of the internal standards that guide your behavior toward others (e.g., Did I live up to my values and standards with the action I took?). Our expectation was that people who had a higher moral perspective-taking capacity would be able to think about the conflicts that others have and help extend themselves to resolve them; they could have their assumptions challenged without fear of losing their self-image, and in fact it would be reinforced; they could go out in advance of others in what they thought and how they acted, without fear that others would not follow; and they would have a set of ideals that could provide them with an internal guide for their behavior and decisions, by definition, regardless of the situation.

In the process of conducting the interviews, something happened that I believe conveys the deep meaning of what we are trying to grasp in this perspective-taking capacity construct, which lies at the base of building the individual and collective force in organizations to make a real difference in performance (see Box 11.3). Perspective-taking capacity is what differentiates the leaders we associate with the term *idealized* versus other leaders who might be referred to as "idolized."[109,110]

We had interviewed several cadets one morning when, during the fourth interview, a cadet asked us whether we had heard of an incident that occurred earlier that morning. The incident was about a cadet who came out for what the upperclassmen call a "sweat party." A sweat party involves waking up the rats for a 5-mile run at 5 a.m., usually with a cannon placed strategically in the barracks courtyard. That morning, one cadet came out of the dorms, limping very badly. He had a doctor's note excusing him from any physical exercise. After presenting the note, he was excused from that morning's "party." And then off went the several hundred cadets running up the hill. Halfway up the hill, someone looked back and noticed the injured cadet limping well behind the

---

BOX 11.3. Moral Development and Transformational Leadership

Lucius and Kuhnert (1998) examined the relationship between the perspective-taking capacity of cadets attending a 4-year military institution and the ratings they received on the MLQ survey. The authors reported that scores generated from using Kegan's subject-object interviews (Lahey et al., 1991) correlated positively with ratings of transformational leadership. Those cadets judged to be higher in moral development were also rated as being more transformational. Turner and Barling (1998) confirmed these results, reporting positive correlations between level of moral reasoning and the transformational leadership ratings of managers.

---

group, obviously in a great deal of pain. Some of his fellow rats called to him to go back, showing appreciation for his efforts, but he continued throughout the morning until he finished. Inspiring, yes, but that isn't the real value of this story.

The first cadet described the incident accurately but was completely clueless as to why this cadet had attempted the run in the first place. He said several times, "He had the excuse, a written excuse. Why would he do such a stupid thing? I don't get it . . . I really don't get it."

In a subsequent interview, another cadet brought up the same incident. He, too, described it in accurate detail, yet his perspective on the event was quite different. He judged the reason this cadet limped the 5 miles was peer pressure. He said the injured cadet would rather suffer the physical pain caused by the run than the psychological pain caused by the condemnation from his peers.

Yes, in case you were wondering, there was a third cadet. He didn't bring up the event right away, but shared another one with us. He was recounting an event for us that had occurred at the end of the previous academic year. Apparently, a group of his friends were out celebrating, and on the way back his best friend was killed. He discussed the week-long drinking binge in which he participated with his buddies and how it had been the first person in his life he was really close to who had died. He then said that, after the week of drinking, he looked at what he was doing with his friends and decided it was of no real benefit to his departed friend or himself to keep drinking. Although many of his friends condemned him for not being "loyal to the cause," he simply chose not to go out and drink another night. He said that, at that point, he made a choice that he would try to learn as much as he could from the incident to improve himself and his relationships with others and that, in his mind, this would be a much better way of honoring his fallen friend. We then asked him about the incident that had occurred that morning, which he, too, had heard about. We asked him for his perspective on the event. He said that he was surprised the cadet continued the run but that he was nevertheless proud of the cadet's choice to do so. He thought that this cadet's behavior had compelled him to ask himself, "Was I doing everything I could do to be the best at what I am capable of doing in this place?" He said it was something he was giving quite a bit of reflection to see what could be learned from these type of events.

In our study, the third cadet was one of the highest-rated cadets in terms of leadership by his peers and was considered for top leadership positions in the institution. He also scored very high on Kegan's interview, suggesting that our observations of his perspective-taking capacity were confirmed by the results of the interview. Perhaps we had a future manager here who would reflect before acting. We will have to wait for the sequel to determine whether this supposition will come true.

Another individual I came to respect highly at this institution was Marty (not his real name). Marty, the commandant, tried tirelessly to enhance the leadership culture in the institution. His goal was to make these cadets the best leaders and followers possible and to do so by providing them with more than one model for leading others, which focused only on maintaining the command and control over others with periodic bursts of inspiration. The cadets, both new and old, saw Marty as an outsider who had gotten soft over time and was trying to submarine a system that had worked well for more than a century. He was fought at every turn, and some might say he tried to change this institution too deeply and too quickly. Probably.

The institution has one of the strongest and most well articulated cultures I have ever witnessed. It was no easy task for any leader to transform it to a more enlightened system. But Marty tried, and he worked to enlist the support of students and colleagues in his efforts. Unfortunately, a heart attack shortened his tenure in the commandant position, along with his 3-year effort to alter the culture. The person who came in after Marty was a Special Forces guy who was very tough and fit very nicely with the prior culture. I should add one thing about Marty: He had the vision to move the institution forward for all the right reasons, but he cared a bit too much about what others thought of him and his efforts. Karl Kuhnert called this the "team player,"[111] the one who is too occupied with what others think about him or her. Marty had this tendency in his perspective that ended up causing him a great deal of pain, but he did survive to go on and do other good things at this institution.

The Special Forces guy had a big picture of himself behind his desk, working his way through some jungle, with eyes blackened and a maniacal look on his face. Near the end of our project, many in the institution seemed to think it was finally returning to "normalcy" after a long period of "insanity." I guess what is normal and insane all depends on one's perspective and goals. I often think, in terms of leadership development, that if it is too comfortable, then it is probably not developing or evolving. As Max Depree, former CEO of Herman Miller, recently recounted, a mentor of his used to say, "Leaders don't inflict pain, they bear it." I don't mean necessarily pain, just a sufficient level of healthy tension that they create and bear for the good of their group or organization.[112]

Like other military organizations that spend a great deal of time on leadership development, this institution of "higher" learning was not much different. Perhaps most striking to me was that, in many ways, the patients were running the institution, and to some degree it was working! Some.

And Now, Another Interesting Place

I turn our attention again to South Africa. We were working for a research and development agency attempting to move toward being fully privatized. This former government agency was seen as being very closely tied to the previous government, the last government to enforce apartheid. Members of this agency were particularly proud in that, during the years that most of the world had an economic embargo against South Africa, they continued to develop and design weapons system that were used in the war against Angola or, indirectly, Cuba and the former Soviet Union.

Unfortunately, since the fall of President de Klerk's government, this agency has been seen as a holdover from the apartheid years with members sympathetic to the old system. Most of its funding came from President Mandela's government, which is not only dominated by blacks but also interested in cutting defense expenditures. All in all, the future looked very dim indeed for this proud group of engineers and scientists, whom I would liken to NASA in the United States.

Our first meeting with the senior management team took place in an African game reserve lodge, where most management training takes place in South Africa these days. Surrounding managers with these natural and sometimes threatening environments is seen as good for opening up discussion . . . an irony I still smile about from time to time. Here we are surrounded by animals that could, without remorse, eat your young for lunch, and their own, talking about leadership development . . . the enlightened approach . . . a "full range." By the way, I still carried my mosquito spray even though the malaria alert was over.

It is probably fair to say that the senior management was suspicious of our presence and what they referred to as the "American model" we were going to present to them on that first day of the retreat. At the outset of the first day of our workshop, the CEO took a very aggressive stance and was obviously impatient with our process. It probably didn't help the situation any when I questioned whether his management team was really a "group" or a "team." He was adamant that it was a team, NOT A GROUP. (That's the way he said it to me, to emphasize his point.) We found out later in our intervention that these senior managers were clearly not a team and barely a functioning group— I know, a nice way of avoiding the word *dysfunctional.* This became readily apparent to us all when we spent nearly half a day creating what we called their compact of understanding and what they called a "freedom of information act." Some had worked together on this leadership "team" for nearly 10 years, and rarely had they had an open exchange of views with each other. Conflict was by no means the highest level of interaction with this team, unless it was described as being completely internalized. And it was typically totally avoided with the senior manager in charge, making him and his decisions highly vulnerable—in the negative sense, of course. He clearly didn't know what he didn't know.

As we usually do in our training workshops, we asked participants to discuss their ideal models of leadership and followed with a presentation of the full range model and cases regarding its application in their context. We proceeded to provide feedback on the MLQ survey, and it became apparent that some managers on the team were not just surprised with their results. It's fair to say that they were shocked and angry. In such a closed organizational system, the managers had little, if any, feedback of how others perceived them in their leadership roles. This lack made them very exposed because they really didn't know what they didn't know. And given the dismal context and future in which they were and would be embedded, they simply could not afford to close any doors to useful ideas and information.

When they evaluated the team in terms of its leadership and culture, the CEO again took the bold and often strong stance that strong and consistent values underlay "his" team's behavior. Unfortunately, the data we collected on the organization's culture looked like someone fired a shotgun at the flip chart. Absolutely no convergence or alignment was found among the scores. They were so disparate on their evaluations of the team and its culture that they finally stopped blowing smoke and began to accept the fact that they were *definitely not a team* (my emphasis this time).

We had finally reached a point where we could begin to reconstruct the group and organization—a significant point of honest reflection. The CEO was struck by the disparities in his team's view of its leadership and culture, and I was struck by his lack of awareness. He simply didn't see it because the script for his organization had been written very differently by him. The script dictated that one should not bring bad news to the boss. This was bad, bad news. A lot of beer was drunk on our night ride into the wild that evening.

From that point of breakdown or tension with respect to the feedback on their cultural data in the workshop to a year later, some remarkable shifts had taken place in perspective about what the team stood for, what businesses they were in and should be in, the type of organization they desired, and how they intended to create the future organizational enterprise. A vast amount of intellectual resources had been released to address some really productive endeavors. Ironically, it started with a discrepancy or common point of tension for the group, which led to an exploration, and in their case the exploration required the development of a compact of understanding. After working together for so many years, they needed to build back trust and develop greater openness. For nearly half of day, they focused on building a set of agreements that would allow them to talk more directly and openly with each other and to be more transparent. The agreement or compact was revised periodically over time as needed, and things changed in the right direction and by many accounts were beginning to take hold in the culture.

Certainly, this group still has many external forces to overcome, but their energy had been renewed in large part by a leader who allowed them to discuss their opinions more freely. What would seem like a very simple gesture to an Introductory Organizational Behavior class was a huge step forward for an organization and society that had lived under such intense control conditions as were in force with the system of apartheid. It had become a culture of never saying what you really thought, which was one of the few color-blind principles of the society for more than 40 years.

> *Know ye by these present that as a member in good standing of the Pitney*
> *Bowes Shipping and Weighing Systems Engineering Organization,*
> *you have the inalienable right to whatever information you need to*
> *do your job.* (John Manzo of Pitney Bowes, "Freedom of
> Information Act")

One Last Story

For this one, we have to take a short trip to Israel. Taly Dvir (her real name)
was a doctoral student in Israel, coming up to the time when she needed to
complete her dissertation. We met at a conference where I was giving a
presentation on leadership and African humanism. She told me afterward that
she was intrigued by the concept of *vital force,* Ubuntu, and the three words *unity*
through diversity. She would say, from time to time, that the three words are very
powerful words, and this has caused me to think even deeper about their
importance and application to my own work and life.

Later that evening, we met at a reception where we talked awhile about my
presentation and her work. She had heard of some work I was doing in Israel
with the military and with the Center for Leadership Studies we were currently
establishing with Drs. Reuvan Gal, Micha Popper, and Giora Ayalon (all real
names) in Zichron. I told Taly that, on a previous visit to Israel, I had promised
a colleague by the name of Eliav Zakay (real name) at the School for Leadership
Development in Netanya that I would be willing to come back on a subsequent
trip to train their consultants in the methods we use within the full range
leadership program. Taly was interested in my work, but we never got to discuss
it much further that evening.

After I returned home, I received an e-mail from Taly, discussing how we
might collaborate on a training project at the School for Leadership Development in Israel. She was interested in providing a definitive test of whether one
could train the full range of leadership and thought the Israeli military would be
a great place to conduct the test because it was already familiar with our work
on transformational leadership. She also thought the military would accept a
training intervention experiment that could examine whether leadership is really
"born versus made."

As the project evolved, we enlisted the help of Professors Dov Eden and
Boas Shamir (more real names), and in the school itself, the research director,

whom I mentioned above, was Eliav Zakay. During the next 2 years, we worked as a virtual team through e-mail to plan a "true" field experiment of leadership development, the most comprehensive experiment to be undertaken in at least the last 20 years. We crossed many, many obstacles of resistance, as diverse as (a) the fear that an "American" model would invade the institution and (b) a very significant difference in philosophies between our group's approach to training, which was highly structured, and the school's approach, which was much more psychodynamic and "here and now." Many consultants saw our structured approach as taking away their freedom to be "psychologists in action."

After some reflection, I guess I could say we wore them down into submission, although publicly let's say we achieved consensus and their commitment to "the cause." My primary job was to train the consultants in the experimental group to conduct our full range training program.[113,114] The comparison group had been offering the school's program for well over 5 years and had become very good at their work. Yet, the growing crisis in the institution was that different consultants were offering programs "their own way," potentially losing some impact and missing their target and mission. There was an obvious lack of alignment among their programs, which Taly positively labeled "eclectic." In addition, the government had recently changed the consultants' contracts, leading to a drop in pay and a great deal of dissatisfaction. The evaluation ratings for their best training programs were dropping quickly.

We had designed a pure field experiment of the most rigorous kind so that any difference we found would have to be a result of the training intervention (see Figure 11.1). Yet, we had to overcome many disadvantages, including the fact that I do not speak Hebrew, although my wonderful mother, Esther Dolly Greenspan, was Jewish. We also had one chance to train the consultants before the experimental group trainers went live. It would be an understatement to say that some consultants were against our intervention. Many were against the intervention because they really thought they would have to give up what they were skilled at doing in training by substituting this new American model. Because I was the outsider and a professor, I was given a lot of leeway and respect. Taly, however, often took the main brunt of abuse yet persisted time and again when she met resistance and outright criticism, which given the conditions in the school, were not beyond our expectations.

Taly went through every training session and provided me with insights I would never have been able to derive on my own. It was an emotionally draining experience for everyone involved, but mostly for Taly because many times she saw her life work just fizzling before her eyes. It was a very important challenge

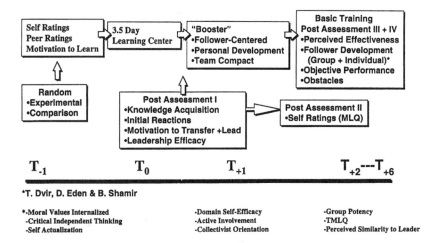

Figure 11.1. Experimental Training Study in Israel

SOURCE: Content based on Dvir (1998).
NOTE: *Moral values internalized: critical independent thinking, self-actualization, domain self-efficacy, active involvement, collectivist orientation, group potency, TMLQ, and perceived similarity to leader.

for me, whereas for Taly it was her dissertation, or the difference between being Ms. Dvir and Dr. Dvir. We finally completed the training of the consultants in Olga, a small training base on the Mediterranean Sea. We gained from the consultants a verbal commitment to do, to the best of their ability, the training with platoon commanders attending a week-long program at the school. We were also able to secure agreements from the school to conduct a 3- to 4-hour booster session 1 month following our initial training intervention to reinforce what was originally learned by the platoon commanders.

After I returned to the United States following the training in Olga, I thought we now at least had a chance to get the training effects we expected. I can't say that everyone agreed with me on this expectation, but then again, given all the obstacles in front of us, I must say for brief moments I also questioned our chances. Brief.

Shortly after I returned home, I heard from Taly that the comparison group of trainers were all fired up and were going to win the competition with the American model because their pride was now on the line. We were all a bit disheartened because we wanted to see what worked best in both programs, not one against the other. But I must admit that their reactions came as no surprise to me. This wasn't my first clambake, and I realized that outsiders have to persist to be successful. Recall my hero worship of President Mandela, one of the great "outsider" success stories of this century.

The week that our commanders were to come to training, the prime minister of Israel, Benjamin Netanyahu, decided to approve the extension of the tunnel in the old city of Jerusalem to bring the Jews closer to the first temple. The tunnel is linked on the other side to the famous Western Wall. Needless to say, all hell broke loose, and 80 people subsequently died. It suffices to say that the meaning of the phrase "all events in Israel are local" took on new meaning for me.

A day before the workshops were to begin, it appeared that the whole effort had to be canceled. Some of our platoons were heading off to Gaza, Lebanon, and the West Bank. There appeared to be no time left for things to cool down and also for us to get the troops in any sort of reasonable condition for leadership training. On the morning of the proposed start of training, I awoke very early to check my e-mail, and it was one of several times I really got emotional about this project. Somehow, an intervention had occurred the evening before, and all our troops had rolled through the gates at 5 o'clock that morning. I was Rocky dancing at the top of the steps in Philly, saying "Yes, Yes . . . YES! Feeling strong now" . . . and again saying to myself, "You gotta believe." Sometimes you just have to believe you can do it.

Although the training started a day late, we again had a chance to pull off this study. Phoenix had risen from the ashes. It was a moment that reflects what I study with my colleagues, something truly inspirational!

Although the trainers were committed to us, many still thought the process was not quite right for them and had difficulty delivering the first edition of the training program. We heard from some of our "internal" sources that the platoon commanders were asking trainers why they had to learn this "American model." We knew that these types of comparisons would only make our efforts more of an uphill battle. No matter what their beliefs, all the trainers came out of the experience very emotionally drained, in part, because the whole nation was on edge and because they all were true professionals. They each knew they could have done a better job if they had just had more practice with implementing the new training program.

We had built into the design a follow-up booster session where trainers met with commanders a month after the initial intervention. I believe in retrospect that these booster sessions may have pushed the training effects over the top. Many platoon commanders had obviously thought about what they had learned from the initial training. The boosters involved one trainer meeting with three or four platoon commanders to discuss the progress they had made on their leadership plans. Also, during these sessions, the commanders discussed problems they had confronted and obstacles they had overcome. An additional purpose of these booster sessions was to debrief on how effective the model of leadership was in application to their roles as platoon commanders. The individual discussions on how they were performing with respect to the feedback they had received on leadership style in the first program appeared to have had a profound impact on these "new" commanders. I should add for clarification that we chose this particular group to study because they became commanders just prior to the training intervention and met their platoons for the first time following training. Thus, our experimental design had no contamination attributable to history effects or familiarity with the units. One problem with some experimental designs is that the participants may have experienced some events over time that could affect how they respond in an experiment. Here, the concern might be that the commanders knew the recruits in an earlier time period, thus affecting how they responded to his leadership. Because the platoons were newly formed, they had no history or familiarity with the platoon commanders.

Taly spent much of the next several months going into the field to collect our posttraining measures. When I say "into the field," I mean this in a very literal sense. She went to the most remote places with staff from the school to collect survey data. The data collection and logistics were extremely complicated to accomplish, often in conditions where the commanders had to fill out survey instruments in front of headlights if they came back from maneuvers after sundown. Invariably, and this is a universal in the military, Taly would show up at a base and the commander would say, "Oh, yes, we heard you were coming, but we need to make some adjustments before collecting this survey data stuff." This was a response on a good day! One remarkable effect of this study is that Taly was able to collect nearly all the data she intended to collect as per the study design. This is another source of inspiration that will remain with me throughout my career.

So, what did we find? First, we found that the comparison group training was rated more satisfactory and effective following the 3.5 days of initial training, as compared with the experimental group, or our training intervention. We also noted that some of our trainers had a difficult time delivering the training, as reflected in their below average ratings on effectiveness, as compared with other training programs they had delivered in the recent past. Yet, as we examined the effects over time, something remarkable happened. The effects of the experimental intervention became significant, whereas no significant effects for the comparison group were found. The comparison group continued to see their ratings drop during 6 months. We had found that leaders could be trained to be more transformational and less corrective in their styles of leadership and that their direct reports and superiors could see it on the basis of their MLQ ratings. Because the study was based on a very rigorous experimental design, the significant effects that were found can only be attributed to the training intervention; all other relevant factors were completely controlled for in the experimental design or, if not, they affected each group equally well or poorly.

Results from this study clearly suggest that training should be designed to unfold over time, as we are fairly confident that the booster session made a big difference in securing the training effects in our study. Second, we believe that, with more practice and concentrated training, the consultants could create even greater training effects with the commanders in the expected direction. This is evidenced by recent evaluations of training instructors that show that after two more pilot versions of our training programs, their evaluations were consistently higher than the average for the last 2 years across all programs.

Third, we believe that by adding 2 or 3 more days toward the middle of basic training, the effects of training would have been significantly enhanced. With those additional days of training, we would have been able to focus more on the relationship of the platoon commander and his NCO officers. In our opinion, this relationship seems key to the significant findings we obtained from the training intervention. Fourth, we were able to train the type of leadership at the high end of the full range and to sustain training effects over an extended period of time and affect platoon performance in addition to ratings of leadership (over more then 3-6 months). A truly remarkable finding!

Finally, we all learned that we must model the model we were trying to test to get the type of results we obtained in this study. At many points, we were under siege and down emotionally, but someone always rose on those occasions to come up with another idea, to inspire each of us to try harder, to pick others up when we had fallen back again, and to keep in mind the ideals we were striving to achieve in this study. And to accomplish this, we were led by another one of my heros, a doctoral student who helped us all fly much higher and longer than most thought possible. At least in this instance, leadership was proved to be made and was exemplified in our "team's" behavior.

In sum, this training project provided us with a basis for exploring in much greater depth the methods that can be used to enhance leadership training along the entire range of leadership development. Given the billions of dollars spent each year on training leaders around the globe, this is a very worthwhile and extremely important foundation for future work to build on and extend. We also learned that, by meeting the individual learner at his or her level of potential through follow-ups and boosters, we can enhance his or her ability to lead others effectively. Not bad for a few years' worth of work with one of the best teams I have ever had the privilege and honor to work with on any project. Okay, okay . . . the best!

In reflection, it is perhaps unusual for an author to discuss his or her own work in the way I've described our training study. I have done so here because this project changed me in ways that I often encourage others in my training programs to work on. And, it is also consistent with a dictum that Kurt Lewin once said, that you never fully understand a phenomenon until you try to change it. I got much closer on this one—much—and sharing with you what we learned is all part of that learning experience we call leadership development.

I've decided to leave the reflections up to you this time and for you to choose what you want to take away from this chapter. It's time.

12

This Is the Last Chapter!
The End/The Beginning

Again, I have come back to the same place, for the first time.
   (T. S. Elliot)

I began this book in a small town called Destin (maybe we can add a *y*). Destin is in the panhandle of Florida on the Gulf of Mexico. I've returned there several times during the course of writing this book to do my Ernest Hemingway "thing" of writing portions of this book on the beach. On many early mornings, I sat at my laptop, typing away while watching people on the beach, inspired by the waters in front of me and Destin's pure white sand that squeaks when you walk on it. I am usually more reflective at the beach, and to write a book about leadership in this situation was truly inspiring for me. It has been a great journey for me in learning about leadership. Although this would never satisfy a publisher, it has been very important for me to learn how my own views about leadership have evolved over the years. I knew these ideas were there somewhere, but when they come out of your fingers and onto the screen, there is something very reflective in that, and very privileged too. I will never stop appreciating the fact that someone out there actually wants to put my thoughts between two covers and call it a book that someday my daughters Casey and Sydney or my son Jake could stumble across in a library. And when that does happen, I would like to think that what I've said in this book will still have some relevance for them; even a chapter's worth would be sufficient.

Maybe if they only picked up the book and looked at the last chapter they could say that something there helped them become more effective followers and leaders. What would I say then? Why do I always have to do this to myself? Shssh . . . I'm doing a little of my own reflection here.

A profound similarity between leading and following often goes over our heads, or we fail to notice what we fail to notice. You have to go inside yourself, step back in order to move forward. Leaders must do this quite often to enable them to understand the past, function in the present, and create the future. And, it is no different with following, except it is likely to be more difficult. We don't tell our children on the way out to school, "Now listen, be the best follower you can be, okay? Now, high five and out the door you go." To reflect on what it takes to be an exemplary follower will require much deeper reflection because we have very little practice in this area. Yet, it is so fundamental to building the vital force in you, in your teams, and in your organization. Followers allow leadership to happen. Leaders have their role in this process too. Yet, the sine qua non of leadership is reflected in the profound accomplishments of the follower. Every great leader knew this and worked to achieve it through her or his own behavior and what she or he encouraged in others. In James McGregor Burns's terms, the transforming leaders were those people who uplifted followers to lead themselves. The leader can only assume a bit part in this "life play," although too often she or he is given much more center stage than deserved.[115]

I believe that at the core of leading others is a solid and complete understanding of one's vulnerabilities and a comfort level to allow them to be exposed. Followers are often asked without forethought to allow themselves to be vulnerable, to listen to the leader, to do their best to make the leader successful, and so on. Well, it's time some of the vulnerability rests with the leader. Recall that we've defined the level of leadership you will see in others (second in command) as being based, in part, on your own behavior. This statement applies to so many things, including how you treat your own failures; how you address criticisms of your most central beliefs, ideals, and values; how you respond when someone challenges your absolutely "best" ideas; and how willing you are to get the hell out the way to let those who should lead, lead.

The sense of vulnerability I have described here can only come through a profound understanding of yourself. You are constantly going through in vivo leadership training, so what are you deriving from those experiences? What types of "boosters" do you build in for yourself? What types of life experiences are you consciously trying to add to your life stream? How do you address the ones that come along in your life stream that are unplanned and very difficult to assimilate?

I know that you might be saying, "Hey, what has gotten into this guy? All along, he is working with me, reflecting together on events, and then, wham! He is challenging the heck out of us." You're right. In honor of all past leaders and followers who put in the necessary effort and sacrifices required to achieve their vital forces and the vital forces in others, I am challenging both of us . . . and I really mean "both of us." Leadership is one of the most profound forces in the universe for good and evil. We must challenge ourselves to make it right. This is not some course on assertiveness training; it's a discussion of leadership on the order of Jesus Christ, Mahatma Gandhi, Nelson Mandela, Mother Teresa, Herb Kelleher, Eleanor Roosevelt, Golda Meir, Eva Perón, Albert Einstein, John F. Kennedy, Abraham Lincoln, Amy Carmichael, and on and on. We can honor great leaders through our own efforts to be exemplary, not just our successes.

The first message I wish to leave with you is to achieve in yourself a level of "confident vulnerability." This will provide others with the space to enter into your reflections, ideas, actions, and accomplishments. It is the space that both leaders and followers require to be successful and to enhance their vital forces over time. *Confident vulnerability* may seem an oxymoron, but exemplary leadership, insights, great discoveries, and adventures are often based on para- doxical thinking. I wonder whether that is why Microsoft's Bill Gates tries to create at his company a learning culture based on what they call an "armed truce" among leaders, among followers, between leaders and followers, and peer-to- peer.

Let's address this issue of vulnerability from another angle. Allowing yourself the space to be vulnerable defines the areas that you may want to develop most. It's not just being vulnerable, it's defining the parameters within which you want to achieve your next level of potential, and the next. Vulner- ability is a profoundly beautiful thing in children, in the loving relationship between husband and wife, and when observed in high-performing teams. It seems quite reasonable to apply it to leadership, to the extent that leadership is a relationship. And it is a relationship of many sorts; thus, working on vulnerability seems a very worthwhile goal to enhance your leadership potential and performance.

No coin should be more profoundly coveted and rewarding in the realm than when we get others to identify with something we and they truly believe in. You have met those people who so firmly identify with what they are doing that you are drawn to them by their example. Their efforts are so deeply rooted in what they identify with that it is almost insulting to them to add in rewards of trivial consequence. Thus, if you really want to ring the bell on leadership, then find something you want to identify with and *need* to accomplish and then develop the reasons that are required to bring others to your way of believing. This requires that you role-model your own beliefs and ideals, that you energize others to put in the effort required to achieve those ideals, that you amend your basic ideas when new insights are brought to the foreground, and perhaps most important, that you understand what each follower will need from you to identify with "the cause" or mission you have chosen to pursue. What will motivate them to be like you and still be willing to disagree for the common good of your group and vision?

Once the doors for greater vulnerability are open, finding the right hooks on which to build identification is a crucially important task of leadership. Yet, it is not a lonely task at all, in that you must know what people can identify with for them to be fully committed. If you listen and observe very carefully, in many cases you will learn what will bring people together. Sometimes it may not always be so obvious, and sometimes people will need to be pushed toward this realization, but in the end, if you know where you want to go, you will get there through their identification with your ideas and, of course, your demonstration of commitment to them over time.

With this process of identification stuff, I know full well that it will require tremendous persistence on your part. Nothing profoundly unique and interesting is adopted at the outset without either question or conflict. Nothing. It can't be, in that beliefs are something we develop in others over time, with some individuals taking more time than others. You have to identify, and then you can persist in bringing others to that level of identification at the truly deep levels where transformational change occurs. This suggests not identifying with everything or nothing, that somewhere in between will suffice.

Once you identify with something, you must convey it to others in a thousand different ways, all nested in your enthusiasm and expressed desire to accomplish something profoundly important. Too often, leaders spread themselves thin and want to identify with any "flavor of the month." Let me be clear about this: "Just don't do it, no matter what Nike said in its ads." The greatest leaders throughout history couldn't do it, and I suggest we use them as a starting point for role modeling. You will know that people identify with what you are trying to present when they come up with examples that are beyond the ones you have been presenting to them to clarify the mission or vision. At that point in their understanding, a true shift in perspective has occurred, and you can now rest a bit easier that your leadership legacy, as well as your shadow, is well on its way to being formed.

You know full well, after reading this book, that what comes next also requires a dogmatic persistence to doing what's right. Trust. No higher control exists in the universe than that based on complete and absolute trust. You will stop and wait, you will never question, you will follow absolutely willingly, and you will place your most precious secrets with those people you trust. It is a battleground in organizations that is won and lost almost every day. We feel the impact of its absence in those organizations with profoundly "obvious" organizational structures that are supposed to "ensure" that employees "comply" with doing the right thing. In those situations, so much energy is dissipated in a system that requires commitment to controls. At the opposite end, it is an amazing feeling to be part of a relationship, team, or organization based on trust. Let me be clear with all those managers who might say, "Trust is a nice soft thing to have." It is NOT nice to have trust; it is part of the fundamental framework required for achieving the vital force in any organization, team relationship, and/or individual. It is a *must have* to sustain success and reinvention of oneself, a group, an organization, communities, and society.

Trust is as fragile as vulnerability, but unfortunately it is too often taken for granted until lost. As a leader, you must know where you are in the process of building trust. At times, you first have to clear the land, so to speak, before you can build the foundation for trust. The more mistrust that pervaded a system before you started your good work, the more likely the clearing process must be put in place. Also frustrating to many leaders is that trust requires continuous replenishment as new people enter the scene, but it is never as difficult as the first time. Trust is part of the essential foundation for accomplishing one's leadership legacy over time. No one carries into the future such things as ideals, principles, and beliefs from someone she or he doesn't trust. So, in the end, if you have a long-term personal vision for leadership success, the choice to build trust is a simple and profoundly meaningful one for everyone, including for your own aims and aspirations (see Box 12.1).

BOX 12.1. Visionary Leadership and Its Impact via Impression Management

---

Holladay and Coombs (1994) examined the contribution that context and delivery make to how effective a leader is seen in delivering a visionary statement. This experimental study examined how the leader delivered the vision (strong vs. weak) and the vision content, including such things as emphasis or mission, core values, and optimism. Both vision *style* and *content* positively affected the leader's charismatic image and perceived effectiveness, although delivery was weighted by raters as far more important to these judgments. Your commitment should determine the quality of your delivery; otherwise, it is just impression management, which is not sustainable.

A few years ago, I interviewed a CEO who said he had been implementing a team-building program in his factory for 2 years. When I interviewed his staff, however, no one had heard of a "team building" program. At the end of the day, I asked him about this discrepancy. He said, "I have spent the last 2 years building trust around here. That's Module 1 in my team-building program." Interesting perspective.

And now we end where we began our discussion concerning perspective. This whole journey together has been about developing, shifting, and reinforcing aspects of each of our perspectives. Leaders who are great have a lens and frame-of-reference through which they view the world that we write about and discuss with colleagues. These leaders view(ed) the world in a way no one else considered, and in so doing they took small steps that contributed to huge steps for humankind. In both leader and follower, the transformation my colleagues and I have studied is fundamentally about a shift in perspective, which ultimately leads to a shift in behaviors, actions, and accomplishments.

Development in its purest sense involves the planned evolution of people's perspectives and the capacity to enlarge those perspectives to understand the needs, abilities, and aspirations of all those around you and those you will meet in the future. In this journey, your perspective will often have to continue to evolve for others around you also to advance and develop to their full potential. Your continuous *personal* improvement (CPI) leads to their CPIs, which in turn ignites the continuous *process* improvement (CPI) for the organization. It is always a works-in-progress with never an end point, just a process sustained by the vital forces we have created in each other. So, you don't get to spike the ball, but just continue to improve.

Before closing, I need to mention one other person. Early on in this book, I talked about the importance of the parent as leader and how the teacher picks up where the parent left off and the manager picks up the rest in terms of developing the full potential of individuals. I think I said that the trainer is the last in the food chain for developing leadership. Everything I've said about leadership at the high end applies to exemplary parenting.

In our research on life streams and their development, we have discovered that one of the most important factors is the ethical standards set by the mother as a role model for her children (see Box 12.2). Recalling that Martin Luther King, Jr., Mahatma Gandhi, and Nelson Mandela were all primarily raised by their mothers, I often joke with people that my best contribution to the leadership potential of my children would be to die young in order to get out of their mother's way. Their mother, Beth, represents one of the most principled people I have ever known, and in every sense she exemplifies all the finest aspects of transformational leadership with our children. She sets for them a very high moral standard, she works with them to do their best, and she challenges the way they think while also supporting them in all their needs. Every day, I see their respect and admiration for her, and her leadership in our family convinced me that everything I study about leadership and followership links directly to the "family team." My highest compliment is to say that the teachers and managers who will work with our children in the future will probably have to afford less time to our children's leadership and followership development. And without any evidence from experiments, meta-analyses, or correlational studies, most of what others will see in our children will be a direct consequence of Beth's long shadow of influence. And for that, I will always be grateful. Always. You can't imagine how profound an experience it is to see such exemplary leadership in one's home every day. Well, I'm sorry, maybe you can, or at least I hope so.

Okay, a final thought for you to reflect on: If all of this leadership stuff still seems overwhelming to you right now, then you may want to take the approach suggested in the story in Box 12.3 from President John F. Kennedy.

And now my journey with you has come to an end. I would like to express my appreciation to you for your patience, for your willingness to work with me, and simply for listening. I have never taken that for granted even though sometimes I was not always sure what you were listening to or why. Yet, in the end, if you have gotten this far, you must have heard something you liked, and for that I have a deep sense of satisfaction. Thanks for listening.

BOX 12.2.   Female and Male Leadership Styles

Eagley (1991) and Eagley and Johnson (1990) provided empirical evidence from a comprehensive meta-analysis of differences in female and male leadership styles, concluding that, on average, women leaders tend to be more democratic and participative than their male counterparts. "Women evidently proceed with more collaboration and sharing of decision-making" (Eagley, 1991, p. 16). Yet, the actual differences were rather small and varied at times, depending on the role held by the leader.

Bass, Avolio, and Atwater (1996) examined female and male differences in leadership style by using the MLQ survey. Generally, the differences across three separate studies between female and male leaders were rather small, although there was a consistent tendency for female leaders to be rated more transformational than their male counterparts by both female and male raters. The mean differences were stronger for managers from larger Fortune 500-type organizations as compared to MLQ data for female and male leaders in not-for-profit, small health care, social service, government, and other local agencies, as well as small businesses. In a fourth sample of leaders who were from educational organizations and held positions such as superintendents, principals, and staff from public school districts, again the differences in leadership style were not very large between female and male leaders rated by their direct reports.

Hackman, Furniss, Hills, and Peterson (1992) reported that both feminine and masculine factors were positively correlated with evaluations of female and male leaders' transactional and transformational leadership. The pattern in these results might suggest that to be optimally effective requires that leaders be both feminine (e.g., empathic) and masculine (e.g., decisive) in their behavior and style. Thus, a balance between the two over time may provide the basis for the highly effective transformational leader.

BOX 12.3.

John F. Kennedy liked to tell about a French marshal who assumed control of France's North African territories: Looking around at the barren hillsides, the marshal said to an aide, "We must plant trees." The aide objected: "In this environment, it will take 100 years for a tree to grow to its full height." "In that case," the marshal said, "We have no time to lose. We must begin this very afternoon."

How about starting this afternoon with building your full leadership potential?

One other thing I want to leave you with to reflect on: *Together, we will each accomplish more. Much more! I really believe that. Let's get to work on making this a much better world.*

Note References

1. Bass, B. M. (1997). Does the transactional-transformational leadership paradigm transcend organizational and national boundaries? *American Psychologist, 52,* 130-139.

2. Christie, P., Lessem, R., & Mbigi, L. (1994). *African management: Philosophies, concepts, and applications.* South Africa: Knowledge Resources.

3. Avolio, B. J. (1995). Integrating transformational leadership and Afrocentric thinking management. *Human Resource Management Journal, 11,* 17-21.

4. Hofstede, G. (1991). *Cultures and organizations: Software of the mind.* New York: McGraw-Hill.

5. Bass, B. M., & Avolio, B. J. (1994). *Improving organizational effectiveness through transformational leadership.* Thousand Oaks, CA: Sage.

6. Avolio, B. J. (1995). Leadership: Building the vital forces in highly developed teams. *Human Resource Management Journal, 11*(6), 10-15.

7. Kelley, R. (1992). *The power of followership.* Garden City, NY: Doubleday.

8. Matusek, L. (1997). *Finding your voice: Learning to lead anywhere you want to make a difference.* San Francisco: Jossey-Bass.

9. Cascio, W. (1995). Whether industrial and organizational psychology in a changing world of work? *American Psychologist, 50,* 928-934.

10. Hamel, G., & Prahalad, C. K. (1994). *Competing for the future: Breakthrough strategies for seizing control of your industry and creating the markets of tomorrow.* Boston: Harvard Business School Press.

11. Manz, C. M., & Sims, H. P., Jr. (1991). *Super leadership: Leading others to lead themselves.* Upper Saddle River, NJ: Prentice Hall.

12. Salas, E., Mullen, B., Rozell, D., & Driskell, J. E. (1997). *Effects of team building on performance: An integration.* Paper presented at the annual meetings of the Society for Industrial and Organizational Psychology, St. Louis, MO.

13. Manz, C. M. (1986). Self-leadership: Toward an expanded theory of self-influence process in organizations. *Academy of Management Review, 11,* 585-600.

14. Popper, M., & Liphshitz, R. (n.d.). *Organizational learning: Mechanisms and feasibility.* Unpublished manuscript, Haifa University, Haifa, Israel.

15. Shamir, B., House, R. J., & Arthur, M. B. (1993). The motivational effects of charismatic leadership: A self-concept based theory. *Organizational Science, 4,* 577-594.

16. Fukujama, F. (1995). *Trust: The social virtues and creation of prosperity.* New York: Free Press.

17. Waldman, D. A., Bass, B. M., & Yammarino, F. J. (1990). Adding to the contingent-reward behavior: The augmenting effect of charismatic leadership. *Group and Organizational Studies, 15,* 381-394.

18. Avolio, B. J., & Bass, B. M. (1988). Transformational leadership, charisma, and beyond. In J. G. Hunt, B. R. Baliga, H. P. Dachler & C. Schriesheim (Eds.), *Emerging leaders' vistas* (pp. 29-50). New York: Pergamon.

19. Bass, B. M., & Avolio, B. J. (1993). Transformational leadership: A response to critiques. In M. M. Chemers & R. Ayman (Eds.), *Leadership theory and research: Perspectives and directions* (pp. 49-80). New York: Academic Press.

20. Bass, B. M., & Avolio, B. J. (1997). *Manual for the Multifactor Leadership Questionnaire.* Palo Alto, CA: Mindgarden.

21. Bass, B. M. (1990). *Bass & Stogdill's handbook of leadership.* New York: Free Press.

22. Frost, P. J. (1997). Cross-roads. *Organizational Science, 8,* 332-347.

23. Bass, B. M. (1998). *Transformational leadership: Industry, military, and educational impact.* Mahwah, NJ: Lawrence Erlbaum.

24. Kuhnert, K. W., & Lewis, P. (1987). Transactional and transformational leadership: A constructive developmental analysis. *Academy of Management Review, 12,* 648-657.

25. Lord, R. G., & Maher, K. J. (1991). *Leadership and information processing: Linking perceptions and performance.* Boston: Rutledge.

26. Atwater, L. A., & Yammarino, F. J. (in press). Self-other agreement: Does it really matter. *Personnel Psychology.*

27. Avolio, B. J., Waldman, D. A., & Yammarino, F. J. (1991). Leading in the 1990's: Towards understanding the four I's of Transformation Leadership. *Journal of European Industries Training, 173,* 571-580.

28. Heifetz, R. A. (1994). *Leadership without any easy answers.* Cambridge, MA: Harvard University Press.

29. Peck, M. S. (1993). *A world waiting to be born: Civility rediscovered.* New York: Bantam.

30. Winston, M. G. (1997). Leadership of renewal: Leadership for the 21st century. *Business Forum, 22*(1), 4-7.

31. Tichy, N., & Devana, M. (1986). *Transformational leadership.* New York: John Wiley.

32. Bass, B. M. (1985). *Leadership and performance beyond expectations.* New York: Free Press.

33. Bennis, W. G., & Nanus, B. (1985). *Leaders: The strategies for taking charge.* New York: Harper & Row.

34. Storm, H. (1994). *Lightning bolt.* New York: Ballantine.

35. Burns, J. M. (1978). *Leadership.* New York: Free Press.

36. Bass, B. M. (1985). Ibid.

37. Sergiovanni, T. J. (1990). *Value-added leadership: How to get extraordinary results in schools.* Orlando, FL: Harcourt Brace.

38. Bass, B. M., & Avolio, B. J. (1998). *Manual for the Multifactor Leadership Questionnaire.* Redwood, CA: Mindgarden, Inc.

39. Sivasubramaniam, N., Murry, W. D., Avolio, B. J., & Jung, D. I. (1997). *A longitudinal model of the effects of team leadership and group potency on performance.* Unpublished manuscript, Binghamton University, Center for Leadership Studies, Binghamton, NY.

40. Howell, J. M., & Avolio, B. J. (1993). Transformational leadership, transactional leadership, locus of control, and support for innovation: Key predictors of consolidated-unit performance. *Journal of Applied Psychology, 78,* 891-902.

41. Avolio, B. J., Howell, J. M., & Sosik, J. J. (1997). *A funny thing happened on the way to the bottom line.* Unpublished manuscript, Binghamton University, Center for Leadership Studies.

42. Avolio, B. J., & Bass, B. M. (1991). *The full range leadership development programs: Basic and advanced manuals.* Binghamton, NY: Bass, Avolio & Associates.

43. Bass, B. M. (1997). Ibid.

44. Eden, D. (1990). *Pygmalion in management: Productivity as a self-fulfilling prophecy.* Lexington, MA: Lexington.

45. Eden, D., & Shani, A. B. (1992). Pygmalion goes to boot camp: Expectancy, leadership, and trainee performance. *Journal of Applied Psychology, 67,* 194-199.

46. Rose, R. J. (1995). Genes and human behavior. *Annual Review of Psychology, 46,* 625-654.

47. Gal, R. (1981). *A portrait of an Israeli soldier.* Westport, CT: Greenwood.

48. Vernon, T. (1996). Personal communication on results concerning the heritability of self-ratings of leadership using the Multifactor Leadership Questionnaire (MLQ).

49. Kuhnert, K. W. (1994). Developing people through delegation. In B. M. Bass & B. J. Avolio (Eds.), *Improving organizational effectiveness through transformational leadership* (pp. 10-25). Thousand Oaks, CA: Sage.

50. Avolio, B. J., & Gibbons, T. C. (1988). Developing transformational leaders: A lifespan approach. In J. A. Conger & R. N. Kanungo (Eds.), *Charismatic leadership: The elusive factor in organizational effectiveness* (pp. 276-308). San Francisco: Jossey-Bass.

51. Avolio, B. J., Bass, B. M., Atwater, L. E., Lau, A. W., Dionne, S., Camobreco, J. & Whitmore, N. (1994). *Antecedent predictors of the full range of leadership and management styles* (Contract MDA 903-91-0131). Binghamton, NY: Binghamton University, Center for Leadership Studies.

52. Yammarino, F. J., & Bass, B. M. (1990). Long-term forecasting of transformational leadership and its effects among naval officers: Some preliminary findings. In K. E. Clark & M. R. Clark (Eds.), *Measures of leadership.* Greensboro, NC: Center for Creative Leadership.

53. Avolio, B. J., & Gibbons, T. C. (1988). Ibid.

54. Frankel, V. E. (1963). *Man's search for meaning: An introduction to logo therapy.* New York: Pocket Books.

55. Kazenbach, R. (1998). *Teams at the top.* Boston: Harvard Business School Press.

56. Cohen, S. G., Chang, L., & Ledford, G. E. (1997). A hierarchical construct of self-management leadership and its relationship to quality of work life and perceived group effectiveness. *Personnel Psychology, 50,* 275-308.

57. Avolio, B. J. (1997). *The great leadership migration to a full range leadership system.* College Park: University of Maryland.

58. Hyatt, D. E., & Ruddy, Y. M. (1997). An examination of the relationship between work group characteristics and performance: Once more into the breech. *Personnel Psychology, 50,* 553-585.

59. Sheff, D. (1996, June/July). Levi's changes everything. *Fast Company,* p. 65.

60. Kotter, J. L. (1992). *Corporate culture and performance.* New York: Free Press.

61. Bass, B. M., & Avolio, B. J. (1993). Transformational leadership and organizational culture. *International Journal of Public Administration, 17*(1), 112-122.

62. Miller, D. (1990). *The Icarus Paradox: How exceptional companies bring about their downfall.* New York: Harper Business.

63. Cascio, W. F. (1995). Ibid.

64. Ungson, G. R., Steers, R. M., & Park, S. (1997). *Korean enterprise: The quest for globalization.* Boston: Harvard Business School Press.

65. Quinn, J. B., Anderson, P., & Finkelstein, S. (1996, March-April). Managing professional intellect: Making the most of the best. *Harvard Business Review,* 71-80.

66. Muio, A. (1998, January). How is your company like a hairball? *USAir Magazine,* pp. 84-86.

67. Bass, B. M. (1990). Ibid.

68. Deming, W. E. (1986). *Drastic changes for Western management.* Madison, WI: Center for Quality and Productivity Improvement.

69. Jackson, S. E., & Associates. (1992). *Diversity in the workplace: Human resource initiatives.* New York: Guilford.

70. Tapscott, D. (1995). *The Digital economy: Promise and peril in the age of networked intelligence.* New York: McGraw-Hill.

71. *Knowledge and speed* (Annual report of the army after the next project to the chief of staff of the army). (1997, July). Washington, DC: Department of Defense.

72. Bass, B. M. (1998, March-April). Leading in the army after next. *Military Review,* pp. 46-57.

73. Hackman, J. R. (1990). *Groups that work (and those that don't): Creating conditions for effective teamwork.* San Francisco: Jossey-Bass.

74. Jehn, K. A. (1997). A qualitative analysis of conflict types and dimensions in organizational groups. *Administrative Science Quarterly, 42,* 530-557.

75. Gersick, C. J. G. (1988). Time and transition in work teams: Toward a new model of group development. *Academy of Management Journal, 31,* 9-41.

76. Kazenbach, J. R., & Smith, D. K. *The wisdom of teams: Creating the high-performing organization.* Boston: Harvard Business School Press.

77. Seltzer, J., Numerof, R. E., & Bass, B. M. (1989). Transformational leadership: Is it a source of more or less burnout or stress? *Journal of Health and Human Resources Administration, 12,* 174-185.

78. Burgess, K. A., Salas, E., Cannon-Bowers, J. A., & Hall, J. K. (1992). *Training guidelines for team leaders under stress.* Paper presented to the Human Factors Society, Atlanta, AL.

79. Avolio, B. J., & Bass, B. M. (1995). Individualized consideration is more than consideration for the individual when viewed at multiple levels of analysis. *Leadership Quarterly, 6*(2), 199-218.

80. Bass, B. M., & Avolio, B. J. (1997). *Platoon readiness as a function of transformational/ transactional leadership squad mores and platoon cultures.* (Army Research Institute contract #DAS W01-96K-008).

81. Avolio, B. J., Jung, D. I., Murry, W., & Sivasubramaniam, N. (1996). Building highly developed teams: Focusing on shared leadership process, efficacy, trust, and performance. In M. M. Beyerlein, D. A. Johnson, & S. T. Beyerlein (Eds.), *Advances in interdisciplinary studies of work teams* (pp. 173-209). Greenwich, CT: JAI.

82. Howell, J. J., & Higgins, C. (1992). Leadership behaviors influence tactics and career experience of champions of technical innovation. *Leadership Quarterly, 1,* 249-264.

83. Daugherty, R. A., & Williams, S. E. (1997). The long-term impacts of leadership development: An assessment of a statewide program. *Journal of Leadership Studies, 4,* 101-115.

84. Conger, J. A., & Kanungo, R. A. (1988). *Charismatic leadership: The elusive factor in organizational effectiveness.* San Francisco: Jossey-Bass.

85. Most, R., & Avolio, B. J. (1997). Utilizing Web-site technology in developing the full potential of organizations. *Industrial Psychologist, 34*(4), 11-13.

86. Hesketh, M. (1997). Dilemmas in transfer of training. *Applied Psychology: An International Review, 46,* 317-386.

87. Weber, M. (1947). *The theory of social and economic organizations* (T. Parsons, Trans.). New York: Free Press. (Original work published 1927)

88. Greenleaf, R. K. (1997). The servant as leader. In R. P. Vecchio (Ed.), *Leadership: Understanding the dynamics of power and influence in organizations.* Notre Dame, IN: University of Notre Dame Press.

89. Kouzes, J. M., & Posner, B. Z. (1991). *Credibility: How leaders gain and lose it. Why people demand it.* San Francisco: Jossey-Bass.

90. Frost, P. J. (1997). Ibid.

91. Quinn, J. B. (1997). *Innovation explosion: Using intellect and software to revolutionize growth strategies.* New York: Free Press.

92. Burns, J. M. (1978). *Leadership.* New York: Free Press.

93. Meindl, J. R., Ehrlich, S. B., & Dukerich, J. M. (1985). The romance of leadership. *Administrative Sciences Quarterly, 30,* 78-102.

94. Bass, B. M., Waldman, D. A., Avolio, B. J., & Bebb, M. (1987). Transformational leadership and the falling dominoes effect. *Group and Organizational Studies, 12,* 73-87.

95. Cohen, G. G., Chang, L., & Ledford, G. E. (1997). A hierarchical construct of self-management leadership and its relationship to quality of work life and perceived group effectiveness. *Personnel Psychology, 50,* 275-308.

96. Drucker, P. (1993). *Managing for the future: The 1990s and beyond.* New York: Truman Tally Books.

97. Koh, W., Terburg, J. R., & Steers, R. M. (1992). *The impact of transformational leadership on organizational commitment, organizational citizenship behavior, teacher satisfaction, and student performance in Singapore.* Paper presented at the Academy of Management, Miami Beach, FL.

98. Shea, C., & Howell, J. H. (1995). *The effects of charismatic leadership and task feedback on self-efficacy, performance quality, and attributes.* Doctoral dissertation, the Richard Ivey School of Business, Western Ontario, Canada.

99. Thite, M. (1997). *Relationship between leadership and information technology project success.* Doctoral dissertation, Swinburne University of Technology, Melbourne, Australia.

100. Howell, J. M., & Higgins, C. A. (1990). Champions of technological innovations. *Administrative Science Quarterly, 35,* 317-341.

101. Avolio, B. J., Jung, D. J., Murry, W., & Sivasubramaniam, N. (1996). Ibid.

102. Howell, J. M., Neufeld, D., & Avolio, B. J. (1998). *Examining leadership close up and at a distance.* Unpublished manuscript. Center for Leadership Studies, Binghamton University.

103. Avolio, B. J., Howell, J. M., & Sosik, J. J. (1997). Ibid.

104. Knouse, S. (1996). *Human resource management perspectives on TQM.* Milwaukee, WI: ASQC Press.

105. Atwater, L. E., Camobreco, J. F., Dionne, S. D., Avolio, B. J., & Lau, A. N. (1997). Effects of rewards and punishment on leader charisma, leader effectiveness, and follower reactions. *Leadership Quarterly, 8,* 133-152.

106. Howell, J. M., & Avolio, B. J. (1993). Ibid.

107. Weick, K. (1991). Educational organizations as loosely coupled systems. *Administrative Sciences Quarterly, 21,* 1-19.

108. Winston, M. G. (1997). Leadership of renewal: Leadership for the 21st century. *Business Forum, 22,* 4-7.

109. Howell, J. A., & Avolio, B. J. (1992). Charismatic leadership: Submission or liberation. *Academy of Management Executive, 6,* 43-54.

110. Howell, J. M. (1988). The two faces of charisma: Socialized and personalized leadership in organizations. In J. Conger & R. Kanungo (Eds.), *Charismatic leadership: The illusive factor in organizational effectiveness.* San Francisco: Jossey-Bass.

111. Kuhnert, K. W. (1994). Ibid.

112. Miller, H. (1997). (1997). Interview with Max Depree. *Leader to Leader, 6,* 18-23.

113. Avolio, B. J., & Bass, B. M. (1998). You can drag a horse to water, but you can't make it drink unless it is thirsty. *Journal of Leadership Studies, 5*(1), 4-17.

114. Dvir, T. (1998). *The impact of transformational leadership training on follower development and performance: A field experiment.* Unpublished doctoral dissertation, Tel Aviv University, Israel.

115. Burns, J. M. (1978). Ibid.

Box and
Research References

Agle, B. R. (1993). *Charismatic chief executive officers: Are they more effective? An empirical test of charismatic leadership theory.* Unpublished doctoral dissertation, University of Washington.

Atwater, L., Lau, A., Bass, B. M., Avolio, B. J., Camobreco J., & Whitmore, N. (1994). *The content, construct, and criterion-related validity of leader behavior measures* (U.S. Army Research Institute Research Note, Washington, DC).

Atwater, L., & Yammarino, F. J. (1997). Self-other agreement: A review and model. *Research in Personnel and Human Resource Management, 15,* 121-174.

Atwater, L. E., Ostroff, C., Yammarino, F. J., & Fleenor, J. W. (in press). Self-other agreement: Does it really matter? *Personnel Psychology.*

Atwater, L. E., & Yammarino, F. J. (1992). Does self-other agreement on leadership perceptions moderate the validity of leadership and performance predictions? *Personnel Psychology, 45,* 141-164.

Avolio, B. J., Bass, B. M., & Jung, D. I. (in press). Reexamining the components of transformational and transactional leadership using the Multifactor Leadership Questionnaire. *Journal of Organizational and Occupational Psychology.*

Avolio, B. J., Howell, J. M., & Sosik, J. J. (in press). A funny thing happened on the way to the bottom line. *Academy of Management Journal.*

Avolio, B. J., Jung, D. I., Murry, W., & Sivasubramaniam, N. (1996). Building highly developed teams: Focusing on shared leadership processes, efficacy, trust, and performance. In M. M. Beyerlein, D. A. Johnson, & S. T. Beyerlein (Eds.), *Advances in interdisciplinary studies of work teams* (pp. 173-209). Greenwich, CT: JAI.

Avolio, B. J., Waldman, D. A., & Einstein, W. O. (1998). Transformational leadership in a management game simulation: Impacting the bottom line. *Group and Organization Studies, 13,* 59-80.

Barling, J., Weber, T., & Kelloway, E. K. (1996). Effects of transformational leadership training on attitudinal and financial outcomes. *Journal of Applied Psychology, 81,* 827-832.

Bass, B. M. (1998). *Transformational leadership: Industry, military, and educational impact.* Mahwah, NJ: Lawrence Erlbaum.

Bass, B. M., & Avolio, B. J. (1997). *First interim report: Platoon readiness as a function of transformational/transactional leadership, squad mores, and platoon cultures.* Washington, DC: U.S. Army Research Institute for the Behavioral and Social Sciences.

Bass, B. M., Avolio, B. J., & Atwater, L. (1996). The transformational and transactional leadership behavior of female and male managers as described by the men and women who directly report to them. *Applied Psychology: An International Review, 45,* 5-34.

Baum, G. J., Locke, E. A., & Kirkpatrick, S. A. (1998). A longitudinal study of the relation of vision and vision communication to venture growth in entrepreneurial firms. *Journal of Applied Psychology, 83,* 43-54.

Berson, Y., Shamir, B., Avolio, B. J., & Popper, M. (1998). *The relationship between vision strength, leadership style, and context.* Unpublished manuscript, State University of New York at Binghamton, Center for Leadership Studies.

Berson, Y., & Yammarino, F. J. (1997). *Followership, leadership, and attachment styles: A developmental approach.* Unpublished manuscript, Binghamton University, Center for Leadership Studies, Binghamton, NY.

Bowlby, J. (1969). *Attachment and loss: Vol 1. Attachment.* London: Hogarth.

Bowlby, J. (1973). *Attachment and loss: Vol 2. Separation.* London: Hogarth.

Brown, J. C. (1994). Leadership education through humanistic texts and traditions: The Hartwick classic leadership cases. *Journal of Leadership Studies, 1,* 104-116.

Bryant, M. A. (1990). *Relationship between nurse managers' perceived transformational versus transactional leadership styles and staff nurse turnover.* Master's thesis, University of Akron, Akron, OH.

Bryce, N. Y. (1989). *Leadership styles of Japanese business executives and managers: Transformational and transactional.* Unpublished doctoral dissertation, Fielding Institute.

Butler, C. (1994). The magnificent seven. *Sales & Marketing Management Performance Supplement,* 41-50.

Bycio, P., Hackett, R. D., & Allen, J. S. (1995). Further assessments of Bass' (1985) conceptualization of transactional and transformational leadership. *Journal of Applied Psychology, 80,* 468-478.

Carless, S., Mann, L., & Wearing, A. (1995). An empirical test of the transformational leadership model. In *Leadership symposium.* Symposium conducted at the Inaugural Australian Industrial and Organizational Psychology Conference, Sydney, Australia.

Cheverton, G. L., & Thompson, B. M. (1996). *Subordinate perceptions of transformational leadership: Relationships with organizational context, formalization, and psychological participation.* Unpublished manuscript.

Clover, W. H. (1988). *Transformational leaders: Team performance, leadership, ratings, and firsthand impressions.* Paper prepared for the Center for Creative Leadership Conference on Psychological Measures and Leadership, Colorado Springs, CO.

Coleman, E. P., Patterson, E., Fuller, B., Hester, K., & Stringer, D. Y. (1995). *A meta-analytic examination of leadership style and selected follower compliance outcomes.* Unpublished manuscript, University of Alabama.

Colin Powell's thoughts on leadership. (1998). *Industry Week, 245*(15), 56-57.

Conger, J. A., & Kanungo, R. N. (1988). The empowerment process: Integration, theory and practice. *Academy of Management Review, 13,* 471-482.

Cowen, S. S. (1990). *A study of the relationships between perceived leadership behaviors of presidents at public 4-year institutions of higher education in the U.S.* Unpublished doctoral dissertation, Gonzaga University, Spokane, WA.

Crookall, P. S. (1989). *Leadership in the prison industry: A study of the effect of training prison shop foremen in situational or transformational leadership on inmates' productivity and personal growth.* Unpublished doctoral dissertation, University of Western Ontario, London, Ontario, Canada.

Curphy, G. J. (1992). An empirical investigation of the effects of transformational and transactional leadership on organizational climate, attrition, and performance. In K. F. Clark, M. B. Clark, & D. P. Campbell (Eds.), *Impact of leadership* (pp. 177-187). Greensboro, NC: Center for Creative Leadership.

Deluga, R. (1997). *Relationship among American presidential proactivity, charismatic leadership, and rated performance.* Paper presented at the National Society for Industrial Organizational Psychology, St. Louis, MO.

Den Hartog, D. N., Van Muijen, E. J., & Koopman, P. L. (1996). Linking transformational leadership and organizational culture. *Journal of Leadership Studies, 3,* 68-83.

Den Hartog, D. N., Van Muijen, E. J., & Koopman, P. L. (1997). Transactional versus transformational leadership: An analysis of the MLQ. *Journal of Occupational and Organizational Psychology, 70,* 19-34.

Densten, I. L., & Sarros, J. C. (1995). *Leadership and burnout in an Australian law enforcement organization.* Doctoral dissertation, Monash University, Melbourne, Australia.

Druskat, V. U. (1994). Gender and leadership style: Transformational and transactional leadership in the Roman Catholic Church. *Leadership Quarterly, 5,* 98-119.

Dvir, T. (1998). *The impact of transformational leadership training on follower development and performance: A field experiment.* Unpublished doctoral dissertation, Tel Aviv University, Israel.

Eagly, A. H. (1991). *Gender and leadership.* Paper presented at the national meeting of the American Psychological Association, San Francisco, CA.

Eagly, A. H., & Johnson, B. T. (1990). Gender and leadership styles: A meta-analysis. *Psychological Bulletin, 108,* 233-256.

Eden, D. (1990). *Pygmalion in management: Productivity as self-fulfilling prophecy.* Lexington, MA: Lexington.

Garcia, E. L. (1995). *Transformational leadership processes and salesperson performance effectiveness: A theoretical model and partial empirical examination.* Unpublished doctoral dissertation, Fielding Institute.

Gardner, W. L., & Avolio, B. J. (1998). Charismatic leadership: The role of impression management. *Academy of Management Review, 23,* 32-58.

Gasper, R. (1992). *Transformational leadership: An integrative review of the literature.* Unpublished doctoral dissertation, Western Michigan University, Kalamazoo.

Geyer, A. L. J., & Steyrer, J. M. (1998). Transformational leadership and objective performance in banks. *Applied Psychology: An International Review, 47,* 397-420.

Gibbons, T. C. (1986). *Revisiting the question of born vs. made: Toward a theory of development of transformational leaders.* Unpublished doctoral dissertation, Fielding Institute.

Gillis, C., Getkate, M., Robinson, D., & Porporino, F. (1995). Correctional work supervisor leadership and credibility: Their influence on offender work motivation. *Forum on Correctional Research, 7,* 15-17.

Gladstein, D. (1984). Groups in context: A model of task group effectiveness. *Administrative Science Quarterly, 29,* 499-517.

Gottlieb, T. W. (1990). *Transactional and transformational leadership styles of chief and associate chief nurses in Department of Veterans' Affairs medical centers: A descriptive study.* Unpublished doctoral dissertation, Columbia University Teachers College, New York.

Hackman, M. R. (1990). *Groups that work (and those that don't): Creating conditions for effective teamwork.* San Francisco: Jossey-Bass.

Hackman, M. R., Furniss, A. H., Hills, M. J., & Peterson, R. J. (1992). Perceptions of gender-role characteristics and transformational and transactional leadership behaviors. *Perceptual and Motor Skills, 75,* 311-319.

Hater, J. J., & Bass, B. M. (1988). Superiors' evaluations and subordinates' perceptions of transformational and transactional leadership. *Journal of Applied Psychology, 73,* 695-702.

Heifetz, R. (1994). *Leadership without any easy answers.* Boston: Harvard Business Press.

Hicks, R. S. (1990). *Effectiveness of transactional and transformational leadership in turbulent and stable conditions.* Unpublished doctoral dissertation, Claremont Graduate School, Claremont, CA.

Holladay, S. J., & Coombs, W. T. (1994). Speaking of visions and visions being spoken. *Management Communication Quarterly, 8,* 165-189.

Horine, J., & Bass, B. M. (1993). *Transformational leadership: The cornerstone of quality* (Report No. 933). Binghamton, NY: Binghamton University, Center for Leadership Studies.

House, R. J. (1995). Leadership in the 21st century: A speculative inquiry. In A. Howard (Ed.), *The changing nature of work.* San Francisco: Jossey-Bass.

House, R. J. (1997). *The GLOBE project.* Wharton: University of Pennsylvania.

Howell, J. A., & Avolio, B. J. (1993). Predicting consolidated unit performance: Leadership behavior, locus of control, and support for innovation. *Journal of Applied Psychology, 78,* 891-902.

Howell, J. M., & Higgins, C. A. (1990). Champions of technological innovations. *Administrative Science Quarterly, 35,* 317-341.

Howell, J. M., Neufeld, D. J., & Avolio, B. J. (1998). *Leadership at a distance: The effects of physical distance, charismatic leadership, and communication style on predicting business unit performance.* Unpublished manuscript, University of Western Ontario, London, Ontario, Canada.

Howell, J. M., & Shea, M. C. (1998). *The effects of champion strengths, boundary activities, and support for innovation on team potency and product innovation.* Unpublished manuscript, University of Western Ontario, London, Ontario, Canada.

HR News. (1997, August). The importance of trust in organizations. (1998). *SHRM Newsletter.*

Jack's men. (1977, July 7). *Industry Week,* pp. 12-17.

Johnson, A. M., Vernon, P. A., Molson, M., Harris, J. A., & Jang, K. L. (1998). *Born to lead: A behavior genetic investigation of leadership ability.* Paper presented at the national meeting of the Society for Industrial Organizational Psychology, Dallas, TX.

Jung, D. I., & Avolio, B. J. (in press-a). Effects of leadership style and followers' cultural values on performance under different task structure conditions. *Academy of Management Journal.*

Jung, D. I., & Avolio, B. J. (in press-b). Examination of transformational leadership and group process among Caucasian and Asian Americans: Are they different? *Research in International Business and International Relations.*

Kahai, S. S., Avolio, B. J., & Sosik, J. J. (1998). Effects of source, participant anonymity, and initial difference in opinion in an EMS context. *Decision Sciences, 29,* 427-460.

Kahai, S. S., Sosik, J. J., & Avolio, B. J. (1997). Leadership and task structure impact on process and outcomes in an EMS environment. *Personnel Psychology, 50,* 121-146.

Kane, T. D., & Tremble, T. R., Jr. (1998). *Transformational leadership effects at different levels of the army.* Unpublished manuscript, U.S. Army Research Institute for the Behavioral and Social Sciences.

Keller, R. T. (1992). Transformational leadership and the performance of research and development project groups. *Journal of Management, 18,* 489-501.

Kelloway, E. K., & Barling, J. (1993). Members' participation in local union activities: Measurement, prediction, and replication. *Journal of Applied Psychology, 78,* 262-279.

Koh, W. L. K. (1990). *An empirical validation of the theory of transformational leadership in secondary schools in Singapore.* Unpublished doctoral dissertation, University of Oregon, Eugene.

Kozlowski, S. W. J., Gully, S. M., Salas, E., & Canon-Bowers, J. A. (1996). Team leadership and development: Theories, principles, and guidelines for training leaders and teams. In M. M. Beyerlein, D. A. Johnson, & S. T. Beyerlein (Eds.), *Advances in interdisciplinary studies of work teams* (pp. 253-291). Greenwich, CT: JAI.

Kumpfer, K. L., Turner, C., Hopkins, R., & Librett, J. (1993). Leadership and team effectiveness in community coalitions for the presentation of alcohol and other drug abuse. *Health Education Research, 9,* 359-374.

Lahey, L., Souvaine, E., Kegan, R., Goodman, R., & Felix, S. (1991). *A guide to the subject-object interview: Administration and interpretation.* Unpublished manuscript, Harvard University, Graduate School of Education.

Laing, R. D. (1981). *Dialogue with R. D. Laing: The man and his ideas.* New York: Praeger.

Lehnen, L. P., Ayman, R., & Korabik, K. (1995). *The effects of transformational leadership and conflict management styles on subordinates' satisfaction with supervision.* Paper presented at the annual conference of the Society for Industrial Organizational Psychology, Orlando, FL.

Leithwood, K., & Jantzi, D. (1990). Transformational leadership: How principals can help reform cultures. *School Effectiveness and School Improvement, 1,* 249-280.

Leithwood, K., Jantzi, D., Silins, H., & Dart, B. (1990). *Using the appraisal of school leaders as an instrument for school restructuring.* Unpublished manuscript.

Leithwood, K., & Steinbach, R. (1991). Indicators of transformational leadership in everyday problem solving of school administrators. *Journal of Personnel Evaluation in Education, 4,* 221-243.

Lord, R. G., & Maher, K. E. (1993). *Leadership and information processing: Linking perceptions and performance.* London: Routledge.

Lowe, K., Kroeck, K. G., & Sivasubramaniam, N. (1996). Effectiveness correlates of transformational and transactional leadership: A meta-analytic review. *Leadership Quarterly, 7,* 385-425.

Lucius, R., & Kuhnert, K. (1997). *Adult development and leadership: Examining tomorrow's leaders today.* Unpublished manuscript, University of Georgia, Athens.

Martin, M. M. (1996). *Leadership in a cultural trust chasm: An analysis of trust-directed behaviors and vision-directed behaviors that lead to positive follower attitude responses.* Unpublished doctoral dissertation, Virginia Commonwealth University, Richmond.

Masi, R. J. (1994). *Transformational leadership and its roles in empowerment, productivity, and commitment to quality.* Unpublished doctoral dissertation, University of Illinois, Chicago.

Matusek, L. R. (1997). *Finding your voice: Learning to lead anywhere you want to make a difference.* San Francisco: Jossey-Bass.

Niehoff, B. F., Eng, C. A., & Grover, R. A. (1990). The impact of top management actions on employee attitudes and perceptions. *Group and Organizational Studies, 15,* 337-352.

O'Connor, J., Mumford, M. D., Clifton, T. C., Gessner, T. L., & Connelly, M. S. (1995). Charismatic leaders and destructiveness: A historiometric study. *Leadership Quarterly, 6,* 529-558.

Onnen, M. K. (1987). *The relationship of clergy leadership characteristics to growing or declining churches.* Unpublished doctoral dissertation, University of Louisville, Louisville.

Pereira, D. F. (1986). *Factors associated with transformational leadership in an Indian engineering firm.* Unpublished manuscript.

Philbin, L. P. (1997). *Transformational leadership and the secondary school principal.* Unpublished doctoral dissertation, Purdue University, Lafayette, IN.

Pile, S. C. (1988). *Visionary leadership: Creating a generative internal map about behavior, belief, and identity.* Unpublished doctoral dissertation, Pepperdine University, Malibu, CA.

Pillai, R. (1993). *The role of structural, contextual, and cultural factors in the emergence of charismatic leadership in organizations.* Unpublished doctoral dissertation, State University of New York at Buffalo.

Pitman, B., III. (1993). *The relationship between charismatic leadership behaviors and organizational commitment among white-collar workers.* Unpublished doctoral dissertation, Georgia State University, Atlanta.

Podsakoff, P. M., Todor, W. D., Grover, R. A., & Huber, V. L. (1984). Situational indicators of leader reward and punishment behaviors: Fact or fiction? *Organizational Behavior and Human Performance, 34,* 21-63.

Popper, M., Mayseless, O., & Castelnovo, O. (1998). *Transformational leadership attachment.* Unpublished manuscript, University of Haifa, Haifa, Israel.

Quinn, J. B., Anderson, P., & Finkelstein, R. (1996). Managing professional intellect: Making the most of the best. *Harvard Business Review, 20,* 72-80.

Rest, J. R. (1986). *Moral development: Advances in research and theory.* New York: Prayer.

Rivera, J. B. (1994). *Visionary versus crisis-induced charismatic leadership: An experimental test.* Unpublished doctoral dissertation, Texas Tech University, Lubbock.

Salas, E., Mullen, B., Rozell, D., & Driskell, J. E. (1997). *The effects of team building on performance: An integration.* Paper presented at the national meeting of the Society for Industrial and Organizational Psychology, St. Louis, MO.

Seltzer, J., Numerof, R. E., & Bass, B. M. (1989). Transformational leadership: Is it a source of more burnout and stress? *Journal of Health and Human Resources Administration, 12,* 174-185.

Shamir, B. (1995). Social distance and charisma. *Leadership Quarterly, 6,* 19-47.

Shamir, B., Zakay, E., Breinin, E., & Popper, M. (1998a). *Diversity and homogeneity of charisma within groups.* Unpublished manuscript, Hebrew University, Jerusalem, Israel.

Shamir, B., Zakay, E., Breinin, E., & Popper, M. (1998b). *Leadership and social identification in military units: Direct and indirect relationships.* Unpublished manuscript, Hebrew University, Jerusalem, Israel.

Silins, H. C. (1992). Effective leadership for school reform. *Alberta Journal of Educational Research, 38,* 317-334.

Sinclair, A. (1992). The tyranny of team idealogy. *Organizational Studies, 13,* 611-626.

Sivasubramaniam, N., Murry, W. D., Avolio, B. J., & Jung, D. I. (1997). *A longitudinal model of the effects of team leadership and group potency on performance.* Unpublished manuscript, Binghamton University, Center for Leadership Studies, Binghamton, NY.

Sosik, J. J., Avolio, B. J., & Kahai, S. S. (1997). The impact of leadership style and anonymity on group potency and effectiveness in a GDSS environment. *Journal of Applied Psychology, 82,* 89-103.

Sosik, J. J., Avolio, B. J., & Kahai, S. S. (in press). Transformational leadership and dimensions of creativity: Motivating idea generation in computer-mediated groups. *Creativity Research Journal.*

Spreitzer, G. M., & Janasz, S. G. (1998). *The transformational capacities of managers.* Unpublished manuscript.

Stewart, G., & Manz, C. C. (1994). *Leadership for self-managing work teams: A theoretical integration.* Paper presented at the national conference of the Society for Industrial and Organizational Psychology, Nashville, TN.

Tepper, B. J. (1993). *Patterns of downward influence and follower conformity in transactional and transformational leadership.* Unpublished doctoral dissertation, University of Kentucky, Lexington.

Thite, M. (1997). *Relationship between leadership and information technology project sources.* Unpublished doctoral dissertation, Swinburne University of Technology, Melbourne, Australia.

Turner, N., & Barling, J. (1998). *Moral reasoning and transformational laadership.* Kingston, Ontario, Canada: Queen's University.

Weierter, S. (1994). *Substitutes for transactional leadership: The impact of transactional leader behaviors on workgroup perceptions at the first line supervisor level.* Unpublished doctoral dissertation, Griffith University, Brisbane, Australia.

Westley, F., & Mintzberg, H. (1991). Visionary leadership and strategic management. In J. Henry & D. Walker (Eds.), *Managing innovation.* Thousand Oaks, CA: Sage.

Winston, M. (1997). Leadership of renewal: Leadership for the 21st century. *Business Forum, 22,* 4-7.

Yagil, D. (1998). *Charismatic leadership and organizational hierarchy: Attribution of charisma to close and distant leaders.* Unpublished manuscript, University of Haifa, Haifa, Israel.

Yammarino, F. J., & Bass, B. M. (1990). Long-term forecasting of transformational leadership. In *Measures of leadership.* West Orange, NJ: Leadership Library of America.

Index

About the Author

Bruce J. Avolio is Professor and Director of the Center for Leadership Studies at Binghamton University, Binghamton, New York (CLS.Binghamton.ed). He received his PhD from the University of Akron in 1982 in industrial/organizational and life span psychology. He has published more than 70 articles and book chapters related to individual, team, and organizational leadership and has coauthored, with Bernard Bass, the book *Improving Organizational Effectiveness Through Transformational Leadership,* as well as two widely used leadership measures: the Multifactor Leadership Questionnaire and the Team Multifactor Leadership Questionnaire. He is writing a third book on how best to develop the full range of leadership potential, focusing on new and innovative ways to embed leadership training in the work context.

Considered an international expert in the area of assessing and developing transformational leadership, Dr. Avolio has conducted training workshops in the United States, Canada, Israel, Italy, Australia, New Zealand, Spain, England, South Africa, Sweden, Austria, Hong Kong, and Belgium. He has worked with CEOs of large companies, senior executive teams, middle-level managers, and project leaders in public and private organizations around the globe, with the goal of enhancing leadership potential at an individual, team, and strategic level.

During the last 5 years, Dr. Avolio has worked with a wide range of colleagues to set up a worldwide network of centers for leadership studies. To date, affiliate centers have been established in Israel, South Africa, Korea, Australia, and New Zealand. Several new centers are planned for inauguration during the next 2 years. He is also working with colleagues to build a leadership development Web site that will help facilitate the continuous training of leaders over time and distance.

His current research interests include assessing transformational leadership potential, examining the impact of computer mediation on leader and follower interactions, and identifying mechanisms to facilitate the development of virtual team leadership.